10X FOR CHRIST

ADVANCE PRAISE

Carlos has masterfully presented God's truth, his Word, to show the way that we can become the champions, the conquerors, the 10X-er that God has destined us to become.

—Bud Handwerk, President, Annamar Associates, Inc.

Discovering Your 10X Lifestyle in Jesus Christ is a powerful devotional for everyone, regardless of spiritual maturity, age, or occupation. It is obvious that Carlos has spent quality one-on-one quiet time with the Lord and has used that experience to create an inspired framework that will guide others on a journey of self-discovery and revelation. His transparency with his own struggles and doubts provides encouragement to all who embark on this journey to walk in the fullness of Jesus Christ.

—Sheryl Clutter, Chief Operations Office, Convene

Discovering Your 10X Lifestyle in Jesus Christ was written by a mentor and friend who has had a large, spiritual impact on my life. His book will be a blessing to those who read it. Each day I spent with the journal I felt like a participant in something. You'll start to feel like you know the heart of the author by first reading a verse and then getting to hear the humble response of Carlos. The Scriptures start to come alive. There's a great interactive aspect to the book that reaches beyond the author's thoughts and perspective. Each day readers are given ample space to be led by the Holy Spirit and to write down their own personal reflections. He also asks us to write a prayer that pertains to the message of the day. This makes me feel as if the book is an heirloom because my family will be able to turn back to my own thoughts and prayers and see the glory of God's will in my life. It's like a spiritual journal that's leading me closer to Jesus. As a businessman, I'm a numbers guy, and I do like the idea of being multiplied in God's Word and wisdom! Who wouldn't want that? Thanks, Carlos, for following the promptings and writing this book, and for sharing it with your friends and the world!

—Ronnie Wills, CEO, Aggregate Technologies, Inc.

Many of us struggle to find time to spend with God—in solitude with Him, prayer to Him, study of Him, and journaling about Him in our lives. My friend Carlos has given us all a solid reason, and a wonderful book, to seek more time with the Father. I'm convinced that is the way to become a 10X-er and leave a legacy that will change the world.

—Harris Wheeler, President, Significance2

I've never been much of a prepared, structured, devotions guy as I am usually working through a specific book or section of the Bible, and then I was introduced to *Discovering Your 10X Lifestyle in Jesus Christ*. This is obviously written by someone who has done some real living, had real-life experiences, struggled, overcome, and would now seem to be living an abundant, joyful life. Each devotion bubbles with the invitation from God through Christ to surrender and live the life of love God intended for us. Enjoy. Be encouraged. Be loved and let Christ's love be yours each day.

—Ed Wekesser, President, Fulcrum Business Solutions, Inc.

From first glimpse, *Discovering Your 10X Lifestyle in Jesus Christ* promises to bring great spiritual growth to the user. It is not just a devotion to read and contemplate—it is a devotion that requires serious action. Contemplate, compare, search, compose/journal. Great steps to spiritual growth. The integration of journaling with the daily devotion is a powerful practice. Many need to begin regular devotions—even more need to begin the practice of journaling. This devotional builds us up on a strong foundation and encourages us to be active and creative in our devotional process—not just doing devotions to get our ticket punched for the day!

—L. Ronald Hoover, PhD, Managing Partner, Hoover Heritage Group, Inc.

Discovering Your 10X Lifestyle in Jesus Christ is an outstanding road map for anyone who wants tangible results through a relationship with Jesus Christ. It leads us on a 52-week journey and draws us to discover our true potential as a follower of our Lord and Savior. Find answers, deepen your faith, and arm yourself to face and overcome what life throws at you. This devotional can give you and others around you undeniable evidence of His wisdom and grace in your life.

—J Scott Baker, Executive Pastor, The Bridge Church

Carlos Rosales answered God's calling and created an exceptional devotional. *Discovering Your 10X Lifestyle in Jesus Christ* allows the reader to experience God's grace by providing a road map to developing the relationship with Jesus Christ we all long for. His honesty and candidness provide the reader with comfort, and his wisdom offers guidance. This devotional is essential for all individuals seeking a closer relationship with Jesus Christ.

—Dr. Patrick A. Laird,
Director-Master of Science in Nursing Program,
Cizik School of Nursing at University of Texas Health

10X means growing well beyond the "average". In *Discovering Your 10X Lifestyle in Jesus Christ*, Carlos takes you deep in a very practical way. Join the journey and 10X your faith each day, becoming more Christlike in character, conduct, and conversation.

—Mark Ross, Thinking Partner, Next Thing Group

There's so much to love about this devotional. Carlos takes us to many delightful passages of Scripture over the course of the year. Because Carlos is a seasoned business coach, his insights and reflections on the text are as challenging yet encouraging as he is in person, and he says just enough to prime the pump and help us make discoveries of our own. I particularly love how he has bookended every devotional with "JJ" and "SDG." With just that simple reminder (which requires reading the introduction to figure out the code), we are daily focused on the big "why" that motivates us to live the 10X life.

—Shelley Leith, Director of Church Relations,
HarperCollins Christian Publishing,
Author of *Character Makeover*

Carlos' collection of devotionals is excellent. There are a lot of strong biblical truths here, presented in an easy-to-understand manner and yet very practical.

—Matthew Fullerton, Principal, Fullerton Consulting, Inc.

What a delightful find in *Discovering Your 10X Lifestyle in Jesus Christ*. If you're interested in growing exponentially and discovering all that God has designed for you, I encourage you to pick up this wonderful devotional and then be prepared to see God work abundantly and joyfully through you in these pages. It's not every day that one comes across both a riveting page-turner *and* also a life changer, but Rosales accomplishes both with this work.

—Brian Horner, Executive Director of Operations Houston 1, Marketplace Chaplains

Carlos Rosales is someone who lives what he believes. His life is a living example of what he writes about. I know it firsthand. I've seen his fathering skills; he loves his kids. I've seen his love for his wife. I've seen his interaction with his Convene CEO clients and I've experienced his influence on my life. Carlos is a man of God on a mission from God who deeply loves God and loves God's people. He lives his life intentionally and deeply. He can write about the 10X life because he lives the 10X life in real time. Carlos' work is practical, loving, hard hitting, and able to be consumed in bite-sized chunks as you live your busy life.

—Greg Leith, Chief Executive Officer, Convene

Carlos Rosales shares the intimate account of his journey beyond a challenging childhood and the uphill battle to a healthy self-image. This story is an inspiration for aspiring men of valor. *Discovering Your 10X Lifestyle in Jesus Christ* is a devotional that speaks truth into lives of men who are in pursuit of becoming their best self in Christ Jesus. This personal journal is a blueprint, process, and tool for every reader to develop a clear, mental picture of who Jesus desires them to become as a 10X-er. More significantly, you will enjoy this genuine experience of the dynamic presence of God's Word at work in our lives. This potential best-selling devotional builds a compelling case for a God-inspired vision of who you can become in Jesus Christ. The daily reading, inspired Scriptures, thinking for a transformation, and prayer provide a daily burst of inspiration and power aimed at helping the reader to accomplish all their faith prompts them to achieve. It is 52 weeks of being energized with joy, peace, and the fulfillment of a 10X-er lifestyle in Jesus Christ. Enjoy the journey as you begin to see yourself as Jesus desires to see you!

—Dr. Larry M. Lindsay, Chief Academic Operating Office, Ron Blue Institute

A powerful journal for the spiritual journey of every Christian business owner or leader.
—Christopher McCluskey, President, Professional Christian Coaching Institute

The 10X daily devotional is a great way to start each workday and a reminder Christ is at the center of each day. It is well written and well organized and a joy to read.
—Steve Parkhill, President, EEPB P.C.

I think the book draws the reader into a daily reading of Scripture, thinking about Scripture, and praying Scripture. Doing those three things will produce God's growth in anyone's life. There can be no greater result from a devotional book!
—W. Mark Lanier, Founder of the Lanier Law Firm,
Author of *Christianity on Trial*

Every now and then a book comes along that is so solid and so pragmatic, there is absolutely no way *not* to be transformed by reading it. *10X4Christ: Discovering Your 10X Lifestyle in Jesus Christ* is such a book. Carlos wields a scalpel to cut to the core issues that stop us from being everything we can be in Christ, while empowering us to risk into new territory in every area of our life. He brings simple, yet potent direction and actionable steps that drive us to grow from live matter, instead of theory and hypothesis. It is genius in its simplicity and focus.
—Dean Del Sesto, CCO, Venthio Brand Group,
Author of *Shift Your Thinking* Series

Discovering Your 10X Lifestyle in Jesus Christ is the preeminent devotional for those who wish to achieve not only success, but also more importantly, significance in life.
—Dr. K. Shelette Stewart, Harvard Business School,
Author of *Revelations in Business: Connecting Your Business Plan
with God's Purpose and Plan for Your Life*

Carlos Rosales has written a personal and very powerful devotional from a Kingdom AND corporate perspective. *10X4 Christ: Discovering Your 10X Lifestyle in Jesus Christ* will guide you in The Word and in prayer every day of the week.
—Dr. David Fleming, Senior Pastor
Champion Forest Baptist Church

10X
FOR CHRIST
DISCOVERING YOUR 10X LIFESTYLE IN JESUS CHRIST

CARLOS E. ROSALES III

MOUNT
TABOR
MEDIA

NEW YORK

LONDON • NASHVILLE • MELBOURNE • VANCOUVER

10X FOR CHRIST

Discovering Your 10X Lifestyle in Jesus Christ

Published in New York, New York, by Mount Tabor Media, LLC, a branded imprint of Morgan James Publishing. Morgan James is a trademark of Morgan James, LLC. www.MorganJamesPublishing.com

ISBN 781642792621 paperback
ISBN 9781642792638 eBook
Library of Congress Control Number: 2018910666

Cover Design & Interior Design by:
Christopher Kirk
www.GFSstudio.com

Unless otherwise noted, Scripture is taken from the New American Standard Bible, copyright © 1960, 1962, 1963, 1968, 1971, 1972, 1973, 1975, 1977, 1995 by The Lockman Foundation.

Scripture marked GNT is taken from the Good News Translation, copyright © 1992 by American Bible Society.

Scripture marked TLB is taken from The Living Bible, copyright © 1971 by Tyndale House Foundation. Used by permission of Tyndale House Publishers Inc., Carol Stream, Illinois 60188. All rights reserved.

Scripture marked NIV is taken from THE NEW INTERNATIONAL VERSION®, NIV® Copyright © 1973, 1978, 1984, 2011 by Biblica, Inc.®.

Morgan James is a proud partner of Habitat for Humanity Peninsula and Greater Williamsburg. Partners in building since 2006.

Get involved today! Visit
MorganJamesPublishing.com/giving-back

And in all matters requiring information and balanced judgment, the king found these young men's advice ten times better than that of all the skilled magicians and wise astrologers in his realm.

Daniel 1:20, TLB

Come on this journey as we explore what it means to be a 10X-er for Jesus Christ. Discover the joy, peace, and abundance Christ offers us.

TABLE OF CONTENTS

East to West

Masterpiece

Abundance

10X

Finish Well

INTRODUCTION

My Journey to This Devotional Study

My sixty-seven-year journey has been filled with ups and downs, joys and heartaches, and victories and defeats. Roughly the first fifty years of my life were filled with self-doubt. I often struggled with feelings of insecurity, with thoughts that I wasn't good enough. The good news is that today, I realize who I am in Jesus Christ. I understand my past is behind me and my future is promised for eternity.

I think it's important for me to share my story so that you, too, can realize that no matter where you are today, there is hope and joy for you.

My story is a testament to God's grace. Growing up in a home with an alcoholic father my life was filled with fear, anxiety, and insecurities, some of which have followed me through most of my adult life. I've made poor decisions too numerous to count.

Even after giving my life to Christ in 1978, I struggled in my faith. Although I knew I was forgiven, I just couldn't accept the fact that God loved me despite my past. I failed to accept God's love and forgiveness.

Realizing this struggle, I finally discovered this truth: before I could truly accept God's love, I had to first completely love myself. Through God's grace, I accepted that I am good enough and am a new creation in Christ.

Today, I am immensely blessed by God's goodness. His faithfulness is new every morning. I truly believe that, as President Ronald Reagan once said, "Everything we need in life is contained in the holy Bible." I know, without a doubt, that if you seriously apply yourself to studying God's Word, you will truly discover joy within that comes from living in the fullness of his love. I know I have!

So, this is where the journey begins. There is one thing I have observed in my own life that has frequently been noticed in lives of other believers: we seem to lack a full understanding of what it means when Jesus said, "I came that they might have life and have it abundantly" (Jn. 10:10, NASB).

Several months ago, I led a devotion based on Daniel chapter 1. I encourage you, right now, to take a few moments to read chapter 1 in the book of Daniel. Basically, the story is about four young men who choose to honor God, rather than serve an earthly king. Here's how the text reads: "And in all matters requiring information and balanced judgment, the king found these young men's advice ten times better than that of all the skilled magicians and wise astrologers in his realm" (Dan. 1:20, TLB).

My prayer for you, if you choose to take this journey with me, is that God will reveal to you, through his Word and through your study, what it means for you to be a 10X-er in your life. I also pray that your life would be fuller, that you would truly experience the abundant life I believe Christ has for all of us. I pray that you would challenge yourself every day to claim God's abundance. May his love and grace radiate through you!

I have two final notes for you. First, this devotional study is in response to the prompting of the Holy Spirit. It is simply my interpretation of the readings with his guidance. My encouragement to you is not to judge my thoughts or my writing but to truly seek your own thoughts, discernment, and direction—to discover, each day, how you can walk in the fullness of Jesus Christ. Second, let me share a story about composer Johann Sebastian Bach:

> Whenever [Bach] began a new piece, he bowed his head and prayed, "Jesus, help me show your glory through the music I write. May it bring you joy even as it brings joy to your people." Without Jesus' help, Johann knew he'd never be able to complete the task. Before writing even one note, Johann carefully formed the letters *J.J.,* which stands for Jesu, Juva in Latin or Jesus help in English, at the top of the page. With that, the music began to pour from his soul and onto the page. When he was finally satisfied, he wrote the letters *SDG* at the bottom of the page: *Soli Deo Gloria*, For the Glory of God Alone. He hoped that when the music was played, it would point toward God.[1]

My prayer all along has been that this devotional book would bring honor and glory to my Lord and Savior, Jesus Christ. Thus, at the top of each page, you will see the two letters *J.J.,* which, in my mind, is not only asking for Jesus' help but also declaring that he would be glorified. At the end of each page, there will be the three letters, *SDG*, for the glory of God alone—which speaks for itself.

Carlos Rosales

HOW TO USE THIS BOOK

I've written this devotional book to be used five days per week over the next fifty-two weeks. My hope for the weekends is that you will put what you've learned that week into action—with your family, your friends, and your church.

Week one is reviewing our foundation, and the next fifty weeks are divided into five sections, which you'll find outlined in the table of contents (East to West; Masterpiece; Abundance; 10X; and Finish Well). The final week will be an action plan.

Each day is divided into five sections:

1. **Today's Verses**: Start by getting into God's Word; read the verse or verses listed. Read in-depth to get context and meaning.
2. **Additional Reading**: To expand your experience, challenge yourself to look up at least one additional verse of the three I suggest on the day's topic.
3. **My Thoughts**: Here, I have provided short reflections on how the Word spoke to me.
4. **Your Reflections**: Take a few moments to reflect on the verses you just read. Capture your thoughts on the lines provided or identify actions to put these verses to use in your daily walk.
5. **Prayer**: I provide a short prayer that captures the main points for the day's study. Pray this prayer or construct your own, but keep the prayer focused on living out what you've read—not your needs. Praying back the verses you just read is also very powerful.

If you will earnestly seek God's presence every day, take the time to read the verses, record your thoughts, and offer your prayer, you will be one step closer to becoming a 10X-er. It's been a blessing to explore God's Word and connect these topics. My prayer is that you will be richly blessed as you journey through the Scriptures to find your true calling.

Feel free to post any comments, thoughts, or additional readings from your daily study at www.10X4Christ.org

WEEK ONE

FOUNDATION

FOUNDATION   DAY ONE

Starting Point

Today's Verses—John 3:16 & Galatians 2:20

For God so loved the world, that He gave His only begotten Son, that whoever believes in Him shall not perish, but have eternal life.

I have been crucified with Christ. It is no longer I who live, but Christ who lives in me. And the life I now live in the flesh I live by faith in the Son of God, who loved me and gave himself for me.

Additional Reading: Exodus 15:2; Acts 4:12; 2 Peter 3:18

My Thoughts

I know that most of us are very familiar with John 3:16. We've consistently heard the verse since childhood, but maybe, for the first time, we can look at what the verse says. This verse starts out very simply: "God so loved the world, that he gave his only son." If you think about that for a minute, that kind of sacrifice must require a tremendous amount of love. As a father, I cannot imagine anything that would cause me to give up a son—especially for people who didn't deserve it. Yet, God willingly sacrificed his son so that he might have an eternal relationship with you and me.

How does the thought of spending eternity with God change the way we live every day? What a powerful thought! When you look at the second verse for today, Galatians 2:20, you see that we not only have hope for an eternal life but we also get to experience the reality that Christ lives in us.

So, as you contemplate these two verses, ask yourself, *How will my daily life reflect an eternal perspective? How will I live, considering this love and sacrifice?*

Your Reflections

_____

_____

_____

_____

_____

Prayer

Father God, keep me ever mindful of your sacrifice and gift of eternal life. May my life and actions reflect an eternal perspective. In Jesus' name I pray, amen.

FOUNDATION

Prayer

Today's Verses—1 Thessalonians 5:16-18 & Colossians 4:2-6

Rejoice always; pray without ceasing; in everything give thanks; for this is God's will for you in Christ Jesus.

Devote yourselves to prayer, keeping alert in it with an attitude of thanksgiving; praying at the same time for us as well, that God will open up to us a door for the word, so that we may speak forth the mystery of Christ, for which I have also been imprisoned; that I may make it clear in the way I ought to speak. Be wise in the way you act toward outsiders; make the most of every opportunity. Let your conversation be always full of grace, seasoned with salt, so that you may know how to answer everyone.

Additional Reading: 2 Chronicles 7:14-15; Psalm 145:18; Mark 11:24

My Thoughts

Prayer is vital to the Christian walk. Prayer is essentially how we communicate with our Savior. In the two verses above, we are encouraged to "pray without ceasing," but what does that mean? Are we to constantly pray about our requests, fears, and anxieties, as well as share our joy?

What is communication like for you with the people you're closest to? Is it mostly about complaints, mostly about your fears, or mostly about the things you want? My requests in all areas of my life are primarily a reflection of my heart: my innermost fears, my needs, my joys.

Prayer must be an integral part of our lives; it must be constant and ongoing. But I don't think prayer should be a laundry list of needs, wants, and desires. Prayer is nothing more than communicating with our Lord. I believe he desires for us to have an open dialogue to share our joys, our fears, and our concerns but also our plans or hopes for the future. Most importantly, he desires for us to share our plans for each day and ask for his guidance.

Your Reflections

_____

_____

_____

_____

_____

Prayer

Father God, I pray 2 Chronicles 7:14. I humble myself and seek your face today. Give me strength to turn from my sinful ways. I ask for your forgiveness and healing for my land, that your name might be glorified. In Jesus' name I pray, amen.

SDG

FOUNDATION   DAY THREE

Others

Today's Verses—Proverbs 15:22; 27:17 & Ecclesiastes 4:9-12

Without consultation, plans are frustrated, but with many counselors they succeed.

Iron sharpened iron so, one man sharpens another.

Two are better than one because they have a good return for their labor. For if either of them falls, the one will lift his companion. But woe to the one who falls when there is not another to lift him up. Furthermore, if two lie down together they keep warm, but how can one be warm alone? And if one can overpower him who is alone, two can resist him. A cord of three strands is not quickly torn apart.

Additional Reading: 1 John 1:3; 1 Thessalonians 5:5, 10-11; Hebrews 10:24

My Thoughts

The central theme in Today's Verses, I believe, is not to go at it alone. As you embark on this journey to live the abundant life Christ promised, find a friend or brother who's willing to take this journey with you. Connect with us on Facebook and become a part of our community.

Too often, we feel like our Christian walk is too personal to share with others. But I believe that to truly grow in your faith, you must be surrounded by others who encourage you and hold you accountable for your walk. Moses had Aaron, his brother, by his side. David had Jonathan to pray with him. Paul had Barnabas as his encourager. Who do you have?

Your Reflections

_____

_____

_____

_____

_____

_____

Prayer

Father God, I am grateful for the men in my life who keep me accountable. And thank you for my family; their love is a source of encouragement. Give me the wisdom and courage to speak truth into the lives of those you have given me to mentor and disciple. In the matchless name of Jesus I pray, amen.

FOUNDATION   DAY FOUR

Perseverance

Today's Verses—James 1:12 & Hebrews 10:36

Blessed is a man who perseveres under trial; for once he has been approved, he will receive the crown of life which the Lord has promised to those who love Him.

For you have need of endurance, so that when you have done the will of God you may receive what was promised.

Additional Reading: Psalm 27:14; Romans 12:12; Colossians 1:11-12

My Thoughts

One thing I know for certain is that Satan will try to defeat you as you seek an ongoing walk with Christ. Along your journey, you will face many obstacles, so it is important at the onset that you have a mind-set of perseverance.

Make a commitment now that no matter what comes your way or what obstacles you face, you will remain steadfast, not only in daily devotion and your walk with Christ but also in your continuing quest to discover the 10X lifestyle. You will be tested to remain faithful and will face many obstacles. The devil will try to render you ineffective, so remain steadfast in the power of Jesus Christ.

Your Reflections

_____

_____

_____

_____

_____

_____

Prayer

Loving Father, I am grateful for your Word that offers me wisdom and gives me hope. I rejoice in your goodness and pray that you will strengthen me daily to persevere. In Jesus' name I pray,

FOUNDATION

DAY FIVE

Devotional Plan

Today's Verses—Proverbs 16:9

The mind of man plans his way, but the Lord directs his steps.

Additional Reading: Proverbs 21:5; Jeremiah 29:11; Matthew 6:33

My Thoughts

This week, we have reviewed the foundations of our faith. We confirmed our faith in our eternal walk with Christ. We examined the idea of prayer and how it can impact our daily walk. We gave thought to enlisting the help of others so that they can stand beside us. And finally, we've committed to staying in the faith—to persevering no matter what Satan throws in our path.

Now, let's look at some practical things you can do to ensure you are faithful in a daily devotional study:

1. Determine the best place for you to spend time daily in prayer and devotion.
2. Decide what time of day or evening you can consistently set aside for your devotional time.
3. Tell someone you love about your commitment to this study and ask him to hold you accountable.
4. Get yourself a good study Bible, which will enable you to find additional verses on the daily topic.
5. Lay your plan before God and ask him to give you the discipline and commitment to complete this journey.

Your Reflections

_____

_____

_____

_____

_____

_____

Prayer

Father God, I am thankful for your presence in my life and for giving me the desire to seek you through this study. Give me the discipline to stay on task and always have a hunger for your Word that my life might glorify you. In Jesus' name I pray, amen.

SDG

EAST TO WEST

WEEK TWO
GOD'S GIFT

GOD'S GIFT
DAY ONE

Today's Verses—Ephesians 2:1-9

And you were dead in your trespasses and sins, in which you formerly walked according to the course of this world, according to the prince of the power of the air, of the spirit that is now working in the sons of disobedience. Among them we too all formerly lived in the lusts of our flesh, indulging the desires of the flesh and of the mind, and were by nature children of wrath, even as the rest. But God, being rich in mercy, because of His great love with which He loved us, even when we were dead in our transgressions, made us alive together with Christ (by grace you have been saved), and raised us up with Him, and seated us with Him in the heavenly places in Christ Jesus, so that in the ages to come He might show the surpassing riches of His grace in kindness toward us in Christ Jesus. For by grace you have been saved through faith; and that not of yourselves, it is the gift of God; not as a result of works, so that no one may boast.

Additional Reading: Romans 3:24; Psalm 51:1-13; 1 Corinthians 12:27

My Thoughts

Ephesians 2:1-9 is a difficult message for me and many people I know. How can I accept God's forgiveness when I know my past? But here is the good news: it's not about me or anything I can do. Rather, it is about God's great mercy and love for me, that he forgave me despite my past. As the passage says, we were dead in our sins, but by his grace, we are alive together with Christ. What great news and great hope!

A gift is offered without the need to give back. However, we have a responsibility to use the gift we have been blessed with. In this case, it's salvation. It's eternal life. It's being a King's kid. It's nothing we did or deserved. It was God demonstrating his great love for us. How will you use this wonderful gift?

Your Reflections

_____

_____

_____

_____

_____

Prayer

Father, hide Thy face from my sins and blot out all my iniquities. Create in me a clean heart, O God, and renew a steadfast spirit within me. Do not cast me away from Thy presence, and do not take Thy Holy Spirit from me. Restore to me the joy of Thy salvation and sustain me with a willing spirit. Then I will teach transgressors Thy ways, and sinners will be converted to Thee. Psalm 51:9-13, NASB

SDG

GOD'S GIFT   DAY TWO

Today's Verses—Romans 5:15-19

But the free gift is not like the transgression. For if by the transgression of the one the many died, much more did the grace of God and the gift by the grace of the one Man, Jesus Christ, abound to the many. The gift is not like that which came through the one who sinned; for on the one hand the judgment arose from one transgression resulting in condemnation, but on the other hand the free gift arose from many transgressions resulting in justification. For if by the transgression of the one, death reigned through the one, much more those who receive the abundance of grace and of the gift of righteousness will reign in life through the One, Jesus Christ. So then as through one transgression there resulted condemnation to all men, even so through one act of righteousness there resulted justification of life to all men. For as through the one man's disobedience the many were made sinners, even so through the obedience of the One the many will be made righteous.

Additional Reading: Ephesians 2:8; Acts 4:12; John 3:11; Ephesians 4:11

My Thoughts

Romans 5:15-19 is one of the many examples of God's gifts to us. Because of Adam's disobedience, we were all condemned. My favorite part of this reading is verse 17, where Paul talks about God's abundant provision of grace and the righteous reign in life through Jesus Christ.

So, how does that apply today to our daily lives? I think, to start with, we need to recognize that a magnificent gift has been bestowed upon us: the gift of eternal life and the hope of spending eternity with our Lord and Savior, Jesus Christ.

I firmly believe that the abundant life Christ promises begins with us fully understanding the responsibility and the joy we have in walking in the righteousness of Christ.

Your Reflections

_____

_____

_____

_____

_____

_____

Prayer

Gracious Father, I am grateful for the gift of salvation and the great sacrifice Jesus made on the cross for me. Give me the strength to walk in a manner that acknowledges this sacrifice and that brings honor and glory to you. In Jesus' name I pray, amen.

SDG

GOD'S GIFT   DAY THREE

Today's Verses—Ephesians 1:3-6

Blessed be the God and Father of our Lord Jesus Christ, who has blessed us with every spiritual blessing in the heavenly places in Christ, just as He chose us in Him before the foundation of the world, that we would be holy and blameless before Him. In love He predestined us to adoption as sons through Jesus Christ to Himself, according to the kind intention of His will, to the praise of the glory of His grace, which He freely bestowed on us in the Beloved.

Additional Reading: Isaiah 41:10; Deuteronomy 28:1-14; Romans 6:23

My Thoughts

As I read Ephesians 1:3-6 this morning, I'm filled with joy. First, it talks about how we are blessed with every spiritual blessing in Christ. Just imagine what that means in our lives on a day-to-day basis and what it can mean for abundant living. There's so much in these verses to encourage us, namely, redemption through his blood and forgiveness of sins.

We rejoice to learn that we are God's adopted children in Jesus Christ. We are to be the message of truth through the gospel.

Now, it's your turn to make the choice to live these verses in your life today. You have been selected to serve the creator of the universe, the King of Kings and Lord of Lords! How does that make you feel, and how will you serve?

Your Reflections

_____

_____

_____

_____

_____

_____

Prayer

Father God, I am thankful for the richness of your blessings and provisions for my life. I pray, dear Lord, that you will give me the strength to walk in these blessings and that I will fully live in your power and not my own. To your glory and in Jesus' name I pray, amen.

GOD'S GIFT   DAY FOUR

Today's Verses—2 Timothy 1:6-11

For this reason, I remind you to kindle afresh the gift of God which is in you through the laying on of my hands. For God has not given us a spirit of timidity, but of power and love and discipline. Therefore do not be ashamed of the testimony of our Lord or of me His prisoner, but join with me in suffering for the gospel according to the power of God, who has saved us and called us with a holy calling, not according to our works, but according to His own purpose and grace which was granted us in Christ Jesus from all eternity, but now has been revealed by the appearing of our Savior Christ Jesus, who abolished death and brought life and immortality to light through the gospel, for which I was appointed a preacher and an apostle and a teacher.

Additional Reading: James 1:7; Romans 8:39; 1 Peter 4:10

My Thoughts

Wow. If these passages don't give you joy and excitement and passion, perhaps nothing will. In 2 Timothy 1:6-11, we're called to kindle afresh the gift of God and not in a timid fashion but with power, love, and discipline. We are reminded not to be ashamed of the gospel and our holy calling.

These passages remind us that Christ has abolished death, and we are appointed as preachers, apostles, and teachers. So, go forth boldly and live the abundant life in his power. Claim the wisdom the Holy Spirit brings to you and be like the young men in Daniel 1:20, ten times wiser.

Your Reflections

_____

_____

_____

_____

_____

_____

Prayer

Thank you, dear Father, that my holy calling is granted to me by Christ Jesus according to his purpose and his grace. Help me to walk in this calling to your honor and glory. In the precious name of Jesus I pray, amen.

GOD'S GIFT

DAY FIVE

Today's Verses—Galatians 2:20

I have been crucified with Christ; and it is no longer I who live, but Christ lives in me; and the life which I now live in the flesh I live by faith in the Son of God, who loved me and gave Himself up for me.

Additional Reading: Romans 8:28, 14:8; Matthew 6:24; 1 Corinthians 12:7

My Thoughts

If Galatians 2:20 isn't a challenge to live a 10X-er lifestyle, I don't know what could be! The living God lives in me, for the Son of God gave his life for us.

If we can walk every day in the power of Jesus Christ that dwells in us, how can we ever despair? I choose today to live: to walk in that power, to claim victory in his Spirit, and to use the gifts he has given me.

How can you impact the people in your life as you walk with the Savior? What influence will you have to turn back the evil one in his quest to defeat the saints? Walk in the power of the Holy One, Jesus Christ, today!

Your Reflections

_____

_____

_____

_____

_____

_____

Prayer

Gracious Father, help me fully yield to your authority and allow your Spirit to work in me, that I might be strengthened to walk in boldness, proclaiming the good news of Jesus Christ. To your honor and glory, amen.

WEEK THREE

FORGIVENESS

FORGIVENESS DAY ONE

Today's Verses—2 Chronicles 7:14

And My people who are called by My name humble themselves and pray and seek My face and turn from their wicked ways, then I will hear from heaven, will forgive their sin and will heal their land.

Additional Reading: Ephesians 4:32; 1 John 1:9; Colossians 3:13; Psalm 103:10-14

My Thoughts

What often keeps us from living the abundant life is a failure to accept God's forgiveness. We also fail to humbly seek our God and pray for the transformation that comes from forgiveness of our transgressions.

What keeps us from fully walking with God? Is it our desire to be part of the world and still try to walk with God? God wants our whole heart. He wants us to turn from our sin, from our wickedness, and seek him every day. He's a God of mercy and lovingkindness, so walk in forgiveness and walk as a 10X-er.

He desires that we walk in his light so we can be the light that displaces the darkness.

Your Reflections

_____

_____

_____

_____

_____

_____

Prayer

Father God, help me to remain humble and to seek your face and your righteousness daily. Give me the strength to walk with you, that I might bring honor and glory to you. In Jesus' name I pray, amen.

FORGIVENESS   DAY TWO

Today's Verses—Isaiah 55:7

Let the wicked forsake his way and the unrighteous man his thoughts; and let him return to the Lord, and He will have compassion on him, and to our God, for He will abundantly pardon.

Additional Reading: James 5:16; Luke 6:37; Psalm 32:5

My Thoughts

Although we have received God's forgiveness, the evil one will attempt daily to draw us back to our old, sinful ways. He will lure us into little sins that lead to bigger sins. Many times, an impure thought will take us places we don't want to go.

As you start your day, commit to be fully dedicated to the Lord. Ask him to guard your heart, your mind, and your deeds. Remember, sin will always take you further than you intended to go, keep you longer than you intended to stay, and cost you more than you intended to pay. Being prepared means being aware and in prayer.

Your Reflections

_____

_____

_____

_____

_____

_____

Prayer

Father God, thank you for your gift of salvation and the forgiveness of my sins. I pray, dear Lord, that you give me the strength to resist temptation and the things of the world that lead me to sin. In Jesus' name I pray, amen.

FORGIVENESS   DAY THREE

Today's Verses—1 John 1:9-10

If we confess our sins, He is faithful and righteous to forgive us our sins and to cleanse us from all unrighteousness. If we say that we have not sinned, we make Him a liar and his Word is not in us.

Additional Reading: Ecclesiastes 7:20; Luke 7:44-50; Psalm 32:5; Acts 2:38

My Thoughts

I wonder, sometimes, if forgiveness is taken for granted. Was that simple act of confessing our sins all it took? Is it that easy? Stop to think about what Jesus did for you to be granted this forgiveness. Because of his great love for us, he was willing to be crucified and die a horrible death on the cross to pay the price for our sins.

My challenge to you is to walk in his righteousness every day, to remain steadfast, to walk in his strength and his discipline that you might sin no more. Rise with wings of eagles! Soar!

Your Reflections

_____

_____

_____

_____

_____

_____

Prayer

Gracious Father, I am so thankful that my salvation in Jesus Christ not only cleanses me from my sin but also offers me a relationship with you, my God. Help me this day to walk in your righteousness. In Jesus' name I pray, amen.

FORGIVENESS

DAY FOUR

Today's Verses—Ephesians 1:7

In Him we have redemption through His blood, the forgiveness of our trespasses, according to the riches of His grace.

Additional Reading: Colossians 1:20-22; Romans 3:24-26; Psalm 111:9-10; Isaiah 44:22

My Thoughts

What do you think about when you hear the word *redemption*? When was the last time you redeemed a coupon or a gift card? What was the value of your redemption? What is the value of your eternal life? Can you put a price on it?

Christ paid the ultimate price for our lives. He redeemed us for all eternity. Think about the price he gladly paid for us to have fellowship with the Savior. Live the abundant life. Walk in his righteousness to honor his sacrifice.

Your Reflections

_____

_____

_____

_____

_____

_____

Prayer

Father God, help me to live a fully committed life to your service, yielding to your will and plan for me. Help me to be ever mindful of the great sacrifice you made for me. In the matchless name of Jesus I pray, amen.

FORGIVENESS

DAY FIVE

Today's Verses—Hebrews 5:7-9

In the days of His flesh, He offered up both prayers and supplications with loud crying and tears to the One able to save Him from death, and He was heard because of His piety. Although He was a Son, He learned obedience from the things which He suffered. And having been made perfect, He became to all those who obey Him the source of eternal salvation.

Additional Reading: Isaiah 44:22; Ephesians 5:1-8; Romans 5:8

My Thoughts

I'm humbled that the son of the living God was obedient unto death for my sins. Our eternal hope and salvation should never be taken lightly.

In our daily walk, we should be ever thankful for our salvation and walk in a manner worthy of the calling (Ephesians 4:1). With our forgiveness assured and our eternity secured, we stand on a firm foundation for the abundant life in Jesus Christ.

Walk as if an enormous debt has been paid for you—it has—and be grateful.

Your Reflections

_____

_____

_____

_____

_____

_____

Prayer

Father God, thank you for the blessings of my salvation and eternal life through my Lord and Savior, Jesus Christ. Give me the strength to remain steadfast in your will and plan for my life, honoring Jesus' great sacrifice. In his name I pray, amen.

WEEK FOUR

OVERCOMING DARKNESS

OVERCOMING DARKNESS   DAY ONE

Today's Verses—1 John 1:5-7

This is the message we have heard from Him and announce to you, that God is Light, and in Him there is no darkness at all. If we say that we have fellowship with Him and yet walk in the darkness, we lie and do not practice the truth; but if we walk in the Light as He Himself is in the Light, we have fellowship with one another, and the blood of Jesus His Son cleanses us from all sin.

Additional Reading: John 11:10; Acts 26:18; I Thessalonians 5:5

My Thoughts

We live in a world surrounded by darkness. At times, the darkness seems to overtake the light—at least on the surface. Our commission is to walk in the light as Jesus walked in the light.

Our family frequently spends time in the woods where the stars shine brightly, lighting up the sky. In the city, light pollution keeps us from having the same experience. The contrast is amazing. The world we live in acts very much the same way; we let it dull our lives and dim our light.

We have the power to overcome the darkness by the power we have in Christ. Where is there darkness in your home, community, or church? Has the darkness taken over areas of your life? We must stand firm and continue to be light in the world and the lives of the people we meet.

Your Reflections

_____

_____

_____

_____

_____

_____

Prayer

Dear Lord, you are the Light of the World that truly casts out the darkness. Help me, Lord Jesus, to walk in your light and cast out the darkness in your strength and power. In your name I pray, amen.

OVERCOMING DARKNESS · DAY TWO

Today's Verses—Luke 1:78-79

Because of the tender mercy of our God, with which the Sunrise from on high will visit us, To shine upon those who sit in darkness and the shadow of death, to guide our feet into the way of peace.

Additional Reading: 1 John 2:8-11; Isaiah 9:2; Psalm 18:28

My Thoughts

Our Lord is commanding us to shine his light on the darkness and those who walk in the shadow of death. We need to extend mercy to those we know who are in darkness and bring them into the marvelous light of Jesus Christ.

How is your light shining in your walk? Are you a beacon of hope to those around you? The light brings clarity. Clarity shows direction, and with direction, you can define God's will for your life. It also offers you strength and love to be a light to others.

Your Reflections

_____

_____

_____

_____

_____

_____

Prayer

Loving Father, thank you that the Light of the World shines in me. Help me to be the light in a dark world. In Jesus' name I pray, amen.

OVERCOMING DARKNESS   DAY THREE

Today's Verses—John 1:4
In Him was life, and the life was the Light of men.

Additional Reading: Luke 1:79; Psalm 139:12; Colossians 1:13

My Thoughts

Jesus is our light. Without him, it is impossible to escape darkness. We are told that Satan is the king of darkness, but he cannot prevail against us.

So, where is darkness defeating you? Where have you allowed it to creep into your life? Are there hidden areas of sin in your life that are ruled by this darkness?

Now is the time to confess your sin. Remove the darkness and claim the light of Christ. You can be victorious as you walk in his light.

Your Reflections

_____

_____

_____

_____

_____

_____

Prayer

Father God, you have delivered me from darkness. Your light shines as a beacon in the world. Help me, dear Lord, to remain in your light and honor you with my light. In your name I pray, amen.

OVERCOMING DARKNESS   DAY FOUR

Today's Verses—John 8:12

Then Jesus again spoke to them, saying, "I am the Light of the world; he who follows Me will not walk in the darkness, but will have the Light of life."

Additional Reading: 2 Corinthians 6:14; Ephesians 6:12; Isaiah 50:10

My Thoughts

Followers of Jesus Christ are called to walk in his light. So, how do we do that? I believe it's by speaking truth in people's life.

Recently, while having lunch with a friend, I was reminded of our call to be light. My friend told me about a play he had attended, in which his daughter had a role. After mentioning that she attends a secular university, he told me that he was appalled by the foul language the students used in their production. I asked him if he was going to speak to someone at the school to express his displeasure; he replied that he wasn't because he didn't want to "cause any trouble." This is the kind of darkness we allow every day in our lives but don't act against—for the same reason.

We must be beacons of light in every area of our life. Our call is to be the lighthouse in a dark world, leading others to the safety and peace of Jesus.

Your Reflections

_____

_____

_____

_____

_____

_____

Prayer

Father God, you have called me into your light, and I am thankful. Help me to keep my light bright by walking in your will and righteousness. May your light cast out the darkness in my life. Keep me faithful and humble, that your light may shine brightly through me. In Jesus' name I pray, amen.

OVERCOMING DARKNESS   DAY FIVE

Today's Verses—Isaiah 2:5

Come, house of Jacob, and let us walk in the light of the Lord.

Additional Reading: 2 Corinthians 4:6; Romans 13:12; Matthew 6:23

My Thoughts

As children of the living God, followers of Jesus Christ, we are of the house of Jacob. Our heritage in Christ is tied to the early saints of the Old Testament.

These early saints struggled with sin and darkness much like we do. They were warned against worshiping idols and being influenced by the world around them. What are our idols today? What gods do we worship that keep us from the light of Christ? Jesus is the Light of the World; where there is light, there is no darkness. Does his light shine in you and through you?

Your Reflections

Prayer

Father God, I realize that your light will only shine through me as I remain faithful and close to you, the source of light and power. Guide me during this day, dear Lord, as I seek to bring your light into the darkness of my world. Help me to have boldness and strength to be your light. In your name I pray, amen.

WEEK FIVE

EAST TO WEST

EAST TO WEST DAY ONE

Today's Verses—Psalm 103:12

As far as the east is from the west, so far has He removed our transgressions from us.

Additional Reading: Acts 2:38; Hebrews 10:26-27; 1 John 1:8-10

My Thoughts

I remember the first time I read this verse. I thought, Cool. Not only have I been forgiven, but I am also separated from my sins. It was a great comfort to know that all my sins and past failures were gone, separated from me as far as the East is from the West.

Now, is this a free ride to continue to sin since you can later ask for forgiveness and those sins will be forgiven as well? Maybe so, but what I have learned is this: that type of understanding only gets you further behind. Sin, forgiveness, sin, forgiveness—or, "rinse and repeat" as it says on a shampoo bottle. In my own life, I have found that once I commit a sin but fail to repent, it impacts my daily walk. I get further and further from the Savior.

The path to the abundant life in Christ is just that: a path, a narrow path. Yes, we can continue to walk in sin, but that just takes us off the path. I believe God forgives us every time we sin, but by staying on the path, our lives become more focused on Kingdom activity.

Your Reflections

_____

_____

_____

_____

_____

_____

Prayer

Gracious God, I am awed at your love and forgiveness. I am grateful that my sins are forgiven and forgotten. Help me, dear Lord, to remain faithful and seek your righteousness daily. In Jesus' name I pray, amen.

EAST TO WEST   DAY TWO

Today's Verses—Ezekiel 18:21-23

"But if the wicked man turns from all his sins which he has committed and observes all My stat-utes and practices justice and righteousness, he shall surely live; he shall not die. All his transgres-sions which he has committed will not be remembered against him; because of his righteousness which he has practiced, he will live. Do I have any pleasure in the death of the wicked," declares the Lord God, "rather than that he should turn from his ways and live?"

Additional Reading: Ephesians 2:1-10; Isaiah 1:18; Malachi 3:17

My Thoughts

God's desire is for us to do what's right, leave our past behind, and walk in his righteousness. As Ezekiel 18:22 says, our sins will not be remembered against us. What a blessing!

Mark Batterson states in his book Chase the Lion that when the devil reminds us of our past, we need to remind him of his future.[2]

If God has forgiven and forgotten our sins, why do we continue to allow them to affect our actions? I feel that, many times, the stain of our past—the stain of our sins—limits our ability to learn how to grow and act. God's plan for our life today and in the future is not impacted by our past unless we allow it to be.

Your Reflections

_____

_____

_____

_____

_____

_____

Prayer

Gracious Father, thank you that my past is forgiven and forgotten. Give me the strength to leave the past behind me and claim a new beginning each day. To your honor and glory, in Jesus' name I pray, amen.

---

2   Mark Batterson, *Chase the Lion: If Your Dream Doesn't Scare You, It's Too Small* (Portland: Multnomah, 2016).

EAST TO WEST

DAY THREE

Today's Verses—Acts 3:19

Therefore, repent and return, so that your sins may be wiped away, in order that times of refreshing may come from the presence of the Lord.

Additional Reading: 1 John 3:2; Isaiah 55:7; Isaiah 61:10

My Thoughts

Think about a new life, a new beginning where your past is totally forgiven. Walking with the Spirit of the living God in you, what will you do with your life? How can you be different than who you are today?

Forget about the old life and start a new relationship with a loving heavenly Father. What kind of relationship do you have with your earthly father?

How much of your relationship is impacted by the past? Now is the time to move into a new relationship with everyone in your life with a clean slate. Offer the same forgiveness you have received.

Your Reflections

_____

_____

_____

_____

_____

_____

Prayer

Father God, I rejoice in your refreshment, the peace and joy that comes in all circumstances because of your presence. Guide me, oh, Lord, to do your will and bring honor to your holy name. In that holy name I pray, amen.

EAST TO WEST DAY FOUR

Today's Verses—Isaiah 43:25

I, even I, am the one who wipes out your transgressions for My own sake, and I will not remember your sins.

Additional Reading: 1 John 1:5-10; 2 Corinthians 5:1; James 1:17

My Thoughts

What a wonderful God we serve, one who sent his only son to die for our transgressions. Once we take our focus off our sin and our past, can we think more like a 10X-er?

Only when we walk fully in the Holy Spirit can we fully walk without fear. God wants us to trust him enough not to follow the ways of the world and, instead, to follow him with abandonment.

As we continue to immerse ourselves in the Word, we will come away with a new sense of hope, confidence, and victory through Jesus.

Your Reflections

_____

_____

_____

_____

_____

_____

Prayer

Father God, once again I come before you with a grateful heart. You are the true and mighty God and have welcomed me into your family through the blood of Jesus. Help me to be ever mindful of this sacrifice. Help me walk in a manner worthy of my calling. In Jesus' name I pray, amen.

EAST TO WEST   DAY FIVE

Today's Verses—Colossians 1:13-14

For He rescued us from the domain of darkness and transferred us to the kingdom of His Beloved Son, in whom we have redemption, the forgiveness of sins.

Additional Reading: Jeremiah 32:27; Revelation 20:12; 1 Corinthians 5:7

My Thoughts

How will you walk in his Kingdom? Too often, we lead our lives as if we have been defeated, yet our redemption in Christ gives us victory in every area of our lives.

What things are holding you back? Where have you allowed your past to keep you from fully entering the service of the living God?

Make a list of all the things that are holding you back; give them to God. He is your champion and will guide you in your quest to serve him in a new and mighty way.

Your Reflections

_____

_____

_____

_____

_____

_____

Prayer

Father God, thank you that I am a new creation in you. My sins are forgiven, and my future is secure. May my life reflect your love and grace, and may it be a sweet fragrance to you. In Jesus' name I pray, amen.

WEEK SIX

ACCEPTANCE

ACCEPTANCE

Today's Verses—Romans 10:8-10

But what does it say? "The word is near you, in your mouth and in your heart"—that is, the word of faith which we are preaching, that if you confess with your mouth Jesus as Lord, and believe in your heart that God raised Him from the dead, you will be saved; for with the heart a person believes, resulting in righteousness, and with the mouth he confesses, resulting in salvation.

Additional Reading: Romans 8:31-39; 2 Peter 3:9; Malachi 3:17

My Thoughts

As we begin our in-depth look at acceptance, ask yourself these questions: Have I fully accepted my salvation and my place in God's master plan? Has my faith led to a new acceptance of challenges and fears?

To live the 10X lifestyle, you must fully accept your calling. Do you think Moses fully accepted his call from God at first? He was certainly doubtful at first, questioning God's judgment: "I'm not a good speaker. Can't you send someone else? Isn't there someone more qualified?"

Moses was focused on what he not could do, not what God could do through him. He failed to accept the full power and strength of the living God. Where are you failing to walk daily in the power and strength of God? Seek him. Accept his authority and live in him!

Your Reflections

_____

_____

_____

_____

_____

_____

Prayer

Father God, I fully accept your salvation and the renewal you offer. I am reminded of these verses in Romans 8:37-39. I offer them as a prayer today: "But in all these things we overwhelmingly conquer through Him who loved us. For I am convinced that neither death, nor life, nor angels, nor principalities, nor things present, nor things to come, nor powers, nor heights, nor depth, nor any other created thing, shall be able to separate us from the love of God, which is in Christ Jesus our Lord." In his name I pray, amen.

ACCEPTANCE

Today's Verses—John 6:35-38

Jesus said to them, "I am the bread of life; he who comes to Me will not hunger, and he who believes in Me will never thirst. But I said to you that you have seen Me, and yet do not believe. All that the Father gives Me will come to Me, and the one who comes to Me I will certainly not cast out. For I have come down from heaven, not to do My own will, but the will of Him who sent Me."

Additional Reading: John 1:12; Acts 4:12; Philippians 4:6-9

My Thoughts

Apparently, the people Jesus addresses in these verses had issues accepting who Jesus was. Jesus was all about doing his father's business. In John 6:35-38, he is reminding his listeners (and us) that if we believe, we will never be cast out.

Where do you hunger or thirst in your walk? Jesus promises to satisfy our spiritual hunger, but are you satisfied? First, we must recognize the fact that God is sufficient to meet all our needs—most importantly, the needs of our soul. When we are hungry, where do we go? When we thirst, what satisfies us?

What does your soul hunger for? Only the Word of God can satisfy this hunger. Jesus is the Bread of Life. Let him satisfy you fully.

Your Reflections

_____

_____

_____

_____

_____

_____

Prayer

Loving Father, your love and grace and forgiveness are all I need. You are a light to my path and a joy to my heart. Thank you for your unending love. In Jesus' name, I pray, amen.

SDG

ACCEPTANCE DAY THREE

Today's Verses—Galatians 5:1

It was for freedom that Christ set us free; therefore, keep standing firm and do not be subject again to a yoke of slavery.

Additional Reading: 1 Corinthians 16:13-14; 2 Timothy 3:12-17; James 5:11

My Thoughts

Experiencing complete freedom can only come from completely accepting God's forgiveness. The yoke of slavery can take many forms. Our thoughts can act as a yoke when they take us away from what is pure and right. Our job or work can be a yoke when it keeps us from serving.

Our hobbies and recreation can be yokes if they keep us from living fully for the Lord. Even our families can be a yoke if we put them above our God. Free yourself from these yokes and stand firm in your salvation.

Your Reflections

_____

_____

_____

_____

_____

_____

Prayer

Gracious Father, I pray this day that I might die to self and live for you. I pray that my life would be radically changed by you. You have given me a new heart. Help me serve you. In Jesus' name I pray, amen.

ACCEPTANCE   DAY FOUR

Today's Verses—Psalm 1:1-3

How blessed is the man who does not walk in the counsel of the wicked, nor stand in the path of sinners, nor sit in the seat of scoffers! But his delight is in the law of the Lord, And in His law, he meditates day and night. He will be like a tree firmly planted by streams of water, which yields its fruit in its season and its leaf does not wither; and in whatever he does, he prospers.

Additional Reading: John 14:6; Galatians 2:20; Proverbs 14:26-27

My Thoughts

Prosperity can mean different things to different people. For many years, I believed prosperity meant having plenty of money in the bank and having the freedom to do whatever I wanted, whenever I wanted. But over the years, the Word has helped me redefine prosperity.

Today, prosperity, for me, is more about living in the richness of God's will, walking with him daily, and seeking his direction for my life. Walking fully in God's presence brings about a prosperity that goes beyond the riches of this world; it is the prosperity of being secure in his love and care. Choosing to study God's Word and to meditate on it gives you a sense of peace and confidence in knowing that God's plan is clear and good for you.

Where is the fruit in your walk and how does it glorify God? Even in calamity, do you radiate his peace and joy? What season of your walk are you in, and what fruit are you yielding?

Your Reflections

_____

_____

_____

_____

_____

_____

Prayer

My Lord, I have been crucified with Christ. It is no longer I who live, but Christ who lives in me. The life which I now live in the flesh is the life I live by putting faith in the Son of God, who loved me and delivered himself up for me (Galatians 2:20, NASB). In his holy name I pray, amen.

ACCEPTANCE DAY FIVE

Today's Verses—Ephesians 1:4-6

Just as He chose us in Him before the foundation of the world, that we would be holy and blameless before Him. In love He predestined us to adoption as sons through Jesus Christ to Himself, according to the kind intention of His will, to the praise of the glory of His grace, which He freely bestowed on us in the Beloved.

Additional Reading: John 5:24; Hebrews 13:5-6; Revelation 3:20

My Thoughts

What a glorious God we serve. From before the creation of the world, we were chosen as sons through Jesus Christ. So, what does it mean to be the King's kid?

Walking in the peace and joy of living for the Kingdom is what we are called to do. What does the Lord's prayer teach us? "Your will be done on earth as it is in heaven" (Matthew 6:10). How can we bring the Kingdom to this earth?

We are God's chosen, working to this end, living by the Spirit to reflect his character and love. Our lives should model God's Kingdom on earth.

Your Reflections

_____

_____

_____

_____

_____

_____

Prayer

Father God, I marvel at your goodness. I join the heavens and the earth to sing your praises. I have passed from death to life. Thank you for your grace and forgiveness. In Jesus' name I pray, amen.

WEEK SEVEN
REPENTANCE

REPENTANCE   DAY ONE

Today's Verses—Matthew 3:8-10

Therefore, bear fruit in keeping with repentance; and do not suppose that you can say to your-selves, "We have Abraham for our father"; for I say to you that from these stones God is able to raise up children to Abraham. The axe is already laid at the root of the trees; therefore, every tree that does not bear good fruit is cut down and thrown into the fire.

Additional Reading: Hebrews 6:1; 2 Corinthians 7:9-10; Acts 26:20

My Thoughts

Repentance must be sincere and from the heart. Once we accept Jesus as our Lord and Savior, it doesn't mean we are free from the temptation to sin. The family we are accepted into is rich in heritage, but we shouldn't become arrogant like the "brood of vipers" John the Baptist refers to in Luke 3:7

We are called not only to repent from our sins but also to bear fruit. Here's the catch: if we don't have a truly repentant heart, we won't bear much fruit. You can walk around like many of the New Testament priests who had rituals full of piety but were still hypocrites. Examine your heart, repent of your sins, and walk according to God's call for your life. You will bear much fruit for the Kingdom.

Your Reflections

_____

_____

_____

_____

_____

_____

Prayer

Loving Father, I am blessed by you and the new life you have given me. Dear Lord, help me to have a repentant heart and strengthen me to bear your fruit for your glory. In your holy name I pray, amen.

REPENTANCE

DAY TWO

Today's Verses—Acts 3:19-21

Therefore, repent and return, so that your sins may be wiped away, in order that times of refreshing may come from the presence of the Lord; and that He may send Jesus, the Christ appointed for you, whom heaven must receive until the period of restoration of all things about which God spoke by the mouth of His holy prophets from ancient time.

Additional Reading: 2 Chronicles 7:14; 2 Peter 3:9; Ezekiel 18:21-23

My Thoughts

God's plan for our lives offers so much joy. We are asked to rejoice always and give thanks in all things (1 Thess. 5:16-18), but without true repentance, our joy will be short-lived. So how do we experience the "times of refreshing" (Acts 3:19)? The message is clear. Repent and return, and your sins are wiped away.

Sin in our lives can zap our energy and leave us depleted. This is never a good place to be. God wants us energized for the work he has called us to. Once we have repented from sin and received God's forgiveness, it brings a new energy and excitement that gives us power to face the battle and come out victorious. Do you feel his energy and power in your walk? How will you make a difference today?

Your Reflections

_____

_____

_____

_____

_____

_____

Prayer

Dear Lord, renew in me each day a passion and hunger for serving you. Your mighty strength and power have delivered me from temptation and given me a new vision of you. In Jesus' name I pray, amen.

SDG

REPENTANCE DAY THREE

Today's Verses—James 4:7-10

Submit therefore to God. Resist the devil and he will flee from you. Draw near to God and He will draw near to you. Cleanse your hands, you sinners; and purify your hearts, you double-minded. Be miserable and mourn and weep; let your laughter be turned into mourning and your joy to gloom. Humble yourselves in the presence of the Lord, and He will exalt you.

Additional Reading: Luke 13:3; Matthew 4:7; Jonah 3:10

My Thoughts

Years ago, as a young believer, I heard Dr. W. A. Criswell teach on John 13:10: "Jesus said to him, 'He who has bathed needs only to wash his feet, but is completely clean; and you are clean, but not all of you.'" Dr. Criswell explained that even though we are clean (from sin), the washing of our feet symbolizes the need for us to daily ask for the forgiveness of our sins.

God gives us the power to resist the evil one. If we draw near to Jesus, the devil has no power over us, and he will flee.

Repentance doesn't mean we won't sin any longer once we accept Jesus as our Savior. It simply means that if we do sin, we need to turn away from that sin and ask for forgiveness. Do your feet need to be washed?

Your Reflections

_____

_____

_____

_____

_____

_____

Prayer

Heavenly Father, you teach us in James 4 that if we submit to you and resist the devil, then he will flee. You also tell us that if we draw near to you, you will draw near to us. Help me, dear Lord, to do these things, that I might be comforted by your nearness. In Jesus' name I pray, amen.

REPENTANCE

DAY FOUR

Today's Verses—Joel 2:13

And rend your heart and not your garments. Now return to the Lord your God, For He is gracious and compassionate, Slow to anger, abounding in lovingkindness and relenting of evil.

Additional Reading: Proverbs 28:13; Romans 2:4; 2 Timothy 2:25

My Thoughts

Dr. Tony Evans says that when you find yourself going in the wrong direction on the road, you need to take the next exit and turn around. Too often, we find ourselves traveling in the wrong direction but can't seem to find the exit to turn around.

Is finding the exit the issue, or is the road we're on too much fun to exit? Are we on the "highway to hell" as the old AC/DC song says? Examine your highways at work, with your family, in your personal habits, and with your friends. If you are headed in the wrong direction, now is the time to find the quickest exit and turn around. God is there waiting for you. He alone offers you the strength to overcome your weakness.

Your Reflections

_____

_____

_____

_____

_____

_____

Prayer

Gracious Father, you are the one and only true God. You are the almighty God, and yet you know and love me. Give me, Lord, a repentant heart and the courage to walk in your light and righteousness in this dark and fallen world. In Jesus' name I pray, amen.

SDG

REPENTANCE

DAY FIVE

Today's Verses—Revelation 3:19

Those whom I love, I reprove and discipline; therefore, be zealous and repent.

Additional Reading: Acts 17:30; Isaiah 44:22; Psalm 38:18

My Thoughts

Newton's third law states that for every action, there is an equal and opposite reaction. Sin is a lot like that in our lives; for every sin, there are consequences. Although we are forgiven, our actions can have consequences. I had a very close friend who constantly told little "white" lies. After a while, it bothered me, so I confronted him. He replied, "I never lied to you!" The result was an end to the friendship. He didn't see it as a lack of integrity.

Our bodies are the temple of the Holy Spirit, so ask yourself, *Is the Spirit having as much fun as I am?* Ultimately, sin separates us from God and keeps us from receiving his full blessings. Are there areas in your life that still need repentance? Ask God to help you overcome these areas and fully walk in his righteousness.

Your Reflections

_____

_____

_____

_____

_____

_____

Prayer

Father God, I praise your holy name. I give thanks for your love, grace, and, most of all, Jesus. Help me to honor your lordship in my life by having a repentant heart. In the matchless name of Jesus I pray, amen.

WEEK EIGHT

RENEWING YOUR MIND

RENEWING YOUR MIND   DAY ONE

Today's Verses—Romans 12:2

And do not be conformed to this world, but be transformed by the renewing of your mind, so that you may prove what the will of God is, that which is good and acceptable and perfect.

Additional Reading: Ephesians 4:23-25; 1 Peter 1:13-15; Psalm 37:1-6

My Thoughts

Our transformation begins at salvation, but, almost immediately, the devil tries to distract us with the things of this world. We are reminded of this in 1 Peter 5:8 NIV, "Be alert and of sober mind. Your enemy the devil prowls around like a roaring lion looking for someone to devour."

Renewing our mind takes a daily commitment to studying God's Word and to praying that God will give us the strength and courage to resist temptation and evil. The Holy Spirit dwells in us, but our free will lets us make choices. Only you can decide the level of your commitment to study and prayer and to remaining steadfast in your transformation.

Your Reflections

_____

_____

_____

_____

_____

_____

Prayer

Gracious Father, I pray the words of 1 Peter 1:15-16: "But like the Holy One who called you, be holy yourselves also in your behavior; because it is written, 'You shall be holy, for I am Holy.'" Father, guide me this day, that I might walk in your holiness. In Jesus' name I pray, amen.

RENEWING YOUR MIND   DAY TWO

Today's Verses—Colossians 1:28

We proclaim Him, admonishing every man and teaching every man with all wisdom, so that we may present every man complete in Christ.

Additional Reading: John 8:3; 1 Corinthians 2:16; Titus 1:15

My Thoughts

"Within the covers of the Bible are the answers for all the problems men face," said fortieth US president, Ronald Reagan. There is little doubt that President Reagan was right, and I believe this is what the verse is speaking of. The ultimate guidebook for our lives was authored by forty different individuals and has sixty-six books, all God-inspired.

This is what makes the journey so exciting. God knows us. He knows our hearts, our fears, and our desires. He's given us the greatest "how-to" guide on the planet. Think about it as a treasure hunt each day, uncovering new nuggets for life and peace. The journey can be arduous and full of traps by the evil one but remember that the battle has already been won. The joy of the Lord is our strength (Nehemiah 8:10).

Your Reflections

_____

_____

_____

_____

_____

_____

Prayer

Almighty God, you are the King of Kings, and you have accepted me into your family. I am a fellow heir with Christ; thank you. Help me, dear Lord, to remain faithful in the renewal of my mind for your honor and glory. In the mighty name of Jesus I pray, amen.

RENEWING YOUR MIND

DAY THREE

Today's Verses—Philippians 4:6-8

Be anxious for nothing, but in everything by prayer and supplication with thanksgiving let your requests be made known to God. And the peace of God, which surpasses all comprehension, will guard your hearts and your minds in Christ Jesus. Finally, brethren, whatever is true, whatever is honorable, whatever is right, whatever is pure, whatever is lovely, whatever is of good repute, if there is any excellence and if anything, worthy of praise, dwell on these things.

Additional Reading: Philippians 2:5; Romans 8:5-6; Colossians 3:10

My Thoughts

I love Philippians 4:6-8, but these verses have always been troubling to me. Is it possible to be anxious for nothing? The answer is no, apart from walking by faith in Jesus Christ. You may become anxious at times. During these moments, do what the verses teach and pray and petition God with a thankful heart.

Praying for God's peace is an ongoing process; we are human, and our minds tend to stray from the strength we have in Christ. Certainly, there are times when we feel anxious: when a loved one is diagnosed with cancer, when we get a letter from the IRS, or when we have a fight with our spouse. However, our anxiety should only be temporary when we remember where our strength lies. God has a plan for our lives. He will see you through whatever you are facing.

Your Reflections

_____

_____

_____

_____

_____

Prayer

Father God, keep me in your Word by giving me a passion and a deep love for you, your teachings, and your wisdom. I pray that I would be daily renewed by your Spirit and bring honor to you. In Jesus' name I pray, amen.

RENEWING YOUR MIND   DAY FOUR

Today's Verses—Colossians 3:17
Whatever you do in word or deed, do all in the name of the Lord Jesus, giving thanks through Him to God the Father.

Additional Reading: Philemon 1:6; Titus 3:5; Psalm 51:10

My Thoughts
Colossians 3:17 has profoundly changed my thinking—or should I say, my behavior. If everything I do, in word or deed, is to be in the name of Jesus, I must guard my mind and my actions. As I yield to the Holy Spirit who lives in me, I feel a closeness to Jesus.

Living with an attitude of gratitude has completely changed my life. Regardless of the circumstances, I thank God that, no matter what, he is in control. Giving thanks in all things is about recognizing who's in control and recognizing that it's not me. Truly believing that God loves me, knows what's best for me, and has a plan for my good, how could I not be thankful? Examine your own life. Who is really in control? Yield to the Savior. Give thanks for his blessings.

Your Reflections

_____

_____

_____

_____

_____

_____

Prayer
Father God, I recognize your authority, not only in heaven and earth but also in my life. May my actions reflect this authority, and may I yield to it. May my words and deeds honor you this day. In the glorious name of Jesus I pray, amen.

RENEWING YOUR MIND   DAY FIVE

Today's Verses—Joshua 1:8-9

This book of the law shall not depart from your mouth, but you shall meditate on it day and night, so that you may be careful to do according to all that is written in it; for then you will make your way prosperous, and then you will have success. Have I not commanded you? Be strong and courageous! Do not tremble or be dismayed, for the Lord your God is with you wherever you go.

Additional Reading: Colossians 1:9; Isaiah 61:1; 2 Peter 1:3

My Thoughts

Once again, the evidence is clear; God wants us in his Word—not just reading it but also meditating on it. When the Word is in us, it offers us strength, faith, and clarity in every way. Whether it be in your family or business life, you will have the answers.

As a lifelong learner, I love reading a variety of topics (business, marketing, fathering, finances, hobbies, etc.), but nothing brings the peace and hope that being in God's Word daily does. The Holy Spirit dwells in us, and he delights in revealing new bits of wisdom and knowledge as we study. He offers the discernment we seek and the guidance we need.

Emboldened by his presence in your life, what can possibly keep you from walking with great courage in his wisdom?

Your Reflections

_____

_____

_____

_____

_____

_____

Prayer

Loving Father, your Word is the source of my strength and courage. Help me keep it in my heart. In Jesus' name I pray, amen.

WEEK NINE

NEW CREATION

NEW CREATION

DAY ONE

Today's Verses—2 Corinthians 5:17

Therefore, if anyone is in Christ, he is a new creature; the old things passed away; behold, new things have come.

Additional Reading: Galatians 2:20; 2 Peter 1:4-7; Ezekiel 36:25-28

My Thoughts

Just think of anything new. It's exciting—whether it be a new car, a new home, or anything that brings you joy. Not only are we new creatures, but the old self is gone.

Here's where many of us fall short, at least in our thinking. We accept Jesus in our heart and ask for forgiveness, but we fail to realize that the old self is gone. Well, that is, if we believe it. It was certainly confusing for Nicodemus when he asked, "How can a man be born when he is old?" (Jn. 3:4).

It doesn't matter how old you are or how much life you lived apart from Christ. At the time of your salvation, you are a new creature. Forget about the past failures, sins, and heartbreaks; they are all gone. Oftentimes, we still carry all the baggage from our old lives. *Hello*: it's called forgiveness. Forget about it! God did! Walk as a new creature, a new warrior for the Kingdom.

Your Reflections

_____

_____

_____

_____

_____

_____

Prayer

Father God, you are mighty and just. I praise your holy name. You are the God of new beginnings. Help me walk as your new creature, rejoicing, praising, and honoring you this day. In Jesus' name I pray, amen.

NEW CREATION

Today's Verses—Isaiah 43:18-19

Do not call to mind the former things, or ponder things of the past. Behold, I will do something new, now it will spring forth; Will you not be aware of it? I will even make a roadway in the wilderness, rivers in the desert.

Additional Reading: Ephesians 2:10; 2 Corinthians 3:17-18; Philippians 2:5

My Thoughts

Getting a do-over in life, how exciting! While we can't relive the past, Christ has given us a new beginning as we walk with him. We are reminded in John 19:26 that with God, all things are possible. So, what's holding you back? If you could do a great work for the Kingdom, what would it be?

Often, we think that if we are going to do something big to advance the Kingdom, we need to become a missionary in Africa. Don't despair; God wants to use you right where you are. He can use you to share the gospel in your workplace and make a difference to the lost souls you work with. He can use you in your family to raise children who will serve him and impact the Kingdom. He can use you in your community to be the salt and light we are called to be in Matthew 5:13-16. Ask God to give you a vision for how you can make a difference right where you are today.

Your Reflections

_____
_____
_____
_____
_____
_____

Prayer

Father God, my new life began at salvation. Your Spirit now lives in me. Help me this day, dear Lord, to walk in your strength, that I might reflect this wonderful, new life you have given me. In Jesus' name I pray, amen.

SDG

NEW CREATION
DAY THREE

Today's Verses—Romans 6:8-11

Now if we have died with Christ, we believe that we shall also live with Him, knowing that Christ, having been raised from the dead, is never to die again; death no longer is master over Him. For the death that He died, He died to sin once for all; but the life that He lives, He lives to God. Even so consider yourselves to be dead to sin, but alive to God in Christ Jesus.

Additional Reading: Colossians 3:9-10; Galatians 4:9-10; Isaiah 64:8

My Thoughts

Why do we often struggle with sin after accepting Jesus into our lives? Is it unbelief, or is it that we don't claim the last part of Romans 6:11: "alive to God in Christ Jesus"? If we understand that Christ is in us and he is light, then darkness cannot remain there at the same time.

Consider areas of your life, thoughts, and habits that draw you to the darkness; turn them over to the Lord. Ask for strength to claim your new identity in him—free from darkness now and for eternity.

The transformation to becoming a new creation in Christ can be a slow process. Old habits die hard. I encourage you to claim this victory in Christ and believe with the power of the Holy Spirit that you will be transformed into his image.

Your Reflections

_____

_____

_____

_____

_____

_____

Prayer

Heavenly Father, your words in Romans 6 tell us that we are dead to sin but alive to God in Jesus Christ. What a glorious gift—thank you! Strengthen me to live in this new life and walk in you. In the holy name of Jesus I pray, amen.

NEW CREATION DAY FOUR

Today's Verses—Ezekiel 11:19-20

And I will give them one heart and put a new spirit within them. And I will take the heart of stone out of their flesh and give them a heart of flesh, that they may walk in My statutes and keep My ordinances and do them. Then they will be My people, and I shall be their God.

Additional Reading: Hebrews 10:16; Isaiah 65:17; Jeremiah 31:33

My Thoughts

Many years ago, my daughter Carla's heart was failing. By God's grace, she received a new heart through a transplant. Having a new heart was a new beginning, enabling her to do many things she previously could not do. It was truly a new life.

When we receive Jesus as our Lord and Savior, we are of one spirit and one heart, not only with him but also with other believers. He replaces our heart of stone (sin) with a new heart that beats a new life of love and service into our very body.

Let your actions reflect this new heart and spirit in how you treat others: your spouse, your children, and your family. Allow this new heart to transform you into the servant Christ has called you to be. Reaching out to others with this new heart will change their lives and yours.

Your Reflections

_____

_____

_____

_____

_____

_____

Prayer

Father God, I am grateful for the new heart that you promise in Ezekiel 11. I pray, dear Lord, that this heart would be a heart filled with your love, your compassion, your joy, and your peace. May my heart overflow with your love and grace for those you bring into my path. In Jesus' name I pray, amen.

NEW CREATION

DAY FIVE

Today's Verses—Titus 3:5-7

He saved us, not on the basis of deeds which we have done in righteousness, but according to His mercy, by the washing of regeneration and renewing by the Holy Spirit, whom He poured out upon us richly through Jesus Christ our Savior, so that being justified by His grace we would be made heirs according to the hope of eternal life.

Additional Reading: Galatians 5:24; Ephesians 2:4-7; Philippians 1:9-11

My Thoughts

It is fantastic to be an heir to the living God—but what a responsibility! Imagine if you were an heir to the richest, most influential family on earth. What impact would you have on the world? Would you feed the poor, build orphanages, or just enjoy life? Consider how much Bill Gates and Warren Buffet have given away.

Guess what? We are heirs of the God who controls the universe and owns the cattle on a thousand hills (Psalms 50:10). What are we doing to continue the legacy of our heritage in Christ? And how will that allow the Spirit to work in us, representing our kinship?

Live daily in this knowledge and may your actions be based on your place in the family. How will you use it to the betterment of others?

Your Reflections

_____

_____

_____

_____

_____

_____

Prayer

Father God, what an honor to be an heir, to be accepted into your family with the promise of eternity with you. Teach me, oh, God. Strengthen me, dear Lord, to walk as an heir and as the King's kid to your honor and glory. In Jesus' name I pray, amen.

WEEK TEN

CONFORMED TO THE WORLD

CONFORMED TO THE WORLD   DAY ONE

Today's Verses—1 John 2:15-16

Do not love the world nor the things in the world. If anyone loves the world, the love of the Father is not in him. For all that is in the world, the lust of the flesh and the lust of the eyes and the boastful pride of life, is not from the Father, but is from the world.

Additional Reading: James 4:4; Colossians 2:8; Ephesians 5:11

My Thoughts

The key to understanding 1 John 2:15-16 is "love for the world." We can live in the world, but we shouldn't love our stuff more than we love God. Remember the story of the rich man who asked Christ what he must do to serve him? Let's read Mark 10:21-22: "Looking at him, Jesus felt a love for him and said to him, 'One thing you lack: go and sell all you possess and give to the poor, and you will have treasure in heaven; and come, follow Me.' But at these words he was saddened, and he went away grieving, for he was one who owned much property."

I don't believe God wants us to give up all we own to serve him, but we must be *willing to*. Examine your heart and ask yourself, *What would I be willing to give up serving Jesus with all my heart?* What are the idols or possessions that I put first, that keep me from a life of service? Turn those over to the Lord and ask him to give you the strength to let them go and reset your priorities. The purity of your heart will allow you to overcome the lust of the flesh and give up your love of the world. Keep in mind, the only things that last are what we have in Christ. The rest can all be gone within an instant.

Your Reflections

_____

_____

_____

_____

_____

Prayer

Gracious Father, I praise your holy name. You alone are holy and just. I pray, dear Lord, that I might walk in your light and righteousness and only covet your love and peace. In Jesus' name I pray, amen.

CONFORMED TO THE WORLD   DAY TWO

Today's Verses—Ezekiel 36:25

Then I will sprinkle clean water on you, and you will be clean; I will cleanse you from all your filthiness and from all your idols.

Additional Reading: Matthew 6:24; 2 Corinthians 4:4-6; Galatians 2:20

My Thoughts

It's unlikely that you have an idol to an unknown god in your backyard, but there may be other ones that keep you from serving our Lord. Idols can take many forms; it could be money, career, or even loved ones. It could even be a pastor or teacher you admire. An idol is anything that takes your eyes off the Savior and keeps you enslaved to worshiping it rather than the living God.

Jesus made it pretty clear when he said, "If anyone comes to Me, and does not hate his own father and mother and wife and children and brothers and sisters, yes, and even his own life, he cannot be My disciple" (Lk. 14:26). Abandon your worldly idols and seek to serve him without limits.

Your Reflections

_____

_____

_____

_____

_____

_____

Prayer

Father God, I pray today the words of 2 Corinthians 4:5: "For we do not preach ourselves but Christ Jesus as Lord, and ourselves as your bond-servants for Jesus' sake." Help me walk as your bond-servant. In Jesus' name I pray, amen.

SDG

CONFORMED TO THE WORLD

Today's Verses—Hebrews 13:5-6

Make sure that your character is free from the love of money, being content with what you have; for He Himself has said, "I will never desert you, nor will I ever forsake you," so that we confidently say, "The Lord is my helper, I will not be afraid. What will man do to me?"

Additional Reading: John 12:46; John 8:12; I Thessalonians 5:21-23

My Thoughts

What a great God we serve. Not only did he create the universe by speaking it into existence, but he is also the Alpha and the Omega, the King of Kings and Lord and Lords. This is who we have as a helper. Remember the words of Romans 8:28: "And we know that God causes all things to work together for good to those who love God, to those who are called according to His purpose."

The key phrase here is "called according to His purpose." When we are focusing on God's purpose for our life, he is there to guide, strengthen, and protect us. This reflects a partnership that builds and gets stronger as we seek him, study his Word, and walk in his will. How can you be a better partner? What are your responsibilities to the partnership? As in any partnership there needs to be trust and accountability. God is faithful, are you?

Your Reflections

_____

_____

_____

_____

_____

_____

Prayer

Father God, I am grateful that you, the God of the universe, are also my helper. Teach me, dear Lord, not to fear man or his actions, but to walk in your strength and faithfulness. In Jesus' name I pray, amen.

CONFORMED TO THE WORLD   DAY FOUR

Today's Verses—Daniel 3:16-18

Shadrach, Meshach and Abednego replied to the king, "O Nebuchadnezzar, we do not need to give you an answer concerning this matter. If it be so, our God whom we serve can deliver us from the furnace of blazing fire; and He will deliver us out of your hand, O king. But even if He does not, let it be known to you, O king, that we are not going to serve your gods or worship the golden image that you have set up."

Additional Reading: Matthew 7:13; Romans 12:1-2; I John 1:7

My Thoughts

I don't know about you, but I have never had to face a fiery furnace to show my allegiance to the living God, but these young men trusted God completely. More importantly, they were willing to stand firm against King Nebuchadnezzar. Wow, that's courage! What a miracle! They were protected through the blaze and lived to praise God.

What opportunities exist where we can stand firm on God's principles and his values? Do you have the courage to face the opposition to the point of the fiery furnace? Our school systems are turning our children from our values and beliefs. Our government is forcing us to forfeit our beliefs. Our workplaces have, in many cases, become a place of crude jokes, sexual harassment, and much more. How brightly is your light shining in your place of business or in your community? We must stand firm, even if it means facing the furnace.

Your Reflections

_____
_____
_____
_____
_____
_____

Prayer

Father God, thank you that you are my fortress and my deliverer. As I live in this fallen world, I know that you alone are true and pure. Strengthen me this day to be faithful to your will and walk in your light, where there is no darkness. In Jesus' name I pray, amen.

CONFORMED TO THE WORLD DAY FIVE

Today's Verses—Revelation 3:17; Matthew 6:19-21

Because you say, "I am rich, and have become wealthy, and have need of nothing," and you do not know that you are wretched and miserable and poor and blind and naked.

Do not store up for yourselves treasures on earth, where moth and rust destroy, and where thieves break in and steal. But store up for yourselves treasures in heaven, where neither moth nor rust destroy, and where thieves do not break in or steal; for where your treasure is, there your heart will be also.

Additional Reading: Romans 8:13-16; 2 Peter 3:9; 2 John 1:9-11

My Thoughts

Our earthly treasures can often give us a false sense of security. My experience has taught me not to rely on my earthly treasures because they can be lost. Our wealth or our possessions too often define us—but not in a good way. Many times, they are just another set of idols. It's clear that the only thing that will last is the treasure we store in heaven.

The investment we make in the Kingdom—the work we do on the Lord's behalf—is the only treasure that has eternal value. Making use of your earthly treasures for the Lord's work can have a multiplier effect; you can bless others through your generosity, and you, too, can receive your rewards in heaven. However, I don't think we should be motivated to do the Lord's work just for heavenly treasures. If our hearts are pure, the heavenly rewards will be there.

When we get to heaven and are greeted by the saints our work or gifts helped bring to salvation, what a reward that will be—not to mention how it will be to stand before the judgment seat (bema) of Christ. Remember Revelation 22:12: "Behold, I am coming quickly, and My reward is with Me, to render to every man according to what he has done." Amen!

Your Reflections

_____

_____

_____

_____

_____

_____

Prayer

Father God, I am confident in your love and grace. I am embraced and protected by your mighty arms. Help me each day to walk in the assurance of eternity with you and not to worry about my earthly treasures. In Jesus' name I pray, amen.

SDG

WEEK ELEVEN

PEACE

PEACE

Today's Verses—Colossians 3:15

Let the peace of Christ rule in your hearts, to which indeed you were called in one body; and be thankful.

Additional Reading: John 16:33; Romans 15:13; Proverbs 12:20

My Thoughts

When I think of all the people God has used to further his purposes, I believe that they all had great peace once they knew that their calling was from God. Peace comes from being in the center of God's will—regardless of the circumstances—and from having a grateful heart.

I am reminded of Daniel, facing the lion's den, or David, as he stood before Goliath. These men knew their calling and stood firm in the face of adversity. Peace can be a fleeting thing, but if we remember whose we are, we can remain in his peace regardless of circumstance. Peace starts with thanksgiving as you focus on where God has you and what you are facing. Give thanks that he is there with you, standing beside you. Where do you lack peace in your life? Is it because you are standing outside of God's will?

Your Reflections

_____

_____

_____

_____

_____

Prayer

Father God, thank you that your peace is all I need to survive and thrive in this fallen world. You have overcome the world, and through your strength and the power of the Holy Spirit, I, too, can overcome. In Jesus' name I pray, amen.

PEACE

DAY TWO

Today's Verses—Isaiah 26:3-4

The steadfast of mind You will keep in perfect peace, because he trusts in you. Trust in the Lord forever, For in God the Lord, we have an everlasting Rock.

Additional Reading: 1 Corinthians 14:33; Isaiah 12:2; Philippians 4:8-9

My Thoughts

God is everlasting and never changes. He is our rock. When I think about rocks, I think about mountains; mountains can be weathered by wind and water, but our God is not weathered by anything. He is steadfast and never changes. So, if we serve the living God who is steadfast, where does our lack of trust come from? I am reminded about the little boy who was frightened by a storm in the night. His father told him not to fear because Jesus was in the room with him. This occurred several times, and finally, the boy replied, "Dad, I want someone with skin on them!"

Is this why we lack trust? Because we can't see God? Because he doesn't manifest himself in bodily form? That's not how it works. God doesn't need to conform to understanding; he is God. He is the one who formed the universe, breathed life into created man, and set this world into motion. But here's the good news about our almighty God: he cares deeply for us; he hurts when we hurt; and he feels our pain. All he wants is for you to reach out to him in your times of need, as well as in the good times. He is faithful and waiting for you to turn to him; he is waiting for you to trust that he will deliver you, stand beside you, guide you, and bring you peace.

Your Reflections

Prayer

Father God, you offer a peace beyond my understanding. I am grateful that I don't need to understand—that I only need to trust and walk in your will. Your peace covers me, calms me, and gives me strength. Help me this day. I pray to you, dear Lord, that I will walk in your peace and strength. In Jesus' name I pray, amen.

SDG

PEACE   DAY THREE

Today's Verses—2 Thessalonians 3:16

Now may the Lord of peace Himself continually grant you peace in every circumstance. The Lord be with you all!

Additional Reading: 1 Peter 3:11; Hebrews 12:14; Proverbs 16:7

My Thoughts

Imagine peace in all circumstances. Peace when you get pulled over by the police for speeding. Peace when you lose your job. Peace when you learn a loved one has a terminal illness. Peace when your business fails. Peace in every circumstance! Where are you experiencing the most peace in your life and why?

If God is the Lord of peace and he dwells in us, how can we not experience the peace that his presence brings? The absence of peace is either from a lack of faith or being outside of God's will for your life. When we are in the center of God's will, his peace is our peace. His hope is our hope. His joy is our joy. I cannot imagine living this life without Christ walking beside me. How frightening it would be to face this world and all the challenges it brings—by myself! Jesus will never leave you or forsake you. Walk with him every day, for his peace is perfect peace.

Your Reflections

_____

_____

_____

_____

_____

_____

Prayer

Gracious God, you are the God of peace and grace. I am grateful that you offer me a perfect peace—a peace that cannot be shaken. Help me, dear Lord, to remain in your will and to experience your perfect peace. In Jesus' name I pray, amen.

PEACE   DAY FOUR

Today's Verses—Psalm 4:8

In peace, I will both lie down and sleep, for you alone, O Lord, make me to dwell in safety.

Additional Reading: Numbers 6:24-26; Job 22:21-22; Psalm 55:18

My Thoughts

What a comfort to rest in the watchful eyes of the Lord! What frightens us in the night? What keeps us awake? If you knew that angels guarded your slumber, would you sleep more soundly? The Lord's safety isn't just provided as we lie down but exists in every aspect of our lives.

I am reminded of the shepherds who are so often referenced in the Bible. Sheep sense when they are under the protection of their shepherd. Shepherds protect, lead, and guide their sheep in safety:

The duties of a shepherd in an unenclosed country like Palestine were very onerous. 'In early morning, he led forth the flock from the fold, marching at its head to the spot where they were to be pastured. Here he watched them all day, taking care that none of the sheep strayed, and if any for a time eluded his watch and wandered away from the rest, seeking diligently till he found and brought it back. In those lands, sheep require to be supplied regularly with water, and the shepherd for this purpose should guide them either to some running stream or to wells dug in the wilderness and furnished with troughs. At night, he brought the flock home to the fold, counting them as they passed under the rod at the door to assure himself that none were missing. Nor did his labors always end with sunset. Often, he had to guard the fold through the dark hours from the attack of wild beasts, or the wily attempts of the prowling thief.[3]

Jesus is the Good Shepherd. Consider his words in John 10:11: "I am the good shepherd. The good shepherd lays down his life for the sheep." Stay close to him, and his peace will dwell in you.

Your Reflections

_____

_____

_____

_____

_____

_____

Prayer

Loving Father, Jesus is the Good Shepherd. He is my protector and my salvation. Keep me this day in his fold and under his watchful eye. In his name I pray, amen.

3   https://www.biblestudytools.com/dictionaries/eastons-bible-dictionary/shepherd.html

PEACE

DAY FIVE

Today's Verses—1 Peter 5:6-8

Therefore, humble yourselves under the mighty hand of God, that He may exalt you at the proper time, casting all your anxiety on Him, because He cares for you. Be of sober spirit, be on the alert. Your adversary, the devil, prowls around like a roaring lion, seeking someone to devour.

Additional Reading: James 3:18; Psalm 29:11; 2 Timothy 2:23

My Thoughts

As a Sunday school teacher, many years ago, I taught part of these verses from 1 Peter 5:7 to preschoolers in a song that went like this: "Cast all your cares on him because he cares for you!"[4] I wanted to teach these young souls that they could trust God with their worries because he loves them. But there is more to this message. We have a responsibility: humbling ourselves.

In our daily walk as we serve our Lord, we must be ever vigilant and know that the devil is working his evil schemes to defeat and destroy us. Remain steadfast in him; remain humble; seek his will through his word; and he will exalt you according to his time. He is the Good Shepherd and will bring you an everlasting peace.

Your Reflections

_____

_____

_____

_____

_____

_____

Prayer

Almighty God, I am grateful for your peace and joy, which give me hope. I praise your name. Thank you for your profound love and protection for me. In Jesus' name I pray, amen.

---

4   Casting all Your Cares on Him, James McGranahan

MASTERPIECE

WEEK TWELVE

MASTERPIECE

MASTERPIECE   DAY ONE

Today's Verses—Ephesians 2:10

For we are His workmanship, created in Christ Jesus for good works, which God prepared before-hand so that we would walk in them.

Additional Reading: Colossians 3:10; Matthew 10:29-31; Isaiah 43:1

My Thoughts

When I think of workmanship, I think of a craftsman. Whether it be a cabinetmaker or a boatbuilder, each of these craftsmen builds with a vision and a purpose in mind. The cabinetmaker envisions his cabinet with the finest of details, reflecting his unique ability and pride in his work. The boatbuilder must build the craft not only to be seaworthy but also to be able to withstand a storm and remain a thing of beauty.

Jesus, being a master carpenter, understood what it took to build something of lasting value. Can you imagine if there were still pieces here today that Jesus, the carpenter, built over two thousand years ago? What a treasure! Granted, none of us are that old, but we are also God's treasures.

What do you think God's plan for your life was when he created you? Imagine the Father's joy as he envisioned the life he created you for. How does God's vision and your vision align? Are you living as the true masterpiece God created? What steps can you take today to be the person God created you to be?

Your Reflections

_____

_____

_____

_____

_____

Prayer

Gracious Father, you created me as a unique masterpiece. I recognize that apart from you, I will remain an incomplete, unfinished work. Guide me this day, dear Lord, to walk with you, that I might truly become who you have created me to be. In the Master's name I pray, amen.

SDG

MASTERPIECE

DAY TWO

Today's Verses—Malachi 3:16-17

Then those who feared the Lord spoke to one another, and the Lord gave attention and heard it, and a book of remembrance was written before Him for those who fear the Lord and who esteem His name. "They will be Mine," says the Lord of hosts, "on the day that I prepare My own possession, and I will spare them as a man spares his own son who serves him."

Additional Reading: Luke 12:7; Colossians 3:17; Ephesians 4:24

My Thoughts

Let me ask you: if you possessed an original painting by a master artist, maybe the *Mona Lisa*, for example, would you value it? Would it be among your most prized possessions? What are your most prized possessions? A car? Your home? Your children? As a father, I consider my children among the top of my prized possessions. They are my flesh and blood, a part of me.

I believe that this is how God sees us; we are his own possession. He created us, and, as such, we are his masterpieces. Does your life reflect a masterpiece, or is your life in pieces? How have you used the resources God has provided you to his glory? Zig Ziglar used to ask, if you had a two hundred thousand dollar racehorse, would you feed it junk food or keep it up all night doing who knows what?

Honor the physical, mental, and spiritual body God created and live as his masterpiece today.

Your Reflections

_____

_____

_____

_____

_____

Prayer

Almighty God, I am overcome with gladness to know that you know me down to the hairs on my head and love me unconditionally. You are my creator and my God. Help me this day to reflect your love and grace while honoring you. In Jesus' name I pray, amen.

MASTERPIECE   DAY THREE

Today's Verses—Psalm 139:13-14

For you formed my inward parts; You wove me in my mother's womb. I will give thanks to you, for I am fearfully and wonderfully made; wonderful are Your works, and my soul knows it very well.

Additional Reading: Jeremiah 1:5; John 15:4-10; Ephesians 1:4

My Thoughts

"What does it mean to have been fearfully and wonderfully made? Here is something I think offers clarity: "The context of the above verse is the incredible nature of our physical bodies. The human body is the most complex and unique organism in the world, and that complexity and uniqueness speaks volumes about the mind of its creator. Every aspect of the body, down to the tiniest microscopic cell, reveals that it is fearfully and wonderfully made."[5]

When I think about Psalm 139:13-14, I don't think it means God was fearful; he was just very precise in forming us. I think about a time when I was building a small model car and working with very small pieces. I literally held my breath to be sure I glued the parts just right.

God took great care in creating us out of love. He also created in us a desire to live for his plan, being guided by the Holy Spirit. Seek the Holy Spirit today. Ask for guidance that you might walk in a manner appropriate for his masterpiece.

Your Reflections

_____

_____

_____

_____

_____

_____

Prayer

Heavenly Father, you knew me before I was born and already had a plan for my life. I wasn't just an afterthought. Guide me—strengthen me—to walk according to your will and not my own, for your honor and glory. In Jesus' name I pray, amen.

---

5   https://www.gotquestions.org/fearfully-wonderfully-made.html

MASTERPIECE DAY FOUR

Today's Verses—Genesis 2:7

Then the Lord God formed man of dust from the ground and breathed into his nostrils the breath of life; and man, became a living being.

Additional Reading: 1 Timothy 4:8; 1 John 4:4; John 6:69

My Thoughts

OK, this is cool. God took dust and made man just by breathing into his nostrils—and not with just any breath but the breath of life! Now, don't try this at home; he's God.

The point here is that God doesn't operate by any rules of physics. Nothing is impossible for him. So, when you think about who God created you to be, don't be limited by your thinking. Allow God to work in your life as he desires and trust him to continuously breathe new life into you.

God created the universe. He made man from the dust of the earth. Think what he can do with a living, breathing human—you. Go, God!

Your Reflections

_____

_____

_____

_____

_____

_____

Prayer

Almighty God, you created the heavens and the earth. You created me from the dust of the ground. Nothing is too difficult for you. Help me this day, dear Lord, to recognize the possibilities to serve you, not based on my limited thinking but on your power. In Jesus' name I pray, amen.

MASTERPIECE DAY FIVE

Today's Verses—Psalm 8:4-8

What is man that You take thought of him, And the son of man that You care for him? Yet You have made him a little lower than God, And You crown him with glory and majesty! You make him to rule over the works of your hands; You have put all things under his feet, all sheep and oxen, and also the beasts of the field, the birds of the heavens and the fish of the sea, whatever passes through the paths of the seas.

Additional Reading: Genesis 1:26-28; Isaiah 43:1; 2 Timothy 3:14-15

My Thoughts

What a magnificent God we serve. He created us over all living creatures. We are crowned with glory and majesty. I get excited when I think of this, not in a prideful sort of way—strutting around, saying, look at me, look at who I am—but I am humbled to know that I am his creation.

I am humbled by how God has entrusted us with this world, and I take the responsibility very seriously. How can I impact this world? I can't do so apart from God.

As we seek to walk as God's workmanship, we must remember that we are his children. We have a responsibility to care for our world and, most importantly, a responsibility to share his love and the gospel of Jesus.

Your Reflections

_____

_____

_____

_____

_____

_____

Prayer

Father God, you created man above all living creatures and gave us the responsibility to care for your world. May your love manifest itself in love and grace for those you bring into my life. In Jesus' name I pray, amen.

WEEK THIRTEEN
FULL ARMOR

FULL ARMOR   DAY ONE

Today's Verses—Ephesians 6:10-17

Finally, be strong in the Lord and in the strength of His might. Put on the full armor of God, so that you will be able to stand firm against the schemes of the devil. For our struggle is not against flesh and blood, but against the rulers, against the powers, against the world forces of this darkness, against the spiritual forces of wickedness in the heavenly places. Therefore, take up the full armor of God, so that you will be able to resist in the evil day, and having done everything, to stand firm. Stand firm therefore, having girded your loins with truth, and having put on the breastplate of righteousness, and having shod your feet with the preparation of the gospel of peace; in addition to all, taking up the shield of faith with which you will be able to extinguish all the flaming arrows of the evil one. And take the helmet of salvation, and the sword of the Spirit, which is the word of God.

Additional Reading: 2 Timothy 4:3-4; Psalm 119:1-8; James 2:20-24

My Thoughts

There is so much in Ephesians 6:10-17 to think about, but the main point is that we are in a battle against the evil one. We are to stand firm in the Lord and rely on his strength.

When we look at the components, we are encouraged to be fully prepared or armored. Our protection comes from truth, righteousness, and the gospel of peace. Our shield comes from faith in our Savior, Jesus Christ, who will protect us from the lies of the devil. The helmet of salvation protects our mind from deceit and false teaching. Finally, the sword of the Spirit, my personal favorite, strengthens us in the daily battles we face to overcome sin and stand firm against the evil one.

Make no mistake. We are in a battle, not against flesh and blood but against the forces of darkness. God has plainly laid out what we are called to do, and that's to stand firm and emerge in triumph. Prepare yourself this day for victory, wearing the full armor of God.

Your Reflections

_____

_____

_____

_____

_____

_____

Prayer

Father God, you are an amazing God, creator of the universe, and my Father. I give thanks that you gave me the tools from your Word to defeat evil. Prepare me this day, dear Lord, to walk fully armored for battle. May my victory be your victory and may I glorify you. In Jesus' name I pray, amen.

SDG

FULL ARMOR DAY TWO

Today's Verses—1 Thessalonians 5:8

But since we are of the day, let us be sober, having put on the breastplate of faith and love, and as a helmet, the hope of salvation.

Additional Reading: 1 Peter 5:8-10; Mark 4:14-20; Jeremiah 23:29

My Thoughts

In my mind, 1 Thessalonians 5:8 is a clear warning to remain vigilant—to remain alert and sober. We are of the day, as opposed to the night or in darkness, and we walk in the light of Christ. Our hearts are protected by our faith and our love and by our hope in our salvation in Jesus Christ. This, too, is what guards our minds.

Remembering that the battle is ongoing and we must be prepared, how will you remain sober and alert? Often, we are poorly prepared. We fail to see the pitfall, so we fall into sin. Think of the innocent flirting with an attractive coworker, the little white lies, or the little sin that leads to bigger sins. Once you put down your armor, you are susceptible to defeat.

Your Reflections

_____

_____

_____

_____

_____

Prayer

Dear heavenly Father, my heritage in you is rich and offers me a joyful life. Guide me, dear Lord, to remain steadfast. May your Word yield much fruit for your Kingdom through my speech and actions, to your glory. In Christ's holy name I pray, amen.

FULL ARMOR   DAY THREE

Today's Verses—2 Corinthians 6:7

In the word of truth, in the power of God; by the weapons of righteousness for the right hand and the left.

Additional Reading: John 14:26; Isaiah 11:5; Job 29:14

My Thoughts

I am amazed at how we get so easily defeated by sin, especially when God's Word is so full of warnings. Why do we need weapons if we are not at war? The devil looks for ways every moment to take us off course.

Truth and righteousness must be your weapon. Use it as a sword to cut out sin and falsehoods. Become a champion for God's Word so that the evil one will not deceive or defeat you.

The way FBI agents are trained to spot counterfeit currency is by studying the real thing. Keeping the Word in our hearts will protect us from the fiery arrows of the devil.

Your Reflections

Prayer

Father God, your truth—your Word—is our weapon in our battle against sin and evil. Prepared for battle, armed by your Word, and guided by the Holy Spirit, our victory is ensured. Keep me, dear Father, faithful to your righteousness. In Christ's holy name I pray, amen.

FULL ARMOR

DAY FOUR

Today's Verses—Hebrews 4:12

For the word of God is living and active and sharper than any two-edged sword and piercing as far as the division of soul and spirit, of both joints and marrow, and able to judge the thoughts and intentions of the heart.

Additional Reading: James 4:7; 1 Corinthians 11:1-2; 2 Timothy 4:3-4

My Thoughts

Have you ever thought to hide something from someone, to keep a secret, which, if found out, you would be ashamed of or embarrassed by? Too many times, we think we can keep these secrets. We often think, *If no one knows, is it really that bad?* Silly question, right?

The inspired Word of God, the living Scripture, has a way of examining every thought we have and everything we do. The Holy Spirit who resides in us reveals to us—to our very soul, to our heart and mind—the error of our ways and gives us a way to correct our actions or thoughts.

Your Reflections

Prayer

Dear heavenly Father, I am grateful that your Word lives in me and reveals to me your righteous path for my life. Strengthen me, dear Lord, to remain faithful to your teachings. Give me ears to hear and eyes to see. In Jesus' name I pray, amen.

FULL ARMOR   DAY FIVE

Today's Verses—Isaiah 59:17

He put on righteousness like a breastplate, and a helmet of salvation on His head; and He put on garments of vengeance for clothing and wrapped Himself with zeal as a mantle.

Additional Reading: Isaiah 49:2-4; Psalm 132:9; Romans 12:1-3

My Thoughts

So, we have come to an understanding that we need to be prepared for battle and armored by God's Word, his salvation, and the sword of the Spirit.

But what about our passion for battle? Do we welcome the opportunity to take on the devil daily? Are we on the offense or just sitting around, waiting for the enemy to overtake us? Be prepared. Ferret out evil when you encounter it. Stand firm on the mighty Word of God!

Your Reflections

_____

_____

_____

_____

_____

_____

Prayer

Father God, I am grateful that I have been called into your service and that you have given me all the weapons for battle against sin and darkness. I am no longer of this world but a warrior for your Kingdom. Surround me, dear Lord, with your angels that I might be victorious and glorify your holy name. In the name of my blessed Savior I pray, amen.

SDG

WEEK FOURTEEN
WINGS OF EAGLES

WINGS OF EAGLES   DAY ONE

Today's Verses—Isaiah 40:31

Yet those who wait for the Lord
Will gain new strength;
They will mount up with wings like eagles,
They will run and not get tired,
They will walk and not become weary.

Additional Reading: Psalm 34:18-22; James 1:17; Romans 8:10-11

My Thoughts

Have you ever seen an eagle soar? What majesty and power! It seems to glide through the air with ease and grace. The metaphor in Isaiah 40:31 is a fitting one for times we are walking fully in the power of the Holy Spirit.

Are you at a point in your walk where you can run and not get tired? I don't think this verse is talking as much about physical strength as it is our spiritual strength. Imagine living your life with the full power of the Holy Spirit, running to do his will and not being defeated. No matter what you face in your daily walk, be strong and run the race. Soar like an eagle!

Your Reflections

_____

_____

_____

_____

_____

_____

Prayer

Father God, it says in James that "every good thing given, and every perfect gift is from above, coming down from the Father of lights, with whom there is no variation or shifting shadow" (1:17). I am grateful that I can trust in you, the only true and living God, with whom there is no variation or shifting shadow. In the holy name of Jesus I pray, amen.

WINGS OF EAGLES

Today's Verses—Philippians 4:13

I can do all things through Him who strengthens me.

Additional Reading: Romans 12:1-2; Isaiah 57:15; Ecclesiastes 9:7-10

My Thoughts

Philippians 4:13 is a simple yet powerful verse. But do we fully believe it? I must often remind myself that this verse is clearly saying that I can do all things through Christ who strengthens me. I often remind my children of this verse when they say they can't do something.

Keep in mind, the verse says, "through Him"; it's not on our own that we can do all things. If we try to do anything without Jesus or outside of his will, we are destined to fail. So, keep your focus on the Savior and rely on him to do all things.

Your Reflections

_____

_____

_____

_____

_____

_____

Prayer

Father God, you promise us in Philippians that we can do all things through you. Dear Lord, help me to remain in your will, and give me the courage this day to fully walk in your strength, to your glory. In the matchless name of Jesus I pray, amen.

WINGS OF EAGLES   DAY THREE

Today's Verses—Isaiah 41:10

Do not fear, for I am with you; do not anxiously look about you, for I am your God. I will strengthen you, surely I will help you, surely I will uphold you with My righteous right hand.

Additional Reading: 2 Corinthians 1:9; Romans 8:37; John 11:16

My Thoughts

"Fear and anxiety—give it up?" When I first read those words, I thought, *Are you kidding me? I can't imagine what my life would be like without these two constant companions.* Most of my life my life has been filled with fear of failure and anxiety over my future. Then it dawned on me: I'm leaning on my own strength, my own wisdom—not on God.

What a glorious gift we have in Christ. God the Father, the King of Kings, the God of the universe is our God! Just the thought fills me with joy. Walk in his strength, and he will lead you to a life without worry or anxiety.

Your Reflections

_____

_____

_____

_____

_____

_____

Prayer

Father God, you are a wonderful, loving father. You understand that I will have worry and fear. I am grateful that your strength comforts me. Help me to rely more on you and draw on your strength—not my own. In Jesus' name I pray, amen.

WINGS OF EAGLES   DAY FOUR

Today's Verses—Nahum 1:7

The Lord is good,
A stronghold in the day of trouble,
And He knows those who take refuge in Him.

Additional Reading: John 10:10-11; Isaiah 40:28-29; Amos 8:11

My Thoughts

Webster defines a *stronghold* as a fortified place or a place of security or survival. So, isn't that just like our God—a fortress for his children?

Where do you turn when you are under attack? What is your stronghold, if not Christ? Is your stronghold money or material things? Is it your education and your own wisdom? Is it a place of refuge built on the sand (Matthew 7:26) or on Jesus, the rock? The promise in Nahum 1:7 is clear. He knows those who take refuge in him. Does he know you?

Your Reflections

_____

_____

_____

_____

_____

_____

Prayer

Gracious heavenly Father, you tell us in Isaiah 40:29 that you give strength to the weary and power to the weak. My heart rejoices in your protection. May I walk in your strength today and not in my own. In Jesus' name I pray, amen.

WINGS OF EAGLES

Today's Verses—Psalm 18:2

The Lord is my rock and my fortress and my deliverer,
My God, my rock, in whom I take refuge;
My shield and the horn of my salvation, my stronghold.

Additional Reading: John 16:33; 2 Timothy 1:7; 1 John 4:4

My Thoughts

OK, bottom line of Psalm 18:2: God is our protector and so much more. He is with us wherever we go. As our rock, he endures forever and is our stronghold. As our fortress, he surrounds us with his love and forgiveness. He arms me with a shield to deflect the fiery arrows of the evil one.

Next time you are in a battle or just feeling anxious, remember that Jesus is your refuge and salvation. Trust him; he never fails.

Your Reflections

_____

_____

_____

_____

_____

_____

Prayer

Lord, I pray the words of Psalm 18:2 and rejoice in your presence in my life: "The Lord is my rock and my fortress and my deliverer, My God, my rock, in whom I take refuge; My shield and the horn of my salvation, my stronghold." In Christ's holy name I pray, amen.

SDG

WEEK FIFTEEN
ROYAL PRIESTHOOD

ROYAL PRIESTHOOD

Today's Verses—1 Peter 2:9-10

But you are a chosen race, a royal priesthood, a holy nation, a people for God's own possession, so that you may proclaim the excellences of Him who has called you out of darkness into His marvelous light; for you once were not a people, but now you are the people of God; you had not received mercy, but now you have received mercy.

Additional Reading: Revelation 1:6; 2 Timothy 1:9-12; Jeremiah 1:5-10

My Thoughts

Growing up, I had very low self-esteem. So, if you had told me that someday I would be a part of a royal priesthood, I would have said, "No way!" To me, that is the miracle of salvation. We are now God's own possession.

We are God's people, whom he called out of darkness into the marvelous light—a light that can never be dimmed or put out unless you let it be so. Live in his mercy. Represent the holy nation with humility and love.

Your Reflections

_____

_____

_____

_____

_____

_____

Prayer

Father God, you are the great high priest. You are the creator and finisher of my faith. I am grateful that you have called me into your priesthood. Help me this day to proclaim your excellences that brought me out of darkness into your marvelous light. In Jesus' holy name I pray, amen.

ROYAL PRIESTHOOD

DAY TWO

Today's Verses—Exodus 19:6

"And you shall be to Me a kingdom of priests and a holy nation." These are the words that you shall speak to the sons of Israel.

Additional Reading: Deuteronomy 7:6; 1 Thessalonians 1:4; Hebrews 10:19-22

My Thoughts

How can we live in the fallen world as a kingdom of priests? Where is our holy nation on earth?

The holy nation begins in our hearts, then in the lives of our families. It then filters to our churches and communities. A modern-day priest of Jesus Christ isn't tied up in rituals and ceremonies. Like Jesus, we must be about the Father's work every day.

Your Reflections

_____

_____

_____

_____

_____

_____

Prayer

Gracious Lord, loving Father, I praise your holy name. You have created in me a new spirit—a new beginning that gives me hope for eternity as your priest in a fallen world. Give me the boldness and courage to proclaim your victory over death and darkness. In your holy name I pray, amen.

ROYAL PRIESTHOOD   DAY THREE

Today's Verses—Revelation 5:10
You have made them to be a kingdom and priests to our God; and they will reign upon the earth.

Additional Reading: Philippians 2:5-8; 1 Peter 2:1-10; Revelation 20:15

My Thoughts
Our salvation and adoption as sons and daughters of God comes with a responsibility. That responsibility is to bring the Kingdom of God to earth.

Let me encourage you, today and every day, to walk in the fullness of God as a priest, bringing about heaven on earth. Let everything about you reflect his love and compassion and his desire to transform this world into a holy nation.

Your Reflections

_____

_____

_____

_____

_____

_____

Prayer
Father God, I cherish you. I love you, Lord. You are my God, worthy of my praises. Help me, dear Lord, to "hold fast to the word of life so that in the day of Christ I many have cause to glory because I did not run in vain nor toil in vain" (Philippians 2:16). In Jesus' name I pray, amen.

ROYAL PRIESTHOOD   DAY FOUR

Today's Verses—Romans 12:1

Therefore, I urge you, brethren, by the mercies of God, to present your bodies a living and holy sacrifice, acceptable to God, which is your spiritual service of worship.

Additional Reading: Mark 4:23-24; 1 Peter 5:2-4; 2 Chronicles 7:14

My Thoughts

Are we willing to die to self and serve our Lord? Our bodies are the temple of the Holy Spirit, so we must keep the temple holy.

Think about Olympic athletes and the sacrifices they must make to be ready for their chosen sport or event. They train and practice for hours upon hours. They change their eating habits and their diets. They virtually give it all for the chance at gold. What are you willing to sacrifice for the ultimate prize?

Your Reflections

_____

_____

_____

_____

_____

_____

Prayer

Gracious and loving Father, you have created the whole earth and everything in it. You created me in your image. I besiege you, dear Lord, to give me the will and discipline to present my body as a living and holy sacrifice so that when the Chief Shepherd appears, I will receive the unfading crown of glory. In Christ's holy name I pray, amen.

ROYAL PRIESTHOOD   DAY FIVE

Today's Verses—Isaiah 42:1

Behold, My Servant, whom I uphold;
My chosen one in whom My soul delights.
I have put My Spirit upon Him;
He will bring forth justice to the nations.

Additional Reading: Hebrews 13:15-16; Romans 8:29-30; Galatians 4:7

My Thoughts

Clearly, Isaiah 42:1 is referring to Jesus, but what is our role in God's plan? I think about being a part of the great army of God. As a soldier, I must train, prepare, and stand firm daily. How does your lifestyle reflect your readiness for the battle?

As a warrior for Christ, you must be vigilant and be on guard. Immerse yourself in God's Word that you might stand firm when the attack comes. Don't be taken by surprise. Like any good solider, you must be trained and ready for action.

Your Reflections

_____

_____

_____

_____

_____

_____

Prayer

Father God, you alone are holy. You alone are majesty. I pray, dear Lord, that I will be conformed to the image of your son (Romans 8:29) and that I might be the firstborn among many brethren to complete your purpose for my life. In Christ's holy name I pray, amen.

SDG

WEEK SIXTEEN
GOD'S COMMANDS

GOD'S COMMANDS   DAY ONE

Today's Verses—1 Samuel 15:15-19

Saul said, "They have brought them from the Amalekites, for the people spared the best of the sheep and oxen, to sacrifice to the Lord your God; but the rest we have utterly destroyed." Then Samuel said to Saul, "Wait, and let me tell you what the Lord said to me last night." And he said to him, "Speak!"

Samuel said, "Is it not true, though you were little in your own eyes, you were made the head of the tribes of Israel? And the Lord anointed you king over Israel, and the Lord sent you on a mission, and said, 'Go and utterly destroy the sinners, the Amalekites, and fight against them until they are exterminated.' Why then did you not obey the voice of the Lord, but rushed upon the spoil and did what was evil in the sight of the Lord?"

Additional Reading: Matthew 36-40; 2 Peter 1:5-7; Revelation 14:12

My Thoughts

God is very clear about how he wants us to live and act. He has given us very specific instructions in his Word. He expects us to follow his laws and be obedient; they are not suggestions to live by. As we learn in 1 Samuel 15:13-23, King Saul thought he could "sort of" follow God's instructions and blame the disobedience on "the people." In the end, it cost him his throne.

Where in your life are you "sort of" following God's rules? Maybe constructing your own version of the law makes it easier on you? After all, these rules are too hard, and rules are meant to be broken, right? Wrong!

God is a loving and forgiving God, but sin has consequences. The penalty may be more than you bargained for. God's laws, big or small, are to be followed—no matter what.

Your Reflections

_____

_____

_____

_____

_____

_____

Prayer

Father God, you are a gracious and loving God—the great creator and finisher of our faith. Out of your love and mercy, you bless us beyond measure. I pray, dear Lord, that you will keep me on the path of righteousness and that I will obey your commands. In Christ's holy name I pray, amen.

SDG

GOD'S COMMANDS

Today's Verses—Deuteronomy 28:1-4

Now it shall be, if you diligently obey the Lord your God, being careful to do all His command-ments which I command you today, the Lord your God will set you high above all the nations of the earth. All these blessings will come upon you and overtake you if you obey the Lord your God: "Blessed shall you be in the city and blessed shall you be in the country. Blessed shall be the off-spring of your body and the produce of your ground and the offspring of your beasts, the increase of your herd and the young of your flock."

Additional Reading: 1 John 2:15-16; Exodus 20:1-17; Zechariah 8:16-17

My Thoughts

Now, here is the flip side of following the rules: blessings! God wants to bless those who follow his commandments.

There is no limit to his blessings: blessings on the city, the country, your offspring, your labor, and your work. Now is the time to examine your life and figure out where you are missing his instructions. What commands are you ignoring or maybe just slightly not following? Unleash his blessing through your obedience.

Your Reflections

_____

_____

_____

_____

_____

_____

Prayer

Father God, you are the great and mighty God who demonstrates a great love for your people. You gave us your commands, not to restrict our lives but to keep us safe and in your loving arms. Keep me this day in your watchful eyes, that I might remain obedient to your will. In Jesus' name I pray, amen.

GOD'S COMMANDS   DAY THREE

Today's Verses—John 14:15, 21

If you love Me, you will keep My commandments.
He who has My commandments and keeps them is the one who loves Me; and he who loves Me
will be loved by My Father, and I will love him and will disclose Myself to him.

Additional Reading: 2 Peter 1:9-11; Psalm 119:10; Jude 1:20-23

My Thoughts

I love these verses from John. God's love throughout the Bible is demonstrated in so
many ways. He sent his son to die on the cross so that we might have fellowship with the holy
and righteous God. He clearly tells us that if we love him, we will keep his promises. Better
yet, he will still love us and reveal himself to us.

Wow, that's intimacy. This is the first and greatest circle of love. I think it's natural that
when you deeply love someone, you also want to honor her. How will you honor our Savior
and show your love today?

Your Reflections

_____

_____

_____

_____

_____

_____

Prayer

Father God, I am amazed daily by your goodness and love for me. Your commands demand my
faithfulness, and following them keeps me on your path of hope and joy. Reveal to me each day,
dear Lord, your will, that I might bring you honor and glory. In the holy name of Jesus I pray,
amen.

GOD'S COMMANDS
DAY FOUR

Today's Verses—Luke 5:5

Simon answered and said, "Master, we worked hard all night and caught nothing, but I will do as You say and let down the nets."

Additional Reading: Deuteronomy 10:12-15; Hebrews 13:5-6; 1 John 2:4-8

My Thoughts

OK, Luke 5:5 captures a mind-set in Simon Peter that is familiar to us all. At the moment when doubt sets in, our thoughts often falter: *I understand what you've told me, Lord, but don't you realize that it hasn't worked before? Will you really do it this time? Will you be faithful if I follow your command?*

Do we doubt because we lack faith? Do we doubt because we lack patience? Or maybe we lack both? We must fully trust God and take him at his Word, regardless of our doubt. Cast your net today because he told you to do it. How will you demonstrate your faith today?

Your Reflections

_____

_____

_____

_____

_____

_____

Prayer

Gracious and loving Father, I am grateful that "the darkness is passing away and the true light is already shining" (1 John 2:8). Jesus is the true light and our Savior. Guide me this day, dear Lord, that I might walk in your light. In his glorious name I pray, amen.

GOD'S COMMANDS

DAY FIVE

Today's Verses—Psalm 119:33-34

Teach me, O Lord, the way of your statutes,
And I shall observe it to the end.
Give me understanding, that I may observe Your law
And keep it with all my heart.

Additional Reading: 1 Peter 3:8-12; Deuteronomy 6:1-9; Revelation 12:17

My Thoughts

In my mind, humility is the key to Psalm 119:33-34. If we are to follow his commands, we must ask for understanding and wisdom. As our understanding of God's commands grows, they become a part of who we are.

In what areas of your life are you lacking wisdom? Where do you not understand his laws? God is waiting for you to seek his wisdom through prayer and studying his Word. Dig deep into your study, and he will reveal it all through his Holy Spirit.

Your Reflections

_____

_____

_____

_____

_____

_____

Prayer

Father God, I pray the words of Psalm 119:33-34: "Teach me, O Lord, the way of your statutes, and I shall observe it to the end. Give me understanding, that I may observe your law and keep it with all my heart." In Jesus' name I pray, amen.

WEEK SEVENTEEN

NEW BEGINNINGS

NEW BEGINNINGS

DAY ONE

Today's Verses—Job 8:7

Though your beginning was insignificant, yet your end will increase greatly.

Additional Reading: Ecclesiastes 3:1-11; Malachi 4:2; 1 Peter 1:3-9

My Thoughts

I love Job 8:7. No matter where we started, God has a plan, and he promises to bless us greatly. What were your beginnings? Were they significant? I am not talking about material wealth, although that is important. What was your spiritual beginning? Today, I talked to a dear friend who told me about a family that was so rich they didn't need God. How sad.

My spiritual beginning was strange, at best. My mom couldn't decide on a church when I was growing up, so we tried them all: Pentecostal, Baptist, Methodist, Mormon, and Jehovah's Witness. But here's the good news: by God's grace, I gave my life to Christ in 1978. In my walk, I continue to grow in his love and grace and enjoy his great blessings. Start a new beginning in Christ today.

Your Reflections

_____

_____

_____

_____

_____

_____

Prayer

Lord God, I pray the words in 1 Peter 1:3-4: "Blessed be the God and Father of our Lord Jesus Christ, who according to His great mercy has caused us to be born again to a living hope through the resurrection of Jesus Christ from the dead, to obtain an inheritance which is imperishable and undefiled and will not fade away, reserved in heaven for you." I give thanks to you, oh, God. In Jesus' name I pray, amen.

SDG

NEW BEGINNINGS   DAY TWO

Today's Verses—Ephesians 4:22-24

That, in reference to your former manner of life, you lay aside the old self, which is being corrupted in accordance with the lusts of deceit, and that you be renewed in the spirit of your mind, and put on the new self, which in the likeness of God has been created in righteousness and holiness of the truth.

Additional Reading: Jeremiah 29:11-14; Job 8:5-7; 1 Peter 5:10

My Thoughts

The best part of salvation is the new self that comes from trusting Jesus Christ as your Savior. As Ephesians 4:22 says, we must lay aside the old self. God doesn't take away your free will. You can choose to either leave your former self behind or just "keep on trucking," as the saying goes.

For me, the hardest thing about receiving a new self was that I still saw the old me. I failed to see myself through God's eyes. It reminds me of a discovery Maxwell Maltz, MD, made after surgery in some of his patients. He discovered that even after removing a scar from a patient's face, they still saw the scar in their mirror reflection.[6] Begin to look at your new self and your new beginning as God sees you. Embrace his plan for your new self.

Your Reflections

_____

_____

_____

_____

_____

_____

Prayer

Father God, I am eternally grateful that you are the God of new beginnings and that my past is forgiven and forgotten. Help me, dear Lord, to live in the new self you have called me to—and not to live in the past, unto your honor and glory. In Christ's holy name I pray, amen.

---

6   Psycho-Cybernetics, Maxwell Maltz, MD

SDG

NEW BEGINNINGS   DAY THREE

Today's Verses—Revelation 21:4-5

And He will wipe away every tear from their eyes; and there will no longer be any death; there will no longer be any mourning, or crying, or pain; the first things have passed away. And He who sits on the throne said, "Behold, I am making all things new." And He said, "Write, for these words are faithful and true."

Additional Reading: Deuteronomy 28:12; Isaiah 40:29-31; Luke 7:47-48

My Thoughts

What a glorious day Revelation 21 describes. No more tears, death, mourning, crying, or pain. Can we have that life now? Sadly, we will still experience grief in this fallen world, but this passage gives me great hope for the future.

Even though we have not yet arrived at that day, our hope is still in the Savior. We may face heartache now, but with Christ by our side, we can endure and give thanks.

Your Reflections

_____

_____

_____

_____

_____

_____

Prayer

Father God, I long for the day you promise in Revelation 21:4: "There will no longer be any mourning, or crying, or pain." You will wipe away every tear. Help me to remain steadfast until that day, sharing the love and hope of Jesus with a dark and broken world. In his holy name I pray, amen.

NEW BEGINNINGS DAY FOUR

Today's Verses—Psalm 40:3

He put a new song in my mouth, a song of praise to our God; Many will see and fear And will trust in the Lord.

Additional Reading: 2 Corinthians 5:15-17; Acts 3:19-20; 2 Chronicles 7:14-15

My Thoughts

Why do you think there are so many passages that relate to the old self or the former things? I believe it is because God knows us. After all, he is the one who created us.

But remember, that old devil is still out there trying to defeat you at every turn, keeping you from doing good work. The easiest way to slip back into old habits is to covet the past, to yearn for the old way. The Christian walk is not easy street. The path is narrow but full of rich blessings. Stay the course. Claim your new beginning in Christ.

Your Reflections

_____

_____

_____

_____

_____

_____

Prayer

Dear heavenly Father, I am grateful that I am called by your name. Help me to humble myself in prayer and to seek your face so that my prayers may be heard and my sins forgiven. In Jesus' name I pray, amen.

NEW BEGINNINGS   DAY FIVE

Today's Verses—Lamentations 3:22-24

The Lord's loving kindnesses indeed never cease,
For His compassions never fail.
They are new every morning;
Great is Your faithfulness.
"The Lord is my portion," says my soul,
"Therefore I have hope in Him."

Additional Reading: Isaiah 58:11-12; Philippians 3:12-16; John 3:3-6

My Thoughts

What a wonderful concept Lamentations 3:22-24 contains. God's blessing and compassion is new every morning. This reminds me of when God provided manna from heaven for the Israelites every day. If they tried to save some for the next day, it spoiled.

God wants us to rely on him daily, to seek his face and enjoy his gracious love and blessings. We have a great hope in his provision. His mercy is new every morning.

Your Reflections

_____

_____

_____

_____

_____

_____

Prayer

Loving Father, help me this day to be blameless and innocent as your child in this wicked and perverse generation. Help me to reflect your light, holding steadfast to you and your Word, that I might not toil in vain, unto your honor and glory. In the holy name of Jesus, I pray, amen.

WEEK EIGHTEEN

GOD'S WORD

GOD'S WORD

Today's Verses—Psalm 119:10-14

With all my heart I, have sought You;
Do not let me wander from your commandments.
Your Word I have treasured in my heart,
That I may not sin against You.
Blessed are You, O Lord;
Teach me Your statutes.
With my lips, I have told of
All the ordinances of your mouth.
I have rejoiced in the way of your testimonies,
As much as in all riches.

Additional Reading: John 14:15-21; Deuteronomy 28:1; Ezekiel 18:9

My Thoughts

When I told people about my plans to write this devotional study, they would say, "Well, you need to read this book or that book to get insight." My reply was simple: "Why do I need to read any books when I have the Word of God? His Word is the source of all learning and wisdom."

Like anything important, the study of Scripture requires diligence. Memorize the verses as a treasure in your heart. Not only does the Bible offer wisdom in all circumstances, but the Bible also offers comfort in a time of need or sorrow. The Word for me is a constant source of joy, understanding, and blessings. Search the Scriptures for his wisdom. Be blessed!

Your Reflections

_____

_____

_____

_____

_____

_____

Prayer

Gracious Father, I pray the words from Psalm 119:10-11: "With all my heart I sought You, do not let me wander from your commandments. Your Word I have treasured in my heart, that I might not sin against You." I am grateful for your Word, oh, God, which gives me hope, joy, and peace. In Jesus' name I pray, amen.

SDG

GOD'S WORD

Today's Verses—Joshua 1:8

This book of the law shall not depart from your mouth, but you shall meditate on it day and night, so that you may be careful to do according to all that is written in it; for then you will make your way prosperous, and then you will have success.

Additional Reading: Matthew 7:21-27; Titus 3:1-5; Hebrews 4:12-14

My Thoughts

Do you obey the law? I'm not talking about God's law but just laws in general. How do you know what laws require? Generally, you know because we have posted speed limits or rules set by local government. My question really is this: if you don't know the law, how can you keep it? The judge will say, "Ignorance of the law is no excuse!"

So, my point here is this: to follow God's laws, you need to know them first. If God's Word is firmly planted in your heart, then the Holy Spirit will caution you when you are stepping outside of God's law and plan.

Your Reflections

_____

_____

_____

_____

_____

_____

Prayer

Father God, thank you that your Word is our guide that keeps us on the path of righteousness and gives us direction on how we should live in this dark and fallen world. Help me to keep your Word locked in my heart and mind, that I might not sin against you. In Jesus' name I pray, amen.

SDG

GOD'S WORD

Today's Verses—2 Timothy 3:16-17

All Scripture is inspired by God and profitable for teaching, for reproof, for correction, for training in righteousness; so that the man of God may be adequate, equipped for every good work.

Additional Reading: Luke 11:28; Psalm 119:97-112; John 6:27-29

My Thoughts

In the modern world, we have become increasingly dependent on the internet for learning. You can find a "how to" on everything imaginable—from apple coring to zebra striping. Wikipedia has become our new source of learning, and the many online courses are too numerous to count.

Don't be deceived. The one true source of knowledge is God's Word, and it is suitable for everything. Ecclesiastes 1:9 says, "That which has been is that which will be, and that which has been done is that which will be done. So there is nothing new under the sun." It's all there for us in the Scriptures.

Your Reflections

_____

_____

_____

_____

_____

_____

Prayer

Father, you are the almighty God—my protector and provider. I am thankful that 2 Timothy 3:16-17 tells us your Word is "profitable for teaching, reproofing, correcting, training, and equipping me in every good work." Continue in me this yearning for your Word, that I might know your will for my life. In Jesus' name I pray, amen.

GOD'S WORD

Today's Verses—Matthew 4:4

But He answered and said, "It is written, 'Man shall not live on bread alone, but on every word that proceeds out of the mouth of God.'"

Additional Reading: Psalm 19:7-11; John 8:31-31; Romans 10:17

My Thoughts

The context for Matthew 4:4 is that Jesus was hungry and the devil was trying to tempt him to sin by turning stones into bread, which was contrary to God's plan and will.

What do we do to thwart God's plan? Are we tempted to take matters into our own hands, rather than waiting on him? As believers in Jesus Christ and, thus, as his disciples, we must live by God's Word as if it is our very substance. If his Word is in us, we will not hunger for this world.

Your Reflections

_____

_____

_____

_____

_____

_____

Prayer

Father God, I pray the words of the psalmist: "Let the words of my mouth and the meditation of my heart be acceptable in Thy sight, O Lord, my rock and Redeemer" (Psalm 19:14). In Christ's holy name I pray, amen.

GOD'S WORD

Today's Verses—Job 23:12

I have not departed from the command of His lips; I have treasured the words of His mouth more than my necessary food.

Additional Reading: 2 Timothy 2:14-19; Ephesians 6:17-18; Genesis 26:4-5

My Thoughts

Not only is God's Word a guidebook for our lives, but it also serves as a reminder of the rich heritage we have as his children. From Genesis to Revelation, it is God's love story for his people. God has laid out every detail for our lives in the richness of his Word.

As I have studied most of the Bible, I marvel at God's complete plan for all of mankind. Nothing surprises God. He wrote the book. He was there in the beginning and will be with us to the end. Our mandate is to study his Word and discover the role we play in this grand adventure.

Your Reflections

_____

_____

_____

_____

_____

_____

Prayer

Gracious God, I marvel at your blessings, your provisions, and the beauty of this world you created by your hand. I praise your holy name. May my life be a sweet fragrance to you, and may my actions and deeds bring honor and glory to you. In the matchless name of Jesus I pray, amen.

SDG

WEEK NINETEEN
GIVE THANKS

GIVE THANKS   DAY ONE

Today's Verses—1 Thessalonians 5:16-18

Rejoice always; pray without ceasing; in everything give thanks; for this is God's will for you in Christ Jesus.

Additional Reading: Psalm 100:1-5; Philippians 4:6-7; 1 Chronicles 29:13

My Thoughts

How is it possible to give thanks in all things? Maybe God didn't understand all possible circumstances or didn't know what we would go through when this was written. Really? No. God understands *all* circumstances and is walking through *every* experience, good or bad, with you.

As a father who lost a daughter when she was twenty-eight, after having watched her endure a major illness, I understand how hard it is to live 1 Thessalonians 5:16-18. I suggest you start with prayer. Then, rejoice in God's goodness and provision for your life. Finally, give thanks for his love, grace, and lovingkindness. Regardless of your circumstance, he's in control. He loves you. Trust him.

Your Reflections

_____

_____

_____

_____

_____

_____

Prayer

Father God, I rejoice in your goodness, in your blessings, and in your presence in my life. I am thankful for the fullness of my life that comes from you. I praise your holy name. In the matchless name of Jesus I pray, amen.

GIVE THANKS DAY TWO

Today's Verses—Colossians 3:17
Whatever you do in word or deed, do all in the name of the Lord Jesus, giving thanks through Him to God the Father.

Additional Reading: Psalm 136:1-3; James 1:17-18; Hebrews 13:15

My Thoughts

What is the condition of your heart? Is it filled with gratitude toward God and his blessings? The key to a thankful heart is forgiveness and acceptance—forgiveness for wrong, for disappointment, and for unmet expectations. If we harbor resentment, anger, or jealousy, it prevents us from being thankful.

Take a moment to examine your heart. Where do you harbor any feeling that keeps you from truly being joyful? Forgive those who have offended or hurt you—move on. Accept God's forgiveness. Embrace his love and experience true joy and happiness.

Your Reflections

_____

_____

_____

_____

_____

_____

Prayer

Father God, my heart rejoices in you. My cup overflows with your goodness. You are my hope and my salvation. You alone are worthy of my praise and thanksgiving. You create in me a thankful heart. In Christ's holy name I pray, amen.

GIVE THANKS

DAY THREE

Today's Verses—Psalm 107:1

Oh, give thanks to the Lord, for He is good, for His lovingkindness is everlasting.

Additional Reading: 2 Corinthians 9:7-8; 1 Chronicles 16:8-9; Daniel 6:10

My Thoughts

What a magnificent God we serve! He created the heavens and the earth and all the beauty within. He created you and me in his image. He sent his only son to die, that he might have a relationship with us.

Contemplate God's lovingkindness toward you. Everything that brings us joy and happiness comes from a loving God. His love never ceases. It is new every morning. Rejoice in him and give thanks.

Your Reflections

_____

_____

_____

_____

_____

_____

Prayer

Father God, I am surrounded by your goodness. Your blessings abound in my life. I give thanks that I am your child and that through my Savior, Jesus Christ, I now have an intimate relationship with you. I am thankful for your Word that is a lamp to my feet. Guide me this day, dear Lord, to serve you and glorify your holy name. It is in this holy name I pray, amen.

GIVE THANKS DAY FOUR

Today's Verses—Ephesians 5:20

Always giving thanks for all things in the name of our Lord Jesus Christ to God, even the Father.

Additional Reading: Psalm 9:1-2; 2 Corinthians 9:15; Romans 1:21

My Thoughts

Take a few moments, right now, to make a list of all the things you are grateful for. That's easy, right? What in your life have you not given thanks for: challenges, hurts, disappointment? Will you thank him for these things as well?

Maybe your challenge is the loss of a spouse or a child, maybe a failed marriage, or maybe a job loss. Could it be an illness you don't understand? Whatever it might be, look for new beginnings. Look for his goodness and give thanks.

Your Reflections

_____

_____

_____

_____

_____

_____

Prayer

Father God, as I focus on your goodness and blessings, I rejoice. I am also grateful for the trials I face, often by my own making, because they teach me to trust you more. Help me this day not to lean on my own understanding but to fully trust you and lean on your strength. Great is thy faithfulness unto me, oh, Lord! In Jesus' name I pray, amen.

GIVE THANKS   DAY FIVE

Today's Verses—1 Chronicles 29:10-11
So, David blessed the Lord in the sight of all the assembly; and David said, "Blessed are You, O Lord God of Israel our father, forever and ever. Yours, O Lord, is the greatness and the power and the glory and the victory and the majesty, indeed everything that is in the heavens and the earth; Yours is the dominion, O Lord, and You exalt Yourself as head over all."

Additional Reading: Isaiah 12:4-5; Philemon 1:4; Jeremiah 1:5-10

My Thoughts
This week, we have been reminded to give thanks in all circumstances. But often, we think about times when things aren't going our way.

Consider King David; he had it all. He had wealth *and* prosperity, and he remembered to give thanks and recognize God for his success. Do you remember to truly give thanks to God for your success, or is your thankfulness intertwined with a little bit of your own pride? God wants a pure heart of thanksgiving and a recognition that all things are the result of his goodness—not our own efforts.

Your Reflections

_____

_____

_____

_____

_____

_____

Prayer
Father God, my words are not sufficient. I fall short in acknowledging your blessings in my life, my health, and my family. Everywhere I turn, I see your mighty hand at work. You are a gracious God who loves your people. Lord, may I always have a grateful heart that recognizes your river of blessings. In Jesus' name I pray, amen.

WEEK TWENTY

GOD'S WORK IN YOU

GOD'S WORK IN YOU

Today's Verses—Philippians 2:12-13

So then, my beloved, just as you have always obeyed, not as in my presence only, but now much more in my absence, work out your salvation with fear and trembling; for it is God who is at work in you, both to will and to work for His good pleasure.

Additional Reading: John 14:12-14; Matthew 5:14-16; Proverbs 3:5-6

My Thoughts

I believe it's time to move into action—God's action plan. As in business, it's one thing to plan, but sooner or later, we must take steps to complete our plan.

In this case, we are a part of God's plan, and we are his emissaries—his soldiers, if you will. The caution in Philippians 2:12-13 is to be ever mindful of our actions, which represent God working in us to his good pleasure. How can we fully let God do his good work in us today?

Your Reflections

_____

_____

_____

_____

_____

_____

Prayer

Father God, I am grateful for your calling on my life and your work in me. Grant me, dear Lord, a renewed spirit and passion for your service. Help me to be salt and light to your honor and glory. In Jesus' name I pray, amen.

SDG

GOD'S WORK IN YOU

Today's Verses—Galatians 2:20

I have been crucified with Christ; and it is no longer I who live, but Christ lives in me; and the life which I now live in the flesh I live by faith in the Son of God, who loved me and gave Himself up for me.

Additional Reading: John 5:19; 1 John 4:12-13; Isaiah 9:6

My Thoughts

In Galatians 2:20, Paul writes, "It is no longer I who live." What does that mean for us today? I'm a living, breathing creature. I get up every day and do my thing—right? So, I must be alive.

The clarion call here is that we die to self and allow Christ to live in us. The hard part is dying to self, right? We still want to hold on to our old bad habits, our selfishness, our sin. However, Christ will not share us with any of these. Truly let him be the ruler of your life.

Your Reflections

_____

_____

_____

_____

_____

_____

Prayer

Loving Father, your immense love for your people was demonstrated by the sacrifice Jesus made on the cross at Calvary. His resurrection offers us a new life. The old self dies, and a new self emerges. Christ now lives in me! Help me, dear Lord, to allow him to work in me for your honor and glory. In his holy name I pray, amen.

GOD'S WORK IN YOU   DAY THREE

Today's Verses—2 Timothy 2:15

Be diligent to present yourself approved to God as a workman who does not need to be ashamed, accurately handling the word of truth.

Additional Reading: John 15:1-8; Romans 8:1-6; Exodus 14:13-14

My Thoughts

As God's workmen, we are his hands and feet in the world. We are called not only to speak the word of truth unashamedly but also to act daily to further his Kingdom on earth.

In John 13:35, Christ says, "By this all men will know that you are my disciples, if you have love for one another." I believe we are called to love in action—to demonstrate God's redemption in service to others. It doesn't mean that you must go to Africa to serve the poor, but it does mean that you ought to demonstrate his love to all. In every chance and encounter, remember that you are his workman, so demonstrate his love.

Your Reflections

_____

_____

_____

_____

_____

_____

Prayer

Father God, you alone are worthy. I praise your holy name and give thanks that you have appointed me as your workman to speak truth to this world. Give me wisdom that comes from you. Give me courage that comes from the Spirit. Give me grace that comes from your son, Jesus, that I might boldly speak truth. In Jesus' name I pray, amen.

SDG

GOD'S WORK IN YOU

Today's Verses—Colossians 3:16

Let the word of Christ richly dwell within you, with all wisdom teaching and admonishing one another with psalms and hymns and spiritual songs, singing with thankfulness in your hearts to God.

Additional Reading: Romans 5:15; Acts 19:4-7; Hebrews 4:10

My Thoughts

Zig Ziglar used to say, "We do not sing because we are happy; we are happy because we sing!" Christ dwelling in us should bubble up as a fountain of joy, causing us to sing praises to his holy name.

What if you won the lottery of maybe a million dollars or more? Would it cause you to sing with joy? We have gained far more than that through our salvation in Christ. Not only does our God own "all the cattle on a thousand hills" (Psalms 50:10), but he also owns all the wealth in the universe. But more importantly, his work in us brings unspeakable peace and joy.

Your Reflections

_____

_____

_____

_____

_____

_____

Prayer

Father God, your presence in my life encourages me to immerse myself in your Word. In turn, you are teaching me, through the Holy Spirit, to teach and admonish others. The richness of your Word that dwells in me brings me unspeakable joy. This joy causes me to sing your praises. In the matchless name of Jesus I pray, amen.

GOD'S WORK IN YOU

Today's Verses—Isaiah 61:1

The Spirit of the Lord God is upon me, Because the Lord has anointed me to bring good news to the afflicted; He has sent me to bind up the brokenhearted, to proclaim liberty to captives and freedom to prisoners.

Additional Reading: Ephesians 2:4-10; Romans 15:14-17; Matthew 16:19

My Thoughts

Is the Spirit of the Lord God upon you? Does his immense joy radiate through you? Are you blessed by his peace? If not, why not? His work in us offers these things and more.

We have his message and the Spirit of the living God, which comforts the brokenhearted and frees those imprisoned by the yoke of sin. Reach out today to someone who needs the good news.

Your Reflections

_____

_____

_____

_____

_____

_____

Prayer

Father God, your unsurpassing love flows free through your Spirit. Your desire is that all may know your love and the hope we have in Jesus Christ. As I experience this great love and immense joy, I pray, dear Lord, that I would remain faithful to share you with others—and that they may experience your everlasting joy. In the holy name of Jesus I pray, amen.

WEEK TWENTY-ONE

ALL THINGS WORK

ALL THINGS WORK   DAY ONE

Today's Verses—Romans 8:28-30

And we know that God causes all things to work together for good to those who love God, to those who are called according to His purpose. For those whom He foreknew, He also predestined to become conformed to the image of His Son, so that He would be the firstborn among many brethren; and these whom He predestined, He also called; and these whom He called, He also justified; and these whom He justified, He also glorified.

Additional Reading: Proverbs 16:9; 1 John 5:4-5; Job 42:2-3

My Thoughts

God has a wonderful plan for the world he created. Here's the best part: that includes *you*. The creator of the universe had you in mind while he was putting his master plan together. Not only does he have a specific path for us to follow, but he also promises things will be good.

As we make our choice every day to follow him and walk according to his purpose, we have a clear mandate to understand his will and purpose. I encourage you to seek his will and walk in it.

Your Reflections

_____

_____

_____

_____

_____

_____

Prayer

Father God, your goodness is too wonderful to fully comprehend. Romans 8:30 tells us that you know us, predestine us, call us, justify us, and glorify us to your service. Romans 8:28 also promises that all things work to together for our good. Help me this day, dear Lord, to remain faithful to your holy calling. In Jesus' name I pray, amen.

SDG

ALL THINGS WORK   DAY TWO

Today's Verses—Jeremiah 29:11

"For I know the plans that I have for you," declares the Lord, "plans for welfare and not for calamity to give you a future and a hope."

Additional Reading: Philippians 4:6-7; Psalm 138:7-8; Hebrews 11:6

My Thoughts

Once again, I am amazed at God's great love for me. As the father of six children, I understand the love of a father for his children. So, if I—fully human, with all my selfishness and frustration—still have wonderful plans for my children, imagine how much greater God's plans are for us, his beloved children.

As his child, and like most children who love their parents, I want to please the Lord. I want to walk in a manner that's worthy of his love and redemption. He offers us a great future full of hope and prosperity.

Your Reflections

_____

_____

_____

_____

_____

_____

Prayer

Father God, your Word tells us that your thoughts are not my thoughts and your ways are not my ways (Isaiah 55:8), and I give thanks for that. You are a mighty God. Your ways are to bless us and to love us unconditionally, despite our rebellion. You, the loving Father that you are, want what's best for us. Guide me this day, dear Lord, to walk in your will, that I might walk in your goodness. In Christ's holy name I pray, amen.

ALL THINGS WORK   DAY THREE

Today's Verses—James 1:2-4

Consider it all joy, my brethren, when you encounter various trials, knowing that the testing of your faith produces endurance. And let endurance have its perfect result, so that you may be perfect and complete, lacking in nothing.

Additional Reading: John 1:12-13; Psalm 32:8-11; Isaiah 55:8-9

My Thoughts

How do we develop endurance? I have a dear friend who, at the age of forty-five, decided to become a trail runner; his next race will be fifty miles! He must train daily and go for long trail runs on most weekends. He is building his endurance for the race. He had to overcome numerous health issues and modify his diet and his running style—all for the love of the sport.

God wants the same from us. First, he wants us to love him enough to persevere through the trials—to stay in the race, despite the setbacks. He is building our endurance so that we might finish strong. Run the race to *his* perfect finish.

Your Reflections

_____

_____

_____

_____

_____

_____

Prayer

Gracious heavenly Father, when I face various trials and the discomfort they produce, I am thankful because I know you are with me to overcome them. I am grateful for the endurance difficulties produce. As James 1:4 tells me, endurance will have perfect results in me. My prayer today is for strength to endure with perfect results. In the matchless name of Jesus I pray, amen.

ALL THINGS WORK   DAY FOUR

Today's Verses—Ephesians 1:9-12

He made known to us the mystery of His will, according to His kind intention which He pur-
posed in Him with a view to an administration suitable to the fullness of the times, that is, the
summing up of all things in Christ, things in the heavens and things on the earth. In Him also
we have obtained an inheritance, having been predestined according to His purpose who works
all things after the counsel of His will, to the end that we who were the first to hope in Christ
would be to the praise of His glory.

Additional Reading: Psalm 23; John 10:9-11; 2 Timothy 2:15

My Thoughts

Many of us hope for an inheritance from our parents, one that will lighten our load and give us additional security. Are we, once again, placing our hope on our earthly father, rather than relying on our heavenly one?

God has predestined us to his inheritance—what a great blessing! He is ready to reveal the mystery of his will to us, that we might claim our rightful place as his children. How will you spend your inheritance?

Your Reflections

_____

_____

_____

_____

_____

_____

Prayer

Dear heavenly Father, I pray that the words of 2 Timothy 2:15 would be true in my life. I
pray that I might be diligent in presenting myself "approved" by you as a worker without shame,
speaking your Word of truth to your honor and glory. I pray in the name of my Lord and Savior,
Jesus Christ, amen.

ALL THINGS WORK   DAY FIVE

Today's Verses—Revelation 4:11

Worthy are You, our Lord and our God, to receive glory and honor and power; for you created all things, and because of your will they existed, and were created.

Additional Reading: Philippians 1:6; Hebrews 4:11-16; Philippians 2:12-16

My Thoughts

Time and time again, we are reminded that our God created us per his plan and for his glory. He could have designed the world any way he wanted to. We could be living in a dry desert or a frozen wasteland. He could have created us to only eat hay or grass like the animals of the field.

God created this planet for his glory, but I believe that he created us to enjoy it and placed us in a beautiful place so that, through our experience, we might see his mighty works. His beauty is all around us. The sky and the earth shout to his glory. Give thanks for his goodness and live to glorify him.

Your Reflections

_____

_____

_____

_____

_____

_____

Prayer

Father God, you indeed are worthy of praise. I give thanks, oh, Lord, for your plans, protection, and provisions in my life. You continue to bless me through your lovingkindness and grace. Keep my eyes on you, Lord, that I might remain on your path and honor you. In Christ's holy name I pray, amen.

SDG

ABUNDANCE

X

WEEK TWENTY-TWO

ABUNDANCE

ABUNDANCE

Today's Verses—John 10:10

The thief comes only to steal and kill and destroy; I came that they may have life and have it abundantly.

Additional Reading: James 1:17-18; Ephesians 3:20; Psalm 36:8

My Thoughts

Abundance is different for most of us. What is it for you? Is your abundance measured by material possessions or your bank account? Don't get me wrong. Proverbs 13:22 says, "A good man leaves an inheritance to his children's children, and the wealth of the sinner is stored up for the righteous."

I think that anything outside of the abundance we have in Christ is short-lived. As John 10:10 says, the thief comes to steal, kill, and destroy. Therefore, if your abundance comes from earthly treasures, it won't bring you true contentment apart from Christ.

How can you experience true fulfillment and abundance in Christ? It all is dependent on your relationship with the Savior. He not only offers perfect peace, but he can also truly help you experience the abundant life in all aspects.

Your Reflections

_____

_____

_____

_____

_____

_____

Prayer

Father God, you are an amazing God. I love to sing your praises. Your blessings are beyond measure and limitless. The abundance we enjoy is provided by your goodness and mighty hand. Thank you, dear Lord, for the abundance I enjoy, not only materially but also the abundance that comes from your presence in my life. In Christ's holy name I pray, amen.

SDG

ABUNDANCE   DAY TWO

Today's Verses—Deuteronomy 28:1-6

Now it shall be, if you diligently obey the Lord your God, being careful to do all His command-
ments which I command you today, the Lord your God will set you high above all the nations of
the earth. All these blessings will come upon you and overtake you if you obey the Lord your God:
"Blessed shall you be in the city and blessed shall you be in the country. Blessed shall be the off-
spring of your body and the produce of your ground and the offspring of your beasts, the increase
of your herd and the young of your flock. Blessed shall be your basket and your kneading bowl.
Blessed shall you be when you come in and blessed shall you be when you go out."

Additional Reading: Matthew 6:33-34; Romans 15:13; Psalm 36:7-9

My Thoughts

Is this passage from Deuteronomy 28 great or what? The almighty God, the creator of the
universe, will bless us beyond all our expectations. There is no area in our lives, businesses, or
families that isn't covered. God wants to bless us and create a legacy to his glory.

So, if you are not experiencing all of God promises, why not?

The key is found in verses 1 and 2. It's very clear that we are called to diligently obey. Right
about now, I hear a collective groan from almost everyone. You might think, *I'm doing OK.*
Do I really have to obey all of God's Word? His Word tells me yes. Your greatest blessing comes
when you yield totally to the Savior, seeking his will and guidance for your life. Blessings will
surely follow.

Your Reflections

_____

_____

_____

_____

_____

_____

Prayer

Gracious heavenly Father, your provision for my life is overwhelming. There is no area of my life
that you do not care about or provide for. Deuteronomy 28:1 promises that I will be set above
all the nations if I diligently obey you. Help me, dear Lord, to obey diligently—to do all you
command, that my words, my actions, and my life will be a sweet song to you and bring you glory.
In Jesus' name I pray, amen.

ABUNDANCE   DAY THREE

Today's Verses—Proverbs 3:9-10

Honor the Lord from your wealth, and from the first of all your produce; So your barns will be filled with plenty and your vats will overflow with new wine.

Additional Reading: Ecclesiastes 6:19-20; Luke 6:43-45; 2 Corinthians 10:6-11

My Thoughts

I am not a big believer in a prosperity doctrine that says, "If you are a follower of Jesus Christ, you will be rich." However, I do believe God wants to richly bless us in every way and that the riches of the sinners are passed on to the godly (Psalm 13:22).

Abundance starts with a belief that God will provide all we need and bless us according to his good pleasure. As he blesses us with good fortune, he expects us to acknowledge him by giving back.

God doesn't need our money, but he does want our hearts. If we give with a willing and generous heart, our lives will be truly blessed, and we will have abundance in Christ.

Your Reflections

_____

_____

_____

_____

_____

_____

Prayer

Father God, you are a righteous and generous God. Your blessings overflow. You fill my storehouse through your goodness and my heart with your love and compassion. Teach me, dear Lord, to give from my wealth—both from my bank account and my heart—with a loving and generous spirit, modeling and honoring your generosity and love to me. In Jesus' name I pray, amen.

ABUNDANCE   DAY FOUR

Today's Verses—Luke 6:38

Give, and it will be given to you. They will pour into your lap a good measure—pressed down, shaken together, and running over. For by your standard of measure it will be measured to you in return.

Additional Reading: Psalm 37:7-11; Exodus 34:6; Philippians 4:18-19

My Thoughts

Although Luke 6:38 can be applied to money, it doesn't stop there. It can be applied to many areas of our lives: love, compassion, and generosity of our time—just to mention a few. How can you give more of yourself to God? How can you love more and share the love of Christ with others? Can you share more compassion with your loved ones, neighbors, friends, or coworkers?

It reminds me of George Baily in that great movie *It's a Wonderful Life*. His love and generosity paid dividends in his time of need. His cup was certainly running over. How will you give more?

Your Reflections

_____

_____

_____

_____

_____

_____

Prayer

Father God, you are the true and almighty God. You alone are worthy of my praises. I give thanks for the abundance in my life and the joy that fills my heart. Your Word is true and speaks of your faithfulness and provision for all who serve you. Help me to remain faithful to your calling and share your love from the abundance of my heart. In Jesus' name I pray, amen.

SDG

ABUNDANCE

DAY FIVE

Today's Verses—Matthew 13:23

And the one on whom seed was sown on the good soil, this is the man who hears the word and understands it; who indeed bears fruit and brings forth, some a hundredfold, some sixty, and some thirty.

Additional Reading: Psalm 66:8-12; Leviticus 26:1-12; John 7:38

My Thoughts

Our abundance is largely a reflection of how God's Word is transforming our lives. When the seed of his Word grows in you, it creates not only an abundant heart but also an abundant spirit. The overflow is what we produce for the Kingdom. When we begin to fully learn more about his grand plan for our lives, it leads to a greater understanding of that plan.

Clearly, his Word is the key to everything in our lives, our finances, and our happiness. The fullness of walking with Christ daily redefines all our thinking; it transforms us into his image. Our walk also brings us to a better understanding of the abundance we have in Jesus.

Your Reflections

_____

_____

_____

_____

_____

_____

Prayer

Gracious heavenly Father, I rejoice in your words in Leviticus 26:12 that say, "I will also walk among you and be your God, and you shall by my people." I am grateful and blessed to be called by you. You are the Lord, my God. Walk with me this day, I pray. In the matchless name of Jesus I pray, amen.

SDG

FRUITS OF THE SPIRIT

FRUITS OF THE SPIRIT

Today's Verses—Galatians 5:22

But the fruit of the Spirit is love, joy, peace, patience, kindness, goodness, faithfulness.

Additional Reading: Matthew 3:8-9; Romans 5:3-5; Ezekiel 18:2-23

My Thoughts

As I contemplate these fruits as they are, I wonder what kind of fruits manifest themselves in my life. But before I go there, I must understand that these fruits come from the Spirit—the Holy Spirit. So, as I walk in the Spirit, all of them should be real and evident in my daily walk.

Love is an easy concept for most of us, especially when you consider the matchless love Christ demonstrated for us, but do we experience real joy and peace? We all battle with the loss of joy and peace, but if we keep our eyes on Christ, his joy is our joy. The other fruits, once again, are an outflow of the Holy Spirit. If you lack any of these, examine how you can walk more fully in the Spirit and yield to his control.

Your Reflections

_____

_____

_____

_____

_____

_____

Prayer

Gracious Father, I rejoice this day in your blessings. I am grateful for the fruits of joy, love, and goodness that are present in my life. Your Spirit that lives in me brings me peace. The knowledge of your salvation teaches me patience because you alone are faithful. Help me this day, oh, Lord, to walk fully in your presence. In the holy name of Christ I pray, amen.

FRUITS OF THE SPIRIT   DAY TWO

Today's Verses—1 Peter 1:21

Who through Him are believers in God, who raised Him from the dead and gave Him glory, so that your faith and hope are in God.

Additional Reading: Matthew 7:11-19;John 15:1-8;Romans 8:28-30

My Thoughts

When I think of faith and hope, I am reminded of these verses in Hebrews 11:8-10: "By faith Abraham, when he was called, obeyed by going out to a place which he was to receive for an inheritance; and he went out, not knowing where he was going. By faith he lived as an alien in the land of promise, as in a foreign land, dwelling in tents with Isaac and Jacob, fellow heirs of the same promise; for he was looking for the city which has foundations, whose architect and builder is God."

What a wonderful responsibility! We must glorify God through our walk, actions, and lifestyle. He is our very hope. Are we willing to trust God enough to follow him—not knowing where we are going, yet trusting him for an inheritance?

Your Reflections

_____

_____

_____

_____

_____

_____

Prayer

Father God, your Word tells us that Jesus is the true vine and you, oh, God, are the vine-dresser (John 15:1). Help me, dear Lord, to abide in you, that I might bear fruit as one of your branches. Produce in me good fruit to draw others to you, unto your honor and glory. In Jesus' name I pray, amen.

SDG

FRUITS OF THE SPIRIT

Today's Verses—1 Corinthians 13:1-2

If I speak with the tongues of men and of angels, but do not have love, I have become a noisy gong or a clanging cymbal. And if I have the gift of prophecy and know all mysteries and all knowledge; and if I have all faith, so as to remove mountains, but do not have love, I am nothing.

Additional Reading: Luke 12:48; Colossians 1:10-14; Psalm 1:1-4

My Thoughts

It might come as no surprise that the word love is found over three hundred times in the Bible. God is love; his Word is a love letter to his people. Time and time again throughout the Old Testament, God demonstrates his great love for a wayward people. No matter how many times the Israelites turned their backs on God, he never wavered in his great love. He loved us so much that he sent his only son to die for us. He continues to show his great love for us today.

How does this fruit manifest itself in you? It is easy to love those who love you, but what about others? Our love for others can be demonstrated in so many ways: in our speech, in our actions, in our generosity, in our patience. What steps can you take to show love to every person God puts in your path today?

Your Reflections

_____

_____

_____

_____

_____

_____

Prayer

Father God, I rejoice in your goodness and give thanks for the many blessings I enjoy. You are the mighty God, worthy of praise. Help me this day to walk in a manner worthy of you, that I might please you in all respects, bearing fruit in every good work and increasing in my knowledge of you. In the wonderful and matchless name of Jesus I pray, amen.

SDG

FRUITS OF THE SPIRIT   DAY FOUR

Today's Verses—Hosea 4:6

My people are destroyed for lack of knowledge. Because you have rejected knowledge, I also will reject you from being My priest. Since you have forgotten the law of your God, I also will forget your children.

Additional Reading: Matthew 6:19-21; Acts 2:38-39; 1 Corinthians 15:48-50

My Thoughts

Wow, the message of Hosea 4:6 is scary! To be rejected or forgotten by God? I can't think of anything that would cause me more fear than to know that my God has rejected me. Here's the good news: that will never happen. In Joshua 1:5, God promises he will never leave us or forsake us.

That promise is something we can always rely on, but the first part of this verse shares what we are responsible for and that is, simply, we must live by his law as quoted above.

Your Reflections

_____

_____

_____

_____

_____

_____

Prayer

Father God, I am grateful for your laws. I give you praise that your Word, the holy Bible, is our guidebook for life and business. Help me, dear Lord, to store your Word in my heart, that I might remain faithful to you, honoring and glorifying your holy name. In your holy name I pray, amen.

FRUITS OF THE SPIRIT   DAY FIVE

Today's Verses—2 Timothy 3:10-12

Now you followed my teaching, conduct, purpose, faith, patience, love, perseverance, persecutions, and sufferings, such as happened to me at Antioch, at Iconium and at Lystra; what persecutions I endured, and out of them all the Lord rescued me! Indeed, all who desire to live godly in Christ Jesus will be persecuted.

Additional Reading: Matthew 13:8-12; Jeremiah 15:16; Hebrews 5:11-14

My Thoughts

Time out, I didn't sign up for this! Persecution? You've got to be kidding me. Too often, we expect, as believers in Jesus Christ, that it's going to be a walk in the park. Thus, we are totally blindsided when challenges come.

The question is, are you able to persevere—to run the race to the finish line regardless? The fruits of the Spirit are not merely applied when things are going well. In all circumstances, we must remain faithful and true to our calling in Jesus.

Your Reflections

_____

_____

_____

_____

_____

_____

Prayer

Lord God, I am blessed by your words in Jeremiah 15:16: "And thy words became to me a joy and a delight of my heart; for I have been called by Thy name, O Lord God of hosts" (NIV). May I continuously study your Word, oh, God, that I might glorify you in all I say and do. In Jesus' name I pray, amen.

WEEK TWENTY-FOUR
BE STRONG

BE STRONG

Today's Verses—Joshua 1:5-6

No man will be able to stand before you all the days of your life. Just as I have been with Moses, I will be with you; I will not fail you or forsake you. Be strong and courageous, for you shall give this people possession of the land which I swore to their fathers to give them.

Additional Reading: 2 Peter 1:3-8; Revelation 1:5-8; Philippians 4:13

My Thoughts

The world looks at strength in physical terms. How much can you bench press? The truth of the matter is, your physical strength doesn't really matter to God. Consider Samson. Where did physical strength get him? The world expects us to "man up" or "woman up" if we are faced with adversity, but this is merely relying on your own strength.

True strength comes from the Holy Spirit who resides in us. Some of the strongest people I know are not all that strong physically. I think about my daughter Carla, who faced seventeen major surgeries; her strength and courage came from Christ. Our strength of character and courage is not dependent on our own human strength but, instead, on the God we serve. Where do you need fortification in your life? Only when you put your trust in the one and only true God will you be able to persevere.

Your Reflections

_____

_____

_____

_____

_____

_____

Prayer

Mighty God, when I am weak, you are strong. I give you thanks, oh, God, because you are a strong tower. Teach me each day to walk in your strength and rely completely on you. Teach me not to try to do things on my own. Work through me, dear Lord, that I might bring honor and glory to you. In Jesus' name I pray, amen.

SDG

BE STRONG   DAY TWO

Today's Verses—Ephesians 6:10
Finally, be strong in the Lord and in the strength of His might.

Additional Reading: Joshua 1:8-9; Romans 8:37-39; Ezekiel 3:8-9

My Thoughts

Being strong in the Lord comes from trusting God to be who he says he is. Knowing that he is the true and mighty God gives us courage. The strength of his might transfers to us as we trust and believe.

When we know we have the strength of our God, we can boldly speak his truth. We can enter the battle without fear, confident in the knowledge that it is his strength and not our own that carries us to victory. Where is your strength lacking? Where do you need your faith fortified? Seek him, and he will answer you.

Your Reflections

_____

_____

_____

_____

_____

_____

Prayer

Gracious heavenly Father, you alone are holy and the one and only true and living God. You are the Almighty. I draw strength from your Word and courage from the Holy Spirit. I give you praise and offer thanksgiving to you. I pray that I would walk in your strength and not my own. Keep me in the battle for your honor and glory. In Jesus' name I pray, amen.

SDG

BE STRONG

Today's Verses—Haggai 2:4

"But now take courage, Zerubbabel," declares the Lord, "take courage also, Joshua son of Joza-dak, the high priest, and all you people of the land take courage," declares the Lord, "and work; for I am with you," declares the Lord of hosts.

Additional Reading: Jeremiah 29:11-13; John 10:28-30; Psalm 110:1

My Thoughts

Why do we need courage? Why do we need to be strong? The answer is clear: we are in a mighty battle with the evil one. The devil loves to see us defeated. He comes to steal our joy, our peace. He attacks the very foundation of our salvation. But remember this: he is a liar.

The Lord reminds us that he is with us and that we have the power to resist the evil one and, finally, to defeat him (Ephesians 6:11). Examine the areas of your life where you need to rely more on God's strength and not your own. God is waiting for you to cry out to him.

Your Reflections

_____

_____

_____

_____

_____

_____

Prayer

Father God, as I prepare for this day, I give you thanks. I praise your holy name. I am grateful that you never grow weary. You never cease. Your watchful eyes and protecting arms never fail. Dear Father, help me this day to remain in your strength—to feel your mighty hand as I seek to do your work in this dark and fallen world. May my efforts bring glory to you, oh, God. In Jesus' name I pray, amen.

SDG

BE STRONG   DAY FOUR

Today's Verses—2 Corinthians 12:9-10

And He has said to me, "My grace is sufficient for you, for power is perfected in weakness." Most gladly, therefore, I will rather boast about my weaknesses, so that the power of Christ may dwell in me. Therefore, I am well content with weaknesses, with insults, with distresses, with persecutions, with difficulties, for Christ's sake; for when I am weak, then I am strong.

Additional Reading: Deuteronomy 31:6; Isaiah 41:10; Psalm 27:11-14

My Thoughts

I love God's Word and his promises. In 2 Corinthians 12:9, Paul tells us God knows that we are weak and in need of his strength so not to worry or be afraid. Think about a time as a child when you were afraid, perhaps of a thunderstorm or the neighborhood bully. How did you feel when your dad came on the scene? For me, it gave me a warm feeling of confidence. God wants the same for us—to feel his mighty arms of protection.

I think the key here is not to try and go it alone; that's not what God wants or expects. His Word says, "power is perfected in weakness." Thank you, Lord! As we learn to admit our weakness, he comes into our lives and replaces our weakness with his strength. He has your back.

Your Reflections

_____

_____

_____

_____

_____

_____

Prayer

Father God, I am grateful for the promises in Deuteronomy 31:6. Help me to "be strong and courageous" and not to "be afraid or tremble," for you, Lord, my God, are with me. You will never fail me or forsake me. Help me to stand firm in this promise and in your strength. In Jesus' name I pray, amen.

SDG

BE STRONG

DAY FIVE

Today's Verses—Isaiah 41:10

Do not fear, for I am with you; Do not anxiously look about you, for I am your God. I will strengthen you, surely I will help you, surely I will uphold you with My righteous right hand.

Additional Reading: 1 Corinthians 16:13-14; James 5:16; Nahum 1:7

My Thoughts

I marvel at God's promises and provisions. Once again, he reminds us we have nothing to fear. He is our strength, enabling us to overcome fear and anxiety. He promises to hold us in his loving hands.

I don't know about you, but just that thought alone gives me hope and courage. His strength gives me courage to enter the battle, to overcome darkness, and to share his love daily. How can he strengthen you today for the battle?

Your Reflections

_____

_____

_____

_____

_____

_____

Prayer

Dear heavenly Father, I am amazed by your goodness, the richness of your blessings, and the depth of your love. You are a good, good father. I am reminded today in your Word that although you are strong and powerful, you are also a merciful father. Help me this day to walk in your strength while being kind and loving. Help me to show strength in love. In Christ's holy name I pray, amen.

WEEK TWENTY-FIVE
AGREEMENT

AGREEMENT

DAY ONE

Today's Verses—1 Corinthians 1:9-10

God is faithful, through whom you were called into fellowship with His Son, Jesus Christ our Lord. Now I exhort you, brethren, by the name of our Lord Jesus Christ, that you all agree and that there be no divisions among you, but that you be made complete in the same mind and in the same judgment.

Additional Reading: Amos 3:3; Colossians 3:15-17; 1 John 5:7-9

My Thoughts

Nothing discourages a follower of Christ as much as disagreements. Whether it be over doctrine, worship styles, prayer, or just sinful pride, quarrelling keeps us from doing what God called us to do. We can get caught up in our petty agendas and dogmas, none of which serve the body of Christ.

My challenge to believers is simple: get over it! We need to be united in who we are in Christ and in sharing the good news of the gospel. In a book I read many years ago, it said, "Don't sweat the small stuff; it's all small stuff!"7 Reach out to other believers in love and find ways to resolve any disagreement or differences into unity, all to God's glory.

Your Reflections

_____

_____

_____

_____

_____

_____

Prayer

Gracious Lord, I praise your holy name. I give you honor and glory. I give you thanks for the unity we have in Jesus Christ; we are one body. Help me, dear Lord, to be a person of unity and reach out to other believers—that in our unity, we might stand firm in sharing the love and good news of our Savior, Jesus, with others. In his holy name I pray, amen.

---

7   *Don't Sweat the Small Stuff and It's All Small Stuff,* Richard Carlson

AGREEMENT   DAY TWO

Today's Verses—1 Timothy 2:3-4

This is good and acceptable in the sight of God our Savior, who desires all men to be saved and to come to the knowledge of the truth.

Additional Reading: 2 Corinthians 6:14-16; Acts 2:1-4; James 4:1-6

My Thoughts

Any agreement must have a foundation in a common cause or purpose. God has called us to his purpose through the death and resurrection of our Savior, Jesus Christ. He is the very foundation of our faith. Apart from that, there is no value in any agreement.

As the body of Christ, a body of believers, so to speak, we must be united in the Great Commission. We must walk arm in arm to defeat the evil one. Our light will overcome the darkness.

Your Reflections

_____

_____

_____

_____

_____

_____

Prayer

Gracious and loving Father, you are an amazing God. Your words in Leviticus 26:12 tell us that you walk among us. You are our God, and we are your people. Hallelujah! I am grateful that I am called by you to be a part of your holy nation. Help me this day, dear Lord, to walk united with your chosen to honor and glorify you. In Jesus' name I pray, amen.

SDG

AGREEMENT

Today's Verses—Matthew 18:19

Again, I say to you, that if two of you agree on earth about anything that they may ask, it shall be done for them by My Father who is in heaven.

Additional Reading: 1 John 4:11-13; Acts 2:38-39; 1 Timothy 2:3-8

My Thoughts

What power and authority God has entrusted to us! His Word tells us that if we agree and ask, it shall be done. Wow, but hold the phone—does that mean *anything*? So, if my wife and I want to win the lottery, all we must do is agree, ask, and receive?

I think we know the answer. It's all contingent on whether we are following God's plan and purpose. I believe that once we yield our will to Christ and deeply commit ourselves to him, our desires and requests will align with his purpose.

Your Reflections

_____

_____

_____

_____

_____

_____

Prayer

Father God, your glory is everywhere. Your majesty is on display in all the earth. You are the great creator and giver of all life. Father, I thank you for your presence in my life. I pray this day, oh, God, that the authority you have given me on this earth will be used to your glory. I pray that your mighty hand would guide me to do your will. In the matchless name of Jesus I pray, amen

AGREEMENT   DAY FOUR

Today's Verses—Colossians 2:8

See to it that no one takes you captive through philosophy and empty deception, according to the tra-dition of men, according to the elementary principles of the world, rather than according to Christ.

Additional Reading: Ecclesiastes 4:9-12; Proverbs 27:17; Hebrews 10:19-25

My Thoughts

The reality is, there will be false teachings, in and out of the church. False doctrine is pervasive in the world today. Matthew 7:15 warns us: "Beware of the false prophets, who come to you in sheep's clothing, but inwardly are ravenous wolves."

Be careful not to get caught up with a religious leader or movement that appears to be from God. The simple litmus test is this: does the teaching hold true to the Word of God? You cannot spot phony teachings or doctrine unless you know the truth. Make a habit of studying God's Word.

Your Reflections

_____

_____

_____

_____

_____

_____

Prayer

Father God, your mercies are new each day. Your love never ceases. You are the everlasting God. I give thanks that you have chosen me to serve you by serving others and by sharing your love and wisdom. Help me this day, dear Lord, to walk with you. Help me keep your Word stored in my heart to guide my thoughts and my words. In Christ's holy name I pray, amen.

AGREEMENT   DAY FIVE

Today's Verses—Philippians 2:1-5

Therefore, if there is any encouragement in Christ, if there is any consolation of love, if there is any fellowship of the Spirit, if any affection and compassion, make my joy complete by being of the same mind, maintaining the same love, united in spirit, intent on one purpose. Do nothing from selfishness or empty conceit, but with humility of mind regard one another as more important than yourselves; do not merely look out for your own personal interests, but also for the interests of others. Have this attitude in yourselves which was also in Christ Jesus.

Additional Reading: 1 Thessalonians 5:14-16; Psalm 133:1-2; 1 Corinthians 3:7-9

My Thoughts

It's hard to have agreement if you are only interested in yourself. Selfishness is not a godly virtue and certainly not a fruit of the Spirit. Jesus is our model; he gave it all for us. That's the ultimate act of unselfishness.

After many years of marriage, my wife's words echo in my mind, "Honey, it's not about you." She's right—she usually is—it's not about me: not in my relationships, not in my service, not in my writing this devotional book. It's about doing for others and loving them with compassion. It's about sacrificially serving others and giving generously of my time and treasures. When you take the focus off yourself and put it onto the Savior, everything changes.

Your Reflections

_____

_____

_____

_____

_____

_____

Prayer

Father, I rejoice in your goodness and in how serving you brings me such joy. I am grateful that I can call you Father; your warm embrace comforts me. I sing your praises, oh, Lord. Help me this day, dear Lord, to share your love, compassion, and grace with others. In Christ's holy name I pray, amen.

WEEK TWENTY-SIX

NEW EVERY MORNING

NEW EVERY MORNING   DAY ONE

Today's Verses—Lamentations 3:22-23

The Lord's lovingkindness indeed never ceases, for His compassions never fail. They are new every morning; Great is Your faithfulness.

Additional Reading: Proverbs 3:5-7; Hebrews 10:22-24; Psalm 51:10-13

My Thoughts

Lamentations 3:22-23 is one of my favorite Bible passages. Why? Because it's true in my life, and it's true in yours. God's lovingkindness is never ending. It flows freely out of his love and compassion. We are surrounded by his creation, the beauty of the world he created for us to enjoy. The rising sun and the blessings of a new day speak of his faithfulness.

Do you see his beauty? Do you recognize his faithfulness? No matter where you are in your life, God is present and faithful. Circumstances such as illness, broken relationships, and financial challenges can cloud our view. Look past these things and know that all things work for good.

Your Reflections

_____

_____

_____

_____

_____

_____

Prayer

Holy Father, I am so grateful that your lovingkindness never ceases. Your compassion never fails. You indeed are faithful. Renew in me a new heart that shouts your praises at the dawn of each new day with hope and love. Let my actions and my deeds reflect your joy and goodness, that it might glorify you. In Jesus' name I pray, amen.

NEW EVERY MORNING   DAY TWO

Today's Verses—Psalm 106:1

Praise the Lord! Oh, give thanks to the Lord, for He is good; For His lovingkindness is everlasting. Who can speak of the mighty deeds of the Lord, or can show forth all His praise?

Additional Reading: Ephesians 1:3-7; 2 Corinthians 5:15-17; Romans 15:4-6

My Thoughts

Are you a morning person? I think it's humorous to think of people that way because, at the end of the day, we are all morning people if we choose to be. Now, I understand that some of us have higher energy levels at different times of the day. Are you dependent on your caffeine to get your day started?

The only thing we should be dependent on is a healthy dose of the Savior. Don't get me wrong; I love a good, strong cup of coffee every morning. I enjoy exercise as well, but it's not what truly gets me going. What energizes me is the knowledge that every morning is a wonderful opportunity to worship and serve the Savior.

Your Reflections

_____

_____

_____

_____

_____

_____

Prayer

Father God, your beautiful creation surrounds me and shouts to your glory. Your faithfulness and blessings are truly new each day with the coming sunrise. Your magnificence brings me encouragement each day to glorify your name and sing your praises. Fill my soul this day with your love and grace, that it would radiate through me. In Jesus' name I pray, amen.

SDG

NEW EVERY MORNING   DAY THREE

Today's Verses—Titus 3:4-5

But when the kindness of God our Savior and His love for mankind appeared, He saved us, not on the basis of deeds which we have done in righteousness, but according to His mercy, by the washing of regeneration and renewing by the Holy Spirit.

Additional Reading: Psalm 89:8; 1 Corinthians 1:4-9; Isaiah 41:10

My Thoughts

What a joy to serve a loving and merciful God who, through his Spirit, offers us a fresh start. And better yet, this is not just a whitewash where your junk gets covered up. Your sin is gone, forgiven and forgotten—as though it never happened.

And even better yet, as we seek to walk with him but stumble, he is quick to forgive. Here's a promise from 1 John 1:9: "If we confess our sins, He is faithful and righteous to forgive us our sins and to cleanse us from all unrighteousness." Will you take a moment today to thank God for your new beginning and recognize that his grace and forgiveness are new every morning?

Your Reflections

_____

_____

_____

_____

_____

_____

Prayer

Loving Father, my heart rejoices in your blessings. Your lovingkindness never ceases. Your Word offers me new insights and wisdom in your plan for my life. Your Holy Spirit guides me and teaches me to do your will. Your Holy Spirit cautions me when I move out of your plan. Strengthen me this day, oh, Lord, that I might walk in your will. In Christ's mighty and wonderful name I pray, amen.

NEW EVERY MORNING   DAY FOUR

Today's Verses—Psalm 51:10
Create in me a clean heart, O God, And renew a steadfast spirit within me.

Additional Reading: 1 Corinthians 1:4-9; Psalm 23:6; 1 John 1:5-9

My Thoughts
God is an amazing God! He can do anything. He can fill a dry well with fresh water. He can bring rain or cover the clouds. He can stop the sun from setting. He can make a donkey speak or part the sea. He can turn water into wine and heal the sick. He can resurrect the dead. He can make the blind see.

There are no limits to what God can do. He is ready to do wonderful and marvelous things in your life if you will yield to him. God is sovereign, so just because he doesn't answer a specific prayer, it doesn't mean he can't. A Bible teacher told me once that we should not expect God to change to meet our needs, but we should, instead, change our requests according to his purpose for our lives.

Your Reflections

_____

_____

_____

_____

_____

_____

Prayer
Father God, I am grateful that you have forgiven me for my sins and they are forgotten. I rejoice that daily, by your grace, I have a fresh start without a blemish from the past. I praise your holy name. Oh, God, you alone are my healer and my deliverer. Help me this day, Lord, to focus on the future, your will for this day, and my walk with you. In the matchless name of my Savior, Jesus Christ, I pray, amen.

SDG

NEW EVERY MORNING DAY FIVE

Today's Verses—Ephesians 4:22-24

That, in reference to your former manner of life, you lay aside the old self, which is being corrupted in accordance with the lusts of deceit, and that you be renewed in the spirit of your mind, and put on the new self, which in the likeness of God has been created in righteousness and holiness of the truth.

Additional Reading: Psalm 24:4-6; Jeremiah 29:11-14; 1 Corinthians 1:4-9

My Thoughts

We were created in the likeness of God for righteousness and truth. Everything about our lives, our family, and our world is made new. We must put aside the old self, along with our old ways, and renew our walk every morning.

What a victory we have in Christ—to know every morning that our relationship with him is fresh. What an adventure to have the living God guide you. How will you celebrate this victory and rejoice in his goodness?

Your Reflections

_____

_____

_____

_____

_____

_____

Prayer

I love you, Lord. I lift my voice to worship you. Oh, my soul rejoices! Take joy, my King, in what you hear. Let it be a sweet, sweet sound in your ear.[8] *Father God, your joy fills my heart. You give me a new song each day. Renew in me this day your love, hope, and grace, that I might glorify you. In Jesus' name I pray, amen.*

---

8   Laurie Klein, "I Love You, Lord" (Nashville: Brentwood Beason, 1978).
SDG

WEEK TWENTY-SEVEN

REJOICE IN THE LORD

REJOICE IN THE LORD   DAY ONE

Today's Verses—Philippians 4:4-5

Rejoice in the Lord always; again, I will say, rejoice! Let your gentle spirit be known to all men. The Lord is near.

Additional Reading: Romans 5:3-5; Zephaniah 3:14-17; Psalm 5:11-12

My Thoughts

Rejoicing with a gentle spirit, I think, simply means that our joy is internal and external. We don't necessarily need to be jumping up and down and acting like a crazy person. To me, it's having a calmness that comes from the strength of the Savior.

How do you act when you're happy? When you get good news, like a promotion or a big tax refund? These events are exciting but only temporary. The kind of joy that this verse speaks of can only come from the unshakable love of Christ. What are new ways you can rejoice in the Lord?

Your Reflections

_____

_____

_____

_____

_____

_____

Prayer

Father God, I love to sing your praises. My rejoicing wells up deep in my spirit. Your love lifts me to new joy. You alone are my rock and my redeemer. I give thanks for your blessings in my life and rejoice. I pray, dear Lord, that your great love would pour through me and that others would see you in me. In Jesus' name I pray, amen.

REJOICE IN THE LORD   DAY TWO

Today's Verses—Luke 10:19-20

Behold, I have given you authority to tread upon serpents and scorpions, and over all the power of the enemy, and nothing shall injure you. Nevertheless, do not rejoice in this, that the spirits are subject to you, but rejoice that your names are recorded in heaven.

Additional Reading: Acts 16:33-34; Romans 12:15; Titus 3:5

My Thoughts

OK, this is cool. It's OK to stomp on spiders and scorpions, which I am glad to learn because I have been smashing them for years. They give me the creeps, to be perfectly honest. But I'm missing what's better. God has given us all the authority and power over the enemy. But wait, there's more. As TV commercials often say, that's not even the best part!

What's even bigger news is that our names are recorded in heaven. Now, that's what I call a wall of honor. I don't think my name will be etched on some wall, but I am confident it will be recorded somewhere. Just the thought of getting there and being in the presence of the Almighty causes me to rejoice.

Your Reflections

_____

_____

_____

_____

_____

_____

Prayer

Gracious heavenly Father, my mouth cannot keep from singing your praises. My soul shouts with the joy of your presence. I rejoice, my King, and praise your holy name. I am reminded in Titus 3:5 that you saved us "according to your mercy." Your goodness is without end. Your blessings surround me, and I give you praise. In the matchless name of Jesus I pray, amen.

SDG

REJOICE IN THE LORD DAY THREE

Today's Verses—Isaiah 65:18

But be glad and rejoice forever in what I create; For behold, I create Jerusalem for rejoicing and her people for gladness.

Additional Reading: Galatians 2:20; Ecclesiastes 3:12; Acts 8:38-39

My Thoughts

God created us for rejoicing; I like that. If we take the time to look around and focus on areas in which we can rejoice, it changes our entire perspective. I personally love to see sunrises and the majesty of the morning sun peeking through the clouds. I love seeing the magnificent hues of orange as my heart sings his praises.

I cannot visit the ocean and see the waves crashing, one right after another, without seeing his glory. God's creation is full of beauty. Take some time today to really look at God's creation. Go for a walk in the woods or on the beach this week. Your soul can't help but sing his praises and rejoice.

Your Reflections

_____

_____

_____

_____

_____

Prayer

Father God, you are an amazing and wonderful God. Everywhere I turn, I see your workmanship. I see you in the beauty of the rising sun. You are present in the serenity of nature. Lord, your blessings are also revealed through the work of your people. I give thanks that your love flows through us for good. We bring hope and light to a fallen world. Strengthen us this day, dear Lord, that we might do your good work. In Christ's holy name I pray, amen.

REJOICE IN THE LORD   DAY FOUR

Today's Verses—Psalm 113:1-9

Praise the Lord! Praise, O servants of the Lord, praise the name of the Lord. Blessed be the name of the Lord. From this time forth and forever. From the rising of the sun to its setting the name of the Lord is to be praised. The Lord is high above all nations; His glory is above the heavens. Who is like the Lord our God, who is enthroned on high, Who humbles Himself to behold the things that are in heaven and in the earth? He raises the poor from the dust and lifts the needy from the ash heap, to make them sit with princes, with the princes of His people. He makes the barren woman abide in the house as a joyful mother of children. Praise the Lord!

Additional Reading: John 1:12-14; Mark 16:15-16; Luke 12:48

My Thoughts

I think Psalm 113:1-9 says it all. We are simply to praise the Lord in everything and always. His majesty is present in every aspect of our lives, whether we choose to see it or not. From Genesis to Revelation, God repeatedly displays his great love for us. His mercy is never ending, and his forgiveness is continuous.

So why do we lack joy? I think it's because we live in a fallen world and allow our thinking and actions to be governed by it. God never intended us to live broken and miserable lives. Our challenge is our free will. God will never force you to walk according to his will or follow him. But from my experience, life can be joyful if we just yield to him. Give him control and let your rejoicing begin.

Your Reflections

_____

_____

_____

_____

_____

_____

Prayer

Blessed be the name of the Lord, from the rising of the sun in the East to its setting in the West. The name of the Lord is to be praised (Psalm 113:2-3). Gracious Father, I lift my voice to give you thanks and rejoice. Your mighty hand is on my life, and I praise you. Give me eyes to see, ears to hear your voice, and opportunities to give you praise. In Christ's holy name I pray, amen.

SDG

REJOICE IN THE LORD

Today's Verses—Job 38:7

When the morning stars sang together, and all the sons of God shouted for joy?

Additional Reading: 1 Thessalonians 5:16-17; Philippians 3:1-3; Galatians 5:22-26

My Thoughts

The Westminster Shorter Catechism states: "Man's chief end is to glorify God and enjoy him forever." So, how can we do that? It sounds easy, but the reality is that when we take our eyes off the Savior, the world clouds our vision. Luke 19:40 reads, "But Jesus answered, 'I tell you, if these become silent, the stones will cry out!' " So, you see, God doesn't need us to shout for joy.

At the end of the day, when you learn to walk fully in God's will, surrender yourself to him, walk by faith, and trust him completely to guide you, encourage you, and prosper you, your very soul will rejoice and shout for joy. Each day is a new adventure, a new opportunity to experience his goodness.

Your Reflections

_____

_____

_____

_____

_____

_____

Prayer

Father God, I see you in my comings and my goings. You surround me with your love, mercy, and lovingkindness. You are my God, and I rejoice. Lord, keep me ever mindful of your goodness, that I might see your hand in everything. Teach me to rejoice in good and bad times, in happiness and in sorrow. Help me to recognize your mighty hand that guides and protects me. You are my comfort and protection. In Jesus' name I pray, amen.

SDG

WEEK TWENTY-EIGHT

MORE THAN CONQUERORS

MORE THAN CONQUERORS DAY ONE

Today's Verses—Romans 8:37-39

But in all these things we overwhelmingly conquer through Him who loved us. For I am convinced that neither death, nor life, nor angels, nor principalities, nor things present, nor things to come, nor powers, nor height, nor depth, nor any other created thing, will be able to separate us from the love of God, which is in Christ Jesus our Lord.

Additional Reading: Ephesians 6:10-12; Revelation 6:2; 2 Corinthians 4:8-11

My Thoughts

When I think of conquerors, I think about an army—especially the ancient Roman army. They certainly had their share of victories, and there was little doubt that they could conquer their enemies. They were well trained, organized, and disciplined and had great strength in numbers.

Unfortunately, any army man builds can and will be defeated. Our calling in Christ is to be conquerors for his Kingdom, which cannot be defeated. We have the almighty God as our supreme commander, and he has a wonderful plan to defeat the enemy. His Word is our training manual, and the Holy Spirit is our battlefield commander. Nothing can separate us from him.

Your Reflections

_____

_____

_____

_____

_____

_____

Prayer

Father God, I welcome this new week of opportunity to stand strong in you. I am more than a conqueror because of you and your presence in my life. I pray, dear Lord, for strength to boldly enter the battle to defeat evil and darkness. I pray that my victory would bring honor and glory to you. In Jesus' name I pray, amen.

MORE THAN CONQUERORS   DAY TWO

Today's Verses—2 Timothy 1:7
For God has not given us a spirit of timidity, but of power and love and discipline.

Additional Reading: Isaiah 46:9-11; John 4-8; Jeremiah 29:11-13

My Thoughts

God's calling is for us to act in his power, exercising compassion while remaining disciplined—much like any good solider. He expects us to be bold in our daily lives, proclaiming his goodness and his glory. He also wants us in the battle.

If God is not your power source and you are easily defeated by the evil one, how can you be a good solider? His boldness and his power must come from inside of us and manifest itself in our daily walk. This victorious outlook will lead others to you, which, in turn, leads them to your power source. Nobody wants to join a defeated army.

Your Reflections

_____

_____

_____

_____

_____

_____

Prayer

Father God, Jesus told me that if I abide in him and his Word abides in me, I can ask anything I want, and it will be done. I rejoice that you abide in me. I pray that I will study your Word daily that it, too, might abide in me. Guide me also that my desires and requests would always be in keeping with your will. Help me to boldly proclaim you and to yield much fruit. In Christ's holy name I pray, amen.

MORE THAN CONQUERORS

DAY THREE

Today's Verses—1 John 5:4

For whatever is born of God overcomes the world; and this is the victory that has overcome the world—our faith.

Additional Reading: Romans 12:1-2; Titus 3:5-7; Ephesians 4:29-32

My Thoughts

It's clear to me that we serve the one and only true and mighty God. As such, he doesn't need us to conquer anything besides our own fears and doubts. He doesn't need us to fight his battles; he has a league of angels. But God has also created this world for us, and he gave us dominion over it.

Where we fall short at times is not trusting in him and not following his battle plan. He gave us free will, and, too often, we think we are smarter than God and can go it alone. Big mistake! God wants us to act in his power and his strength. If we follow his battle plan, we cannot be defeated. We can overcome fear, the evil one, and the world.

Your Reflections

_____

_____

_____

_____

_____

_____

Prayer

Gracious Father, you have given me victory and authority to overcome the world. As your emissary, I pray for the courage and faith to stand boldly in the gap as an overcomer. Your great love and mercy are present in me. Teach me to share it each day as I conqueror darkness. In Jesus' name I pray, amen.

MORE THAN CONQUERORS   DAY FOUR

Today's Verses—1 Corinthians 15:57
But thanks be to God, who gives us the victory through our Lord Jesus Christ.

Additional Reading: Isaiah 41:10-13; Romans 16:20; James 1:12

My Thoughts
I love the fact that we do not have to face life's battles alone. We have the Son of God beside us. Jesus is God, and his mission was to come to the earth in bodily form to lead us in the fight against evil. He cannot and will not be defeated, and he welcomes you to the battle.

Are you engaged? Are you preparing for the fight? God has a very clear path to victory that's clearly laid out in his Word. Take time today to go beyond your basic training and advance your knowledge so that none of the fiery arrows of the devil can pierce your soul.

Your Reflections

_____

_____

_____

_____

_____

_____

Prayer
Father God, your words in Isaiah 41:13 tell me that "you are the Lord my God, who upholds my right hand." You also tell me not to fear because you are with me. This gives me hope and courage to enter your service with boldness and in assurance of victory. Keep me on your path, dear Lord, that I would remain in your will to do your good work. In Christ's holy name I pray, amen.

SDG

MORE THAN CONQUERORS   DAY FIVE

Today's Verses—Deuteronomy 20:4

For the Lord your God is the one who goes with you, to fight for you against your enemies, to save you.

Additional Reading: Romans 8:11; 1 John 4:4; Psalm 60:12

My Thoughts

With God by our side, how can we be defeated? Our victory is assured if we follow the Savior. He has given his angels charge to protect us, and we have the Holy Spirit to guide us.

What is it that defeats you? What is it that keeps you in the battle that leads to victory? Satan doesn't want you to fight; he wants you defeated before you even engage. Is there sin in your life, or is it fear? You must repent of your sin and trust God to keep his promise to bring you victory. He will not leave you, and he is always by your side. Trust him!

Your Reflections

_____

_____

_____

_____

_____

_____

Prayer

Father God, as I start my day, I recognize that the battle I face is not against flesh and blood but against the ruler of darkness and spiritual wickedness in high places (Ephesians 6:12). With you by my side, victory is assured. Keep me ever vigilant against the schemes of the enemy, Lord God. Help me to be fortified with your Word and filled by your Spirit that victory would be certain. To you be the glory, oh, Lord! In Jesus' name I pray, amen.

WEEK TWENTY-NINE
GOD'S QUALITIES

GOD'S QUALITIES

DAY ONE

Today's Verses—Romans 1:20

For since the creation of the world His invisible attributes, His eternal power and divine nature, have been clearly seen, being understood through what has been made, so that they are without excuse.

Additional Reading: Hebrews 13:8; 2 Peter 3:8-9; Isaiah 40:28-31

My Thoughts

This is a big topic. How can you describe the indescribable, the one true God? What I will share this week is the God I know, based on some of his names, characteristics, attributes, and sovereignty. It is only a display of my thoughts and in no way limits who God is.

God is Jehovah, the name of the independent, self-complete being. "I AM WHO I AM" (Exodus 3:4) only applies to Jehovah God. For me, God is my all in all; there is nothing I lack or need besides him.

God is El-Shaddai. This name means God Almighty, the God who is all-sufficient and all-bountiful in the source of all blessings. He is my only source for hope and blessings. Once we understand and recognize him for who he is, all else pales in comparison.t

Your Reflections

_____

_____

_____

_____

_____

_____

Prayer

Father God, you are without equal; nothing can compare with you. You are eternal and all-powerful—the creator of the universe. Yet you are not a cold and distant deity. You are a loving and compassionate God who loves me deeply. You are the true and living God who cares for my soul. I give you thanks, dear Lord, that I can approach your throne of grace and call you Father. I love you, Lord. In your holy name I pray, amen.

SDG

GOD'S QUALITIES DAY TWO

Today's Verses—Isaiah 9:6

For a child will be born to us, a son will be given to us; and the government will rest on His shoulders; And His name will be called Wonderful Counselor, mighty God, Eternal Father, Prince of Peace.

Additional Reading: 1 John 4:7-10; Psalm 18:30-31; 1 Peter 1:15

My Thoughts

Although God sent his son born of a human mother, he sent him to set the world right. Everything rests on his shoulders, and he is God. Jesus emanates the qualities of the Father: love, compassion, wisdom, forgiveness, mercy, and truth.

Jesus walked on the earth and experienced hunger and thirst. He was fully human, so he understands us. He was tempted but did not sin. He had the power to heal the sick, cause the lame to walk, and give sight to the blind. He is the Prince of Peace and welcomes us into his loving arms.

Your Reflections

_____

_____

_____

_____

_____

_____

Prayer

Father God, your attributes are unparrelled. They are too great for me to fully comprehend, yet still you are a loving and intimate God. Your mighty hand created the world but also gently guides me, your child. You are never too busy to hear my prayers or show your grace. You are the same Holy God yesterday, today, and tomorrow. I pray this day, oh, Lord, that my actions would be in keeping with your will and that your character would shine through me. In Christ's holy name I pray, amen.

GOD'S QUALITIES   DAY THREE

Today's Verses—Colossians 1:16

For by Him all things were created, both in the heavens and on earth, visible and invisible, whether thrones or dominions or rulers or authorities—all things have been created through Him and for Him.

Additional Reading: Psalm 30:5; Micah 7:18-19; Exodus 34:67

My Thoughts

God is eternal and infinite. He created everything in heaven and on earth for his glory. Be it the air we breathe, the water we drink, or the food that sustains us, it all comes from him. He causes kings to rise and kingdoms to fall. He blesses nations and promises to protect all who believe and follow his commands.

The world is at his command, and nothing is out of his domain. God, out of his great love for us, sent his only son to die on the cross so that we might have an intimate relationship with him. God controls the universe but still has a plan for you. He knows the hairs on your head and cares deeply for you. Reach out to him today. He's waiting.

Your Reflections

_____

_____

_____

_____

_____

_____

Prayer

Father God, I marvel at your promises and praise your holy name for your amazing love and protection. Everything in heaven and earth was created by you. You are all-knowing and all-seeing. You never sleep. Your watchful eye keeps us safe, and your loving arms comfort us. Help me this day, oh, Lord, to walk in your will, that I might stay in your warm embrace. In your wonderful and holy name I pray, amen.

SDG

GOD'S QUALITIES

DAY FOUR

Today's Verses—1 Chronicles 29:11

Yours, O Lord, is the greatness and the power and the glory and the victory and the majesty, indeed everything that is in the heavens and the earth; Yours is the dominion, O Lord, and You exalt Yourself as head over all.

Additional Reading: John 4:24; Proverbs 30:5-6; Psalm 89:8-14

My Thoughts

God is sovereign. He is the mighty God and King, worthy of our praise. Nothing stands against his mighty throne. He will never be defeated, and, best of all, we are included in the victory.

Has his power transferred to you? Are you easily defeated by worry or fear? Is sin keeping you from completing God's will in your life? Has the evil one defeated you and taken you out of the fight? We are his warriors. He is our champion. Call on him!

Your Reflections

_____

_____

_____

_____

_____

_____

Prayer

Almighty God, righteousness and justice are the foundation of your throne. I am grateful that you have accepted me into your Kingdom. Teach me your righteousness and justice. I rejoice in our divine partnership. Guide me this day, oh, Lord, that I might truly speak in your holy name and act in your righteousness. In your holy name I pray, amen.

SDG

GOD'S QUALITIES

DAY FIVE

Today's Verses—Ephesians 1:19-21

And what is the surpassing greatness of His power toward us who believe. These are in accordance with the working of the strength of His might which He brought about in Christ, when He raised Him from the dead and seated Him at His right hand in the heavenly places, far above all rule and authority and power and dominion, and every name that is named, not only in this age but also in the one to come.

Additional Reading: Psalm 18:30-31; Job 12:9-10; John 14:17-19

My Thoughts

Seminary professor Wilburn Smith is credited for saying, "If you try and understand the Trinity, you will lose your mind. But if you deny the Trinity, you will lose your soul!" I won't try to explain the Trinity because understanding God with the human mind is very difficult.

I do believe, however, that God the Father, God the Son, and God the Holy Spirit are one. They may all play a separate role, but they are still God. I often pray to God the Father but end my prayers, "In Jesus' name," as recognition to both members of the Trinity. I believe the Holy Spirit resides in me and is my daily guide, instructing me and reminding me when I am about to step out of God's will. So, understanding the Trinity is not the key but believing in a triune God is.

Your Reflections

_____

_____

_____

_____

_____

_____

Prayer

Almighty God, you are my rock and my shield. You alone are my refuge. I praise your name, oh, Lord, for you alone are good. You are my king, and all power and glory is yours. Father, teach me to recognize your hand in every aspect of my life, that I might give you honor and praise. In Jesus' name I pray, amen.

WEEK THIRTY

SERVE OTHERS
WITH JOY

SERVE OTHERS WITH JOY   DAY ONE

Today's Verses—Romans 12:11-13

Not lagging in diligence, fervent in spirit, serving the Lord; rejoicing in hope, persevering in tribulation, devoted to prayer, contributing to the needs of the saints, practicing hospitality.

Additional Reading: 1 Peter 4:8-10; Acts 20:34-35; Matthew 20:25-28

My Thoughts

I believe we could spend the rest of our lives serving the Lord and it wouldn't be enough. With service comes honor, so as we serve, we honor our God. Our service must come from an attitude of gratitude. If we are truly thankful for God's goodness, provisions, and blessings, service comes naturally.

How do we serve our Lord and Savior? We serve him with our prayers, recognizing his glory and majesty. We serve him through our obedience to his commands. We serve him by our worship and our praises. We serve him by recognizing his authority in our lives. Do you have a servant's heart? Do you openly look for ways to serve our king?

Your Reflections

_____

_____

_____

_____

_____

_____

Prayer

Lord God, you are a mighty and wonderful God. You are the King of the universe, yet you are an intimate God. I give you praise. I am grateful that as your child, I can model Jesus in his service to others. Help me to be ever mindful that he came to serve and not to be served. Help me to find ways to serve others and share your love. In Jesus' name I pray, amen.

SDG

SERVE OTHERS WITH JOY

Today's Verses—Mark 10:45

For even the Son of Man did not come to be served, but to serve, and to give His life a ransom for many.

Additional Reading: Philippians 2:1-4; Proverbs 11:25; 1 John 3:17-18

My Thoughts

Jesus was a model of service. He was the ultimate servant leader. He served by healing the sick and giving sight to the blind. He broke bread with the slave and the sinner. He washed his disciples' feet. His service was on display as he preached and taught us the only path to eternal life. He prayed for his disciples and the people he was in contact with.

He served the Father by doing his will. He served the Father by giving him the glory. Jesus' life was dedicated to service, service to the Father, service to people. How can you model Jesus in your service?

Your Reflections

_____

_____

_____

_____

_____

_____

Prayer

Gracious and loving Father, I praise your holy name. You alone are worthy of my praises. You gave me a heart of love and compassion to serve others, and I am grateful. Give me this day, dear Lord, your compassion for others. Give me your discernment to reach out to the sick and hurting. Help me to model you, that your love would shine through me, unto your honor and glory. In Christ's holy name I pray, amen.

SERVE OTHERS WITH JOY   DAY THREE

Today's Verses—Ephesians 6:7
With good will render service, as to the Lord, and not to men.

Additional Reading: Proverbs 19:17; Matthew 5:16; James 2:14-1

My Thoughts

As we serve, we must do it as though we are serving God. Serving others reflects the model Christ gave us, and it must be personal. We have the greatest impact on people when we serve them out of love and compassion, serving out of the joy that God has given us and sharing his love as we serve.

If Christ came to serve and not to be served, shouldn't we have the same mind-set? How can we serve our families, our friends, and our coworkers/staff? Are we the first person our friends think of when they have a need? Are you inconvenienced by serving others? Christ wasn't, so why should you be?

Your Reflections

_____

_____

_____

_____

_____

_____

Prayer

Father God, the heavens sing of your glory. You alone are magnified by the praises of your people. You have given me a grateful heart for your presence in my life. You are my God, my protector, and provider. I praise your name, oh, Lord. Help me, dear Lord, to have a heart for service to the hurting and lost. Give me the wisdom to reach out in love and share your goodness. In Christ's holy name I pray, amen.

SERVE OTHERS WITH JOY DAY FOUR

Today's Verses—Galatians 5:13

For you were called to freedom, brethren; only do not turn your freedom into an opportunity for the flesh, but through love serve one another.

Additional Reading: 1 Corinthians 9:19; Proverbs 31:8-9; Deuteronomy 15:11

My Thoughts

How are you serving in your community, your church, or in missions? Service is the greatest demonstration of God's love I can think of. Often, we think that if we just give of our finances, that is enough. Not that giving money is wrong, but what has the most impact is personal touch—our personal service.

Jesus walked among the people. He made it personal. Your presence is often what a lonely person needs. Your loving words serve the brokenhearted. Your prayers over the sick or grieving are comforting. Going to the needy, whether it be in your community or a foreign land, is service in action. How can you demonstrate the love of Jesus in your service?

Your Reflections

_____

_____

_____

_____

_____

_____

Prayer

Father God, you are love. You created me in your image. Give me a heart of love and compassion just like your own. Help me this day to be aware of the needs of others and to demonstrate your love to them, that my service would bring you honor and glory. In Jesus' name I pray, amen.

SERVE OTHERS WITH JOY DAY FIVE

Today's Verses—Joshua 24:15

If it is disagreeable in your sight to serve the Lord, choose for yourselves today whom you will serve: whether the gods which your fathers served which were beyond the River, or the gods of the Amorites in whose land you are living; but as for me and my house, we will serve the Lord.

Additional Reading: Matthew 25:35-40; Ephesians 2:10; Romans 12:6-7

My Thoughts

Have you created a culture of service in your home? Does your family see the model of a loving servant in you? Does this service reflect your love for Jesus?

Often, our service is determined by our schedule or our finances, but I think God wants us to serve regardless of either. Schedule time with your family to visit an elderly friend or relative. Work in a food kitchen over the holidays. Volunteer at an old-age home. Be Christ in action!

Your Reflections

Prayer

Father God, I rejoice in you this day for giving me the gift of service. I am grateful to have been created in Christ Jesus for good works (Ephesians 2:10). Dear Lord, please give me clear direction about whom to serve and help me remember that everyone in my path needs you. Help me to be your emissary of love, compassion, and service. In the matchless name of Christ Jesus I pray, amen.

WEEK THIRTY-ONE
HEALED

HEALED DAY ONE

Today's Verses—Isaiah 53:5

But He was pierced through for our transgressions, He was crushed for our iniquities; The chastening for our well-being fell upon Him, and by His scourging we are healed.

Additional Reading: Jeremiah 17:14; 1 Peter 2:24; James 5:15

My Thoughts

In the beginning, God had fellowship with Adam and Eve. He walked with them. He provided all their needs. What a wonderful time for them! But with the discontent that Satan put in Eve's head, both she and Adam disobeyed God. Thus, we were forever separated from fellowship with God.

Throughout the Old Testament, God shows his grace to his people. He blessed them and forgave them. Time after time, they turned their backs on God and suffered the consequences. Through the death and resurrection of Jesus Christ, forgiveness is available to all who accept him as Savior. As believers, we can walk in the light of his healing and salvation.

Your Reflections

_____

_____

_____

_____

_____

_____

Prayer

Father God, each new day, I give you praise, for you alone are great. Your love and compassion sustain me and strengthen me. Your healing is complete, and your restoration is for all eternity. You have healed me from the sickness of my sin. You have healed me from the depravity of my soul. As I walk in your redemption, I sing your praises and give you thanks, oh, Lord, my God. In Jesus' holy name I pray, amen.

HEALED   DAY TWO

Today's Verses—James 5:16

Therefore, confess your sins to one another, and pray for one another so that you may be healed. The effective prayer of a righteous man can accomplish much.

Additional Reading: Luke 4:40; Psalm 103:3; 1 John 3:8-9

My Thoughts

I love the fact that we are called to pray for one another. It comforts me when I know others are lifting me up in prayer for my needs and for my family. We are truly a spiritual family that deeply cares about each other's well-being. We get to model God's love and the compassion of our Lord Jesus.

The best part of James 5:16 is that it tells us God hears our prayers. We have a direct line of communication to the King of Kings, the mighty God. How would your prayers change if you believed without a doubt that God hears your prayers? He may not always answer prayers in the way we want, but he does hear our prayers and will bring about our healing according to his will and his purpose.

Your Reflections

_____

_____

_____

_____

_____

_____

Prayer

Father God, you are too amazing for me to fully comprehend. Your magnificence covers all the earth. Your love and compassion are available to all, and your healing touch is ever present. You have the power to heal illness and disease. More importantly, you heal our souls. Your healing offers us eternal life in your son, Christ Jesus. Help me this day to be your ambassador to a hurting world that needs your divine healing. In your holy name I pray, amen.

SDG

HEALED   DAY THREE

Today's Verses—1 Peter 1:18-19

Knowing that you were not redeemed with perishable things like silver or gold from your futile way of life inherited from your forefathers, but with precious blood, as of a lamb unblemished and spotless, the blood of Christ.

Additional Reading: Matthew 18:18-20; Deuteronomy 7:15; Revelation 21:4

My Thoughts

No barrier was too great to bring us into a right relationship with our God—not even the foolishness of our past or the belief that the wealth of the world could save us in any way. Only the precious blood of Jesus has the power to cleanse us of our sins.

Our redemption gives us a new life in which to maximize the wonderful gift of healing and the new beginning we've received. The challenge is not to return to our old self but to walk every day in the light of salvation, which gives us hope and joy to proclaim God's goodness and salvation.

Your Reflections

_____

_____

_____

_____

_____

_____

Prayer

Dear Lord Jesus, you are the Alpha and Omega. You are the beginning and the end. You are the Bright Morning Star. Nothing is greater than you. I praise your name, oh, Lord. You are the great healer, who offers eternal hope and healing to the world. Use me this day, oh, Lord, as an instrument of your healing touch. You alone offer eternal wellness and everlasting hope. In your holy name I pray, amen.

HEALED

Today's Verses—Ephesians 2:8-9

For by grace you have been saved through faith; and that not of yourselves, it is the gift of God; not as a result of works, so that no one may boast.

Additional Reading: 1 John 5:14-15; Matthew 10:8; Psalm 107:20-21

My Thoughts

If you've ever played the game Monopoly, you know that playing a "get out of jail" card or paying a fine will free you. Often, we think the same is true in life, but the ultimate "get out of jail" card only comes through the blood of Jesus.

We can't buy our salvation. We can't earn it by good works or by being a good person. The Bible clearly says that we are all sinners and fall short of God's glory. There is nothing on your own that you can do to be healed. Only by accepting Christ can you walk with God.

Your Reflections

_____

_____

_____

_____

_____

_____

Prayer

Father God, thank you for this day. I rejoice in your goodness and blessings. I am grateful that your healing and forgiveness have transformed me for eternity. Father, guide me this day to be your hands and feet to reach out to those who need your healing touch. Help me to allow the Holy Spirit to flow through me for your glory. In Christ's holy name I pray, amen.

SDG

HEALED

DAY FIVE

Today's Verses—Revelation 21:4

And He will wipe away every tear from their eyes; and there will no longer be any death; there will no longer be any mourning, or crying, or pain; the first things have passed away.

Additional Reading: 2 Peter 3:8-9; Galatians 2:20; 2 Chronicles 7:14

My Thoughts

God's ultimate plan is to bring healing to his people—healing from sin, illness, and ultimately death. He will heal the hurting, the grieving, the lonely, and the lost. Everything will be new, no more sorrow, no more pain.

Our role as disciples of Christ is to share this healing now with those who are hurting. Jesus is the great healer, and he alone can bring true peace. Share his love and healing by sharing his salvation. We are his workers who bring the good news.

Your Reflections

_____

_____

_____

_____

_____

_____

Prayer

Father God, every day is a new day as I walk with you. Your goodness is new every morning. Your immense love sustains me. Your loving arms comfort me. Your grace encourages me. Lord, your heart must break at the site of this fallen world. Give me the courage and the boldness to share you with everyone I can—to share your message of love, hope, and salvation. You alone offer complete and eternal healing. In the matchless name of Christ Jesus I pray, amen.

10X

WEEK THIRTY-TWO

10X

10X   DAY ONE

Today's Verses—Daniel 1:20

As for every matter of wisdom and understanding about which the king consulted them, he found them ten times better than all the magicians and conjurers who were in all his realm.

Additional Reading: 2 Timothy 2:15; 1 Corinthians 15:57-58; Philippians 1:9-11

My Thoughts

Daniel 1:20 is the verse that motivated me to write this entire devotional book. Imagine four young Jewish boys, in captivity, taken by King Nebuchadnezzar from Jerusalem to Babylon. They were second-class citizens at best and slaves at worst—but God had a great purpose for them. They were chosen to serve at the king's court, with access to rich food from the king's table. Yet they chose a diet of vegetables and water to avoid defiling themselves or dishonoring their God.

How easy would it have been to simply eat the king's food and drink the wine? They were in captivity. Who would blame them? I wonder what I would have done under these circumstances. I might not have been as strong, to be honest.

What would it be like if we had that kind of conviction and trust in God? I believe that in many ways we are in a foreign land—maybe not in captivity but surrounded by darkness. The whole idea here is to stand firm on the promises of God and honor him. What is keeping you from being ten times better?

Your Reflections

_____

_____

_____

_____

_____

_____

Prayer

Father God, my heart rejoices at your wisdom and knowledge, which is transferred to your followers. Your Word is filled with that same wisdom and knowledge for us to live by. Help me, oh, Lord, to run to you—to immerse myself in your learning. May your wisdom help me to succeed in your work, which brings victory in Jesus Christ. In his holy name I pray, amen.

10X

DAY TWO

Today's Verses—Colossians 3:23

Whatever you do, do your work heartily, as for the Lord rather than for men.

Additional Reading: Matthew 5:13-16; Romans 12:1-2; 2 Chronicles 15:7

My Thoughts

Living life as a true 10X-er means giving your all, first to God and then to everything else. Whether you are an employee or a business owner, you must strive to be the best—not the best you can be, because that relies on you, but the best God created you to be. Follow the example of the heroes of the Bible. Once they understood their calling, they were all in—even to the point of death. That's our model.

What are you good at? What makes you stand out among your peers? Do others clearly see the joy of the Lord in you? Do you shine because of his Spirit that lives in you? To truly excel in anything, it must be through the power of the Holy Spirit.

Do everything in your life with passion to God's glory. Live each day to the fullest and give it your all. He expects nothing less.

Your Reflections

_____

_____

_____

_____

_____

_____

Prayer

Father God, you are an excellent God. You created us to be like you and do your good work as your children. Your will is good, acceptable, and perfect. Help me this day, oh, Lord, to walk in your will with passion and excellence, that my actions might glorify you, my loving God. Through the strength of Christ Jesus and in his name I pray, amen.

10X

Today's Verses—2 Corinthians 8:7

But just as you abound in everything, in faith and utterance and knowledge and in all earnestness and in the love we inspired in you, see that you abound in this gracious work also.

Additional Reading: Galatians 5:16; 1 Peter 2:9; Philippians 3:13-15

My Thoughts

Just like the young men in Daniel 1:20, we are given the wisdom to excel in every manner of faith and knowledge. With this knowledge comes the responsibility to become a student, a scholar of God's Word. I do believe the Holy Spirit will unlock our minds to wisdom and knowledge, but we must constantly be in the Word.

Our mandate is to then take the knowledge we receive to make a difference and to be different—using our learning to teach, to disciple others, and to be a living example of God's grace and love. It's one thing to be filled with knowledge and grace, but unless we share it, it won't be glory to the Kingdom. Our role is to become disciples and lead others to the saving knowledge of Jesus Christ.

Set your sights on learning and growing in your knowledge of God's Word. Look for new ways every day to share his love. Be salt and light.

Your Reflections

_____

_____

_____

_____

_____

_____

Prayer

Father God, you alone are the mighty God, my fortress in times of trouble. Whom shall I fear? When I am fearful, you give me courage. When I am discouraged, you give me hope. I sanctify Christ as Lord of my heart. May I live this day in you, proclaiming with boldness the hope of my calling in Christ Jesus. In his holy name I pray, amen.

10X

Today's Verses—2 Peter 1:3-4

Seeing that His divine power has granted to us everything pertaining to life and godliness, through the true knowledge of Him who called us by His own glory and excellence. For by these He has granted to us His precious and magnificent promises, so that by them you may become partakers of the divine nature, having escaped the corruption that is in the world by lust.

Additional Reading: Ephesians 1:3-6; Colossians 1:18-19; 2 Corinthians 10:15

My Thoughts

The model Jesus gave us when he lived on the earth is one we should emulate. He walked the earth teaching, admonishing, and loving people. He prepared his disciples to continue his work long after his resurrection. He was all wisdom and knowledge, but he remained humble.

He was the epitome of strength and humility. He was, in fact, God. He chose restraint over violence. He chose love over hate. He showed grace to those who condemned him. Until Jesus returns, others must see him in us. How can we live each day in loving strength, boldly sharing the love and salvation of Jesus Christ?

Your Reflections

_____

_____

_____

_____

_____

Prayer

Almighty God, I give you praise. I magnify your mighty name. I give you thanks for empowering me with every spiritual blessing pertaining to life and godliness. I am grateful that I was predestined as a son through Jesus Christ. Help me this day, dear Lord, to dwell in you and to be bold in my proclamation of your love and grace. In Christ's holy name I pray, amen.

10X   DAY FIVE

Today's Verses—Psalm 119:99

I have more insight than all my teachers, for your testimonies are my meditation.

Additional Reading: Galatians 5:16; Colossians 1:27-28; Matthew 28:18-20

My Thoughts

As a 10X-er, we must continuously be in God's Word. Only then can we truly walk in our calling. Regardless of your gender, your education, your career, or business, and regardless of your family of origin, you are now a child of the living God. To fully mature into who God made you to be, you must be a student of his Word. It's not about scholarly work or being a great preacher; it's about the Bible.

Often, we get a little of God's Word and then charge off into the battle, later realizing we are woefully unprepared. It's like the parable of the sower in Matthew 13; we must be planted in firm, rich soil, which is God's Word. If you are going to be a warrior in God's army, then you must be trained and prepared for the battle. False doctrines and false teachers will only be revealed by the light of truth.

Your Reflections

_____

_____

_____

_____

_____

_____

Prayer

Gracious and loving Father, I rejoice in you this day for the anointed in me: Jesus. He is our liberating King. Give me an insatiable hunger for your Word and a love for your people. Give me your wisdom, dear Lord, to walk in you and boldly proclaim this anointing, which is available to all who believe in you. In the name of the liberating King, Christ Jesus, I pray, amen.

WEEK THRITY-THREE

WISDOM

WISDOM   DAY ONE

Today's Verses—Colossians 1:27-28

To them God has chosen to make known among the Gentiles the glorious riches of this mystery, which is Christ in you, the hope of glory. He is the one we proclaim, admonishing and teaching everyone with all wisdom, so that we may present everyone fully mature in Christ.

Additional Reading: James 1:5; Ephesians 5:15-17; Proverbs 10:23

My Thoughts

What are we to do with this great blessing if we don't teach others? What a wonderful responsibility to be entrusted by the living God to teach and admonish others to his glory. It can be a little overwhelming at times, especially if we walk in our own knowledge or strength. But with the Holy Spirit living in us and the living God directing us, there is no way to fail.

Our mission is to prepare the hearts of men for the day Christ returns. It's a big undertaking, but as we walk, grow, and study, God will strengthen and protect us as we share. God has a master plan and has chosen his people to execute it. God doesn't need us. He could do it on his own, but he desires us to get involved in personal relationships with others. Through our witness, we can bring others to Christ.

Your Reflections

_____

_____

_____

_____

_____

_____

Prayer

Father God, I praise your wonderful name. You are wisdom. Apart from you, there is only foolishness. The richness of your Word is our guide for all knowledge and instruction. Help me this day, oh, Lord, to walk in your wisdom and not my own folly. Help me to be a man of understanding, that I might lead others to you. In the matchless name of Christ Jesus I pray, amen.

WISDOM

DAY TWO

Today's Verses—Ephesians 1:7-9

In Him we have redemption through His blood, the forgiveness of our trespasses, according to the riches of His grace which He lavished on us. In all wisdom and insight, He made known to us the mystery of His will, according to His kind intention which He purposed in Him.

Additional Reading: Proverbs 18:15; Colossians 3:16-17; Luke 21:15

My Thoughts

One of the richest men who ever lived, at least in biblical times, was King Solomon. It was also said that he was the wisest man who ever lived, but why? Simply because he asked for and received wisdom and knowledge from God. You can read the story for yourself in 2 Chronicles 1:7-12. It reminds me of the old "genie in a bottle" question: what would you wish for? Solomon asked for wisdom so he could rule his people. God not only rewarded him with what he asked for, but he blessed him with riches as well.

Here is the wonderful part about God: he is offering you and me the same thing. Read Ephesians 1:7-9 again. God promises to reveal to us all manner of wisdom and knowledge. We must have an insatiable thirst for the truth of God's Word. Spending time in his Word daily not only offers us the wisdom of the ages but also offers us great hope and joy as we see his grand plan for all of mankind.

Your Reflections

_____

_____

_____

_____

_____

_____

Prayer

Father God, your goodness and mercy are too great for me to fully grasp. You are faithful and loving beyond measure. Your wisdom is a gift that is offered freely to all who believe. Help me this day, dear Lord, to seek your wisdom, that I might bring honor to you. As Colossians 3:17 says, may all I do in word or deed be in the name of Jesus with a thankful heart. In his holy name I pray, amen.

WISDOM   DAY THREE

Today's Verses—James 3:12

Can a fig tree, my brethren, produce olives, or a vine produce figs? Nor can salt water produce fresh.

Additional Reading: Job 12:12-13; 2 Timothy 2:7; Colossians 2:8-10

My Thoughts

James 3:12 makes me smile. God makes it so simple and so plain that even I can understand. The answer to these questions is no. Fig trees bear figs; vines produce grapes; and salt water is just that—salty. There are many things to be learned here. First and foremost is that apart from the salvation of Jesus Christ, we cannot produce anything good. We are a sinful and depraved people.

Jesus said he is the vine and we are the branches, and, thus, it is only through him that we produce good fruit (John 15:5). We are no longer the dead and dying; our souls are renewed. The caution here is that we are still capable of producing rotten fruit because we still have free will. Only when we allow the blood of Jesus to cleanse us and the wisdom of the Holy Spirit to fill us will we bear meaningful fruit for the Kingdom.

Your Reflections

_____

_____

_____

_____

_____

_____

Prayer

Gracious heavenly Father, I rejoice that I am your child through the blood of Jesus. I also give thanks that, as your child, I can produce good fruit for your Kingdom. Keep me this day, oh, Lord, by your side, that I might yield much fruit for you. Help me to store your Word in my heart, which produces wisdom and understanding in me. In the wonderful name of Jesus I pray, amen.

SDG

WISDOM   DAY FOUR

Today's Verses—Proverbs 3:13-18

How blessed is the man who finds wisdom and the man who gains understanding. For her profit is better than the profit of silver and her gain better than fine gold. She is more precious than jewels; nothing you desire compares with her. Long life is in her right hand; in her left hand are riches and honor. Her ways are pleasant ways and all her paths are peace. She is a tree of life to those who take hold of her, and happy are all who hold her fast.

Additional Reading: Jeremiah 33:3; Galatians 4:9; James 3:13-17

My Thoughts

I believe that once you gain true, godly wisdom, you no longer desire gold, silver, or jewels. I don't believe any of these things are bad, but it's the condition of your heart and what motivates you that causes problems. His wisdom clearly establishes that only through the pursuit of God's will for your life can you be at peace.

James 3:17 says, "But the wisdom that comes from heaven is first of all pure, then peace-loving, considerate, submissive, full of mercy and good fruit, impartial and sincere" (NIV). Ask God for wisdom, and he will give it to you. Pursue him with abandon. Seek his face. He is waiting.

Your Reflections

_____

_____

_____

_____

_____

_____

Prayer

Father God, your wisdom is pure, peaceable, gentle, reasonable, full of mercy and good fruit, unwavering, and without hypocrisy. You are the creator of wisdom, and I am grateful and praise your holy name. Give me this day, dear Lord, a pure heart so that I will walk in your truth and model your grace, that others may come to know you. In Jesus' name I pray, amen.

WISDOM   DAY FIVE

Today's Verses—Luke 21:15

For I will give you utterance and wisdom which none of your opponents will be able to resist or refute.

Additional Reading: Ecclesiastes 8:1-5; Daniel 12:3; 1 Corinthians 3:18-19

My Thoughts

This is where we can now take the wisdom we have gained to go and change the world. God is looking for a revival, and we are to be his champions. From the beginning of creation, God has relied on his people to be salt and light and transform others. Unfortunately, the world, at times, influences us more that we influence the world.

Our effectiveness starts with us. Only by defeating our own discouragement and despair and instead relying on the wisdom of the written Word can we boldly move forward. Christ is by our side as we proclaim the victory available to all through his redeeming blood. The wisdom we possess by the power of the Holy Spirit makes us fearless in the face of darkness. We are the light of Christ. Pierce the darkness today!

Your Reflections

_____

_____

_____

_____

_____

_____

Prayer

Father God, I sing your praises; you alone are worthy. You created our minds to be a storehouse of your wisdom. Your wisdom is pure and true, without contradiction or falsehoods. Your gift of this truth is for our benefit, that we might defeat false doctrine and false teachings. Help us this day, oh, Lord, to pierce the darkness with your words and your truth. Make us instruments of grace to your glory. In Christ's holy name I pray, amen.

WEEK THIRTY-FOUR

CHRIST IN YOU

CHRIST IN YOU

Today's Verses—Philippians 2:13

For it is God who is at work in you, both to will and to work for His good pleasure.

Additional Reading: 1 John 2:15-17; Ephesians 1:3-8; 1 Corinthians 6:14-17

My Thoughts

This week, as we look at "Christ in You," we begin to put together everything else we've looked at over the previous thirty-three weeks. A true 10X lifestyle comes from the transformation of a self-centered life to a life that fully recognizes the total dominion of Christ. This reminds me of old sci-fi movies where an alien completely takes over an earthling's body. All actions, thoughts, and speech are no longer the human's but, instead, that of the alien possessor.

The wonderful blessing is that we don't have some creature from outer space possessing our body. We have the resurrected King! The Holy Spirit that now lives in us is God, one part of the triune God. Think about that for a moment; contemplate the impact of this truth on your daily life. Once we fully yield to Jesus Christ, our thoughts are no longer our own but Christ's, who lives in us.

Your Reflections

_____

_____

_____

_____

_____

_____

Prayer

Father God, I rejoice this day as your child who is overwhelmed by your blessings. Your great love for me has given me a new life through the redemption I have in Christ Jesus. As your child, I am blessed with every spiritual blessing, and I am one with Christ. I pray this day, dear Lord, that you will work in me to your good pleasure, that I might glorify you. In the matchless name of Christ Jesus I pray, amen.

CHRIST IN YOU   DAY TWO

Today's Verses—2 Corinthians 13:5

Test yourselves to see if you are in the faith; examine yourselves! Or do you not recognize this about yourselves, that Jesus Christ is in you—unless indeed you fail the test?

Additional Reading: Philippians 3:9-14; Romans 6:11-14; John 14:10-14

My Thoughts

How do you feel about tests? Does the thought give you anxiety? What if you fail? What are the consequences? Can you take the test again, or is it now or never? Taking a test in not an issue if you know the material. If you studied, reviewed, and studied some more, you should ace it.

What is the most important test you've ever taken? How did you do? Well, 2 Corinthians 13:5 is about the *most* crucial test. Have you prepared? How can you test yourself to reveal your passing grade? A simple blood test doesn't show it. You could recite Scripture or tell others about your faith, but that's not enough either.

Passing this test simply reflects the condition of your heart. If Christ is in you, everything you do and every aspect of your life will reflect him. Your courage and your hope when you face difficulty will reflect Christ in you. The love and grace you show others reflects Christ in you. When people no longer see you but, instead, Christ living through you, you know you've aced it.

Your Reflections

_____

_____

_____

_____

_____

_____

Prayer

Gracious Father, I rejoice and give thanks that Christ is in me, and with his presence, your righteousness is in me. I no longer live, but, instead, it is Christ who lives in me. Help me this day to let Christ be more and me be less, that your love and goodness would radiate through me. Help me to yield to your way and your will for your honor and glory. In Christ's holy name I pray, amen.

CHRIST IN YOU

DAY THREE

Today's Verses—Romans 8:10

If Christ is in you, though the body is dead because of sin, yet the spirit is alive because of righteousness.

Additional Reading: 1 John 2:5-6; 2 Peter 1:3-4; 2 Timothy 2:11-13

My Thoughts

God has a wonderful plan of redemption for us; it comes in the form of Jesus Christ. We are dead because of our sin—in the sense that we cannot have fellowship with a divine and righteous God apart from Jesus. But once we accept Jesus as our personal savior and ask for forgiveness of our sin, we are forgiven for all of eternity.

Our old self is gone, and we are a new creation—with a new spirit that comes from God. Here's the challenge: we must believe and claim the new spirit. We still have free will and can hold on to the junk from our past. But through the power of the Holy Spirit, we can choose to walk away from the past and start fresh. Claim your victory in Christ and walk in him.

Your Reflections

_____

_____

_____

_____

_____

_____

Prayer

Loving Father, I praise you for the victory over sin and death that was granted me when I accepted Jesus into my heart. I give you thanks that, with Christ in me, I am now a partaker of his divine nature. Give me boldness to walk according to his nature and proclaim your victory over darkness. In Christ's holy name I pray, amen.

CHRIST IN YOU
DAY FOUR

Today's Verses—Galatians 2:20

I have been crucified with Christ; and it is no longer I who live, but Christ lives in me; and the life which I now live in the flesh I live by faith in the Son of God, who loved me and gave Himself up for me.

Additional Reading: Colossians 3:10-14; Philippians 2:5-8; 1 John 2:28-3:3

My Thoughts

What a wonderful act of love that God would send his only begotten son to die for us. Christ's obedience unto death is also an unspeakable act of love. God's depth of love for us is beyond comprehension, and I don't know about you, but I am grateful for it.

Now, it's our turn to no longer live in the old flesh but to, instead, live each day with the Savior. Don't waste his ultimate sacrifice on a life of mediocrity. Live every day to the fullest—to the glory of the living God who now lives in you. Walk by faith and in the boldness that comes with living for the Lord.

Your Reflections

_____

_____

_____

_____

_____

_____

Prayer

Loving Father, what a wonderful gift you have given us: to not only be called your children but also to be renewed in true knowledge of Christ, our Savior. I no longer live, but, instead, it is Christ who lives in me (Galatians 2:20). Help me this day to be transformed by your presence and to be true to your will and calling. Lord, may I be a voice to the world that does not know you—a voice that offers hope and eternal life with you. In Christ's holy name I pray, amen.

CHRIST IN YOU   DAY FIVE

Today's Verses—Ephesians 3:17

So that Christ may dwell in your hearts through faith; and that you, being rooted and grounded in love.

Additional Reading: Revelation 3:20-21; 1 Corinthians 12:13; Colossians 3:1-4

My Thoughts

God's Word is very clear: his ultimate plan for the lives of mankind is fellowship with him. Since the fall of man in the book of Genesis, God has faithfully provided a way to gain forgiveness and enter into his fellowship. In the Old Testament, the only way to receive forgiveness for sins was through blood. The blood of the sacrifices covered the sins of the people, but the Law required sacrifices to be done again and again. Countless animals were slain over time.

The New Testament introduces us to the New Covenant in the form of Jesus Christ. God sent his son to die on the cross for the sins of the world. The wonderful news is that this sacrifice doesn't have to be repeated. Christ's death on the cross paid the price once and for all—for all the sins of the world, for the sins that come from you and me. There is no longer any need for rituals or slaying animals.

Jesus Christ paid the ultimate price that we might have fellowship with the only true and living God. The very creator of the universe, the King of Kings, is waiting for you to reach out to him. Once you do, you will experience the overwhelming joy of Christ in you.

Your Reflections

_____

_____

_____

_____

_____

_____

Prayer

Father God, I rejoice that I have the living God in me. It's not just a phrase, "Christ in me," but a reality. My thoughts, my hopes, and my dreams are now directed by your Spirit. My daily renewal comes from you as I seek things from above and not of this world. Guide me this day, oh, God, to fully walk in your authority with boldness and compassion. In the matchless name of my Savior, Christ Jesus, I pray, amen.

SDG

WEEK THIRTY-FIVE
JESUS SAID SO

JESUS SAID SO   DAY ONE

Today's Verses—John 14:15

If you love Me, you will keep My commandments.

Additional Reading: Matthew 28:19-20; Mark 3:24-25; Luke 4:18-19

My Thoughts

God's Word is very simple and easy to understand. His commands are clear and easy to follow. The challenge is often that we really don't want to obey what he asks of us. We either ignore his teaching or pretend we don't understand.

John 14:15 is simple enough: if we love Christ, we will keep his commandments. My sixteen-year-old daughter recently received her driver's license and wasn't following the rules dictated by the state. Her response when I confronted her about the infraction: "Everyone else does it!" Isn't that what we see in Christendom today? Everyone else does it, so why shouldn't we?

The answer is clear. God commands us, and Jesus said it, so we must obey. If Jesus said so, that is all I need to know. It's not a matter of whether it pleases me or if it's convenient. I don't even have to like it. God's commandments are there for our own good, that we might fully enjoy his blessings. Keep his commandments!

Your Reflections

_____

_____

_____

_____

_____

_____

Prayer

Gracious and merciful Father, I give you thanks that Christ Jesus came to this earth to die for our sins and to give us his teaching and a model of obedience to you. Give me, dear Lord, ears to hear and a mind to understand that I might walk in obedience to the commands of Christ. May my actions and speech reflect Christ in me, that they might bring others to know you. In Christ's holy name I pray, amen.

JESUS SAID SO
DAY TWO

Today's Verses—Matthew 5:43-45

You have heard that it was said, "You shall love your neighbor and hate your enemy." But I say to you, love your enemies and pray for those who persecute you, so that you may be sons of your Father who is in heaven; for He causes His sun to rise on the evil and the good, and sends rain on the righteous and the unrighteous.

Additional Reading: Luke 5:4-5; John 16:31-33; Mark 9:35

My Thoughts

God is a just God, and he doesn't show favoritism. He loves all his people equally. It's easy to show love to our family, friends, or neighbors, but what about our enemies? For me, this is a tough call because, most of the time, it's hard for me to love someone who is persecuting me or is my enemy. But it's not our role to judge; it is only our duty to love others.

The Bible tells us in the book of 1 John that we will be known by our love. So, the bottom line is that if we are to share the good news of salvation in Jesus Christ, it must be done in love. Love is the one thing that can break down barriers of racial divide. It can also overcome fear and build trust. Christ gave his life for you out of love. Who can you show that same love and compassion to today?

Your Reflections

_____

_____

_____

_____

_____

_____

Prayer

Lord God, you have modeled for us perfect love to all people. You cause the sun to rise on the evil and the good, and you send rain on the righteous and the unrighteous (Matthew 5:45). Dear Lord, please give me your heart, that I might love others as you have commanded me. Help me to see them through your eyes and not my own. In the mighty name of Jesus Christ I pray, amen.

JESUS SAID SO   DAY THREE

Today's Verses—Mark 4:34
And He did not speak to them without a parable; but He was explaining everything privately to His own disciples.

Additional Reading: Matthew 5:16; Luke 4:8; John 4:12-14

My Thoughts

Jesus was one of the greatest teachers who ever lived, and he used parables to illustrate his messages. A parable is a simple story that illustrates a moral or spiritual principle. Jesus spoke in parables to help listeners understand his teachings. Many times, his disciples long with nonbelievers would not fully grasp the message or principle that the parable was illustrating. God's Word is not meant to be difficult, but it can be confusing without a mentor to guide you in understanding.

The Holy Spirit, who lives in us, will explain everything to us. Think about the way you teach a child. You tell a story and then guide her in the meaning or moral of the story. The same applies here: we have a gentle, loving Spirit who is fully God as our teacher. Seek him. Seek his teaching so that the mysteries of God's Word will be revealed to you.

Your Reflections

_____

_____

_____

_____

_____

_____

Prayer

Father God, you are an amazing and wonderful God who sent your son Jesus so that we might have eternal life through his death and resurrection. He offers us a living water that never ends and assures us a place in heaven with you. Dear Father, give me a heart for others, that I might share your living water and hope for all eternity. May my life shine in good works so that you would be glorified. In Christ's holy name I pray, amen.

JESUS SAID SO

Today's Verses—Luke 12:15

Then He said to them, "Beware, and be on your guard against every form of greed; for not even when one has an abundance does his life consist of his possessions."

Additional Reading: Matthew 16:18-19; Mark 4:21-23; John 5:24

My Thoughts

The story in Luke 12 is about a man who prides himself in his wealth and builds bigger storage facilities to hedge against future calamity. The bad news is that he dies before he can enjoy the fruits of his labor. Unfortunately, his focus was on his material wealth. I don't believe there is anything wrong with wealth, but I do believe that you shouldn't lose sight of your spiritual health because of it.

Whether you are rich or poor doesn't matter to God. It's the condition of your heart that concerns him. If you are only concerned with growing your material possessions and personal wealth, you do so at your own spiritual peril. Is it possible to do both? Yes, but seeking God must be first! Remember these words from Matthew 16:26: "For what will it profit a man if he gains the whole world and forfeits his soul? Or what will a man give in exchange for his soul?"

Your Reflections

_____

_____

_____

_____

_____

_____

Prayer

Father God, you are the giver of all good and perfect gifts. Our wealth is not measured by our material possessions or our bank account but in our position in you. Lord, teach me and renew in me a spirit to pursue the everlasting wealth that comes from serving you. All my earthly possessions and wealth will pass away and only what I have in you will last for eternity. In Jesus' name I pray, amen.

JESUS SAID SO   DAY FIVE

Today's Verses—Matthew 26:40-41

And He came to the disciples and found them sleeping, and said to Peter, "So, you men could not keep watch with Me for one hour? Keep watching and praying that you may not enter into temptation; the spirit is willing, but the flesh is weak."

Additional Reading: Mark 8:34-36; Luke 6:44-49; John 5:39-44

My Thoughts

At the very moment Christ was depending on his disciples, they let him down. Peter and some of the other disciples couldn't stand watch for just one hour. These are men who walked with Jesus, lived with him, and broke bread with him—yet they fell asleep. If these men grew weary, what's it like for us?

I think the message in Matthew 26:40-41 is that we need to stand guard every day—to keep watch, so to speak. The words of Christ here are very clear: "the spirit is willing, but the flesh is weak." Only through continuous prayer and study can we overcome our weakness and be ready when the Master calls. Think about it as spiritual fitness: if we take better care of our spiritual health, our eternity is secure.

Your Reflections

_____

_____

_____

_____

_____

_____

Prayer

Father God, you made us and know our innermost being. You know that we are weak and grow weary. We are not unlike the disciples; we fall asleep when we should be awake to the evil that surrounds us. Please keep me this day, oh, Lord, close to you, that I might remain vigilant and draw my strength from you. Help me to remain engaged in the battle for your honor and glory. In Christ's holy name I pray, amen.

SDG

WEEK THIRTY-SIX

BEAR FRUIT

BEAR FRUIT   DAY ONE

Today's Verses—Joshua 3:5

Then Joshua said to the people, "Consecrate yourselves, for tomorrow the Lord will do wonders among you."

Additional Reading: Matthew 7:17-20; 2 Timothy 2:15; Ephesians 4:11-15

My Thoughts

Preparation is only a part of consecrating ourselves to the Lord's service. It's one thing to study and prepare for service, but consecration is more of a declaration—a formal commitment to service. In fact, I believe this comes first. We must decide we are going to serve and declare our intentions, at least to God.

Once we have made the declaration to devote ourselves to serving God and to prepare our hearts and our minds, he will do wonders in our lives. Our most productive time in harvesting is when we are at the center of God's will and dedicated to him. How are you preparing for the harvest? Have you planted good seed, watered your crop, weeded, and pruned? A bountiful yield is allowing God to work through you, but you cannot forget to work the fields yourself.

Your Reflections

_____

_____

_____

_____

_____

_____

Prayer

Father, you are an amazing God who uses your people to be your disciples to bear fruit for your Kingdom. Help me this day, oh, Lord, to be approved as your workman (2 Timothy 2:15)—steadfast in all I do and openly sharing your love and hope for eternity in Christ Jesus. In his holy name I pray, amen.

SDG

BEAR FRUIT   DAY TWO

Today's Verses—Colossians 1:10

So that you will walk in a manner worthy of the Lord, to please Him in all respects, bearing fruit in every good work and increasing in the knowledge of God.

Additional Reading: Jeremiah 15:16; 1 Corinthians 2:12-13; Romans 8:14-17

My Thoughts

God's Word is full of references to bearing fruit, so as his disciples, we should be focused on just that. What does that mean? Am I to start planting orange trees? Not really, but the thing to keep in mind is that an orange tree will not bear apples nor will a poisonous plant bear eatable fruit. "You reap what you sow" is especially true. The fruit takes many forms, such as sharing his love and grace or performing discipleship or service.

Jesus tells us that he is the vine and we are the branches, so, as such, the fruit we bear will reflect him. It's not that simple though. It's not a one-and-done type of experience. To yield much for the Kingdom, we must, as Colossians 1:10 says, "Walk in a manner worthy of the Lord." To do that, we must be students of his Word, that it might transform us into his likeness. Unless the seed of Christ is in us, our fruit will be of no value.

Your Reflections

_____

_____

_____

_____

_____

_____

Prayer

Father, I rejoice in your goodness and knowledge. You have chosen me to be your representative as a disciple through my Savior, Christ Jesus. Help me this day, oh, Lord, to walk in a manner worthy of you. Give me a heart for your people so that I might share your love, your grace, and, most of all, your son, Jesus, that others might walk with you in eternity. In Christ's holy name I pray, amen.

BEAR FRUIT   DAY THREE

Today's Verses—John 15:16

You did not choose Me, but I chose you, and appointed you that you would go and bear fruit, and that your fruit would remain, so that whatever you ask of the Father in My name He may give to you.

Additional Reading: 2 Peter 3:18; 1 Timothy 2:1-8; Colossians 1:5-6

My Thoughts

Could you imagine if a farmer knew that his crop would last for all of eternity? Would it change how he cared for his crop? What excitement at harvesttime! John 15:16 is so cool. We are to produce fruit that lasts for all eternity—exciting! This gives a whole new meaning to the word *legacy*. The only lasting fruit comes from the seeds that are planted in people. And that is the seed of salvation in Jesus Christ. As servants, we are responsible to invest in the people God has put in our lives.

This is where discipleship comes into play. As you learn and grow in your understanding of God's character, his will, and his Word, you must begin to share it with others. They, in turn, will do the same as they grow in their walk. Think about the ripple effect that you can have on your generation and the generations to follow. Imagine the saints who will greet you in heaven, those who show the results of your discipleship and mentoring of others.

Your Reflections

_____

_____

_____

_____

_____

_____

Prayer

Gracious and loving Father, you have given us an outlook for eternity. The fruit we bear in others for you has eternal ramifications. Please give me wisdom, dear Lord, to be an effective witness for the gospel. Give me hope, love, and grace that I might share you with others. To your eternal Kingdom and glory I pray, amen.

SDG

BEAR FRUIT

Today's Verses—Matthew 13:8

And others fell on the good soil and yielded a crop, some a hundredfold, some sixty, and some thirty.

Additional Reading: 1 Peter 2:13; Isaiah 54:13; Psalm 139:23-24

My Thoughts

What is good soil anyway? My experience tells me that good soil is rich in nutrients and feeds the plant. But without the proper amount of water and sunlight, good soil can produce very little. We are the good soil that this verse speaks of, but without the watering of the Word of God and the Son shining in us, our output will be nil.

What's your yield goal? Is it thirty or one hundred? Like some fields that produce more than others, God's people have different yields. Why does someone like Billy Graham reach millions when others struggle to speak to one person about Christ? I am convinced it's a condition of the heart and a matter of desire to see others come to know the Savior. Examine your heart. Do you have a burning desire to rescue the lost, love the forgotten, and share God's grace? If you do, you, too, can yield one hundredfold!

Your Reflections

_____

_____

_____

_____

_____

Prayer

Dear heavenly Father, your Word tells us that through you, we can yield one hundredfold for the Kingdom. You have planted in me the seed of salvation. Help me to be good soil, that the harvest would be great. I pray these words from Psalm 139:23-24: "Search me, O God, and know my heart; try me and know my anxious thoughts; and see if there be any hurtful ways in me and lead me in the everlasting way." Father, I sing your praises and glorify your holy name. In Christ's name I pray, amen.

BEAR FRUIT   DAY FIVE

Today's Verses—Jeremiah 15:16

Your words were found, and I ate them, and Your words became for me a joy and the delight of my heart; For I have been called by Your name, O Lord God of hosts.

Additional Reading: Matthew 28:19-20; John 6:44-45; Ephesians 5:9

My Thoughts

Do you love the Word of God so much that you hunger for it? Is it your joy and delight? Think about your favorite food. Is your appetite insatiable for it? Does your mouth savor the flavors? How about your favorite activity or hobby—don't you long for times to enjoy it?

The idea here is to develop such an appetite for God's Word that you can never get enough. It becomes your first food every day. It nourishes your soul and gives you sustenance. As you feed your mind with the holy Word, the Holy Spirit increases your hunger for learning and enhances your understanding. Only then can you bear the fruit that lasts for eternity. The good news is that the more you learn, the more you want to learn. It's an amazing privilege to be able to study the God we love.

Your Reflections

_____

_____

_____

_____

_____

_____

Prayer

Father God, I give you praise for the Scriptures that give us hope, wisdom, and instruction so that we might walk as children of light. Keep me close to you, dear Lord. Give me an insatiable hunger for your Word, that I might walk in your righteousness and bring you honor and glory. In the matchless name of Christ Jesus I pray, amen.

WEEK THIRTY-SEVEN

NO WEAPON

NO WEAPON   DAY ONE

Today's Verses—Isaiah 54:17

"No weapon that is formed against you will prosper; And every tongue that accuses you in judgment you will condemn. This is the heritage of the servants of the Lord, and their vindication is from Me," declares the Lord.

Additional Reading: Luke 10:19; James 4:7-10; 2 Timothy 1:7

My Thoughts

The more I learn about God's provision and protection, the more excited I get about serving him. Living in Texas, we are big on weapons. You name it, we have it. Estates are measured by the size of the gun collection. But I digress. The weapons spoken of in Isaiah 54:17 are not the same. They are the weapons of the evil one—weapons that will be used against you to defeat you in your quest to do the will of God.

The wonderful news is that nothing—let me say it again, nothing—will prevail against you. Be it lies told about you, false accusations, or just plain deceit, they cannot harm you. Why? Because we have the power and protection of the living God in us. Our heritage in serving the living God is assured. But there is a catch: we must stay in his will and follow his commands.

Your Reflections

_____

_____

_____

_____

_____

_____

Prayer

Dear heavenly Father, you are truly the mighty and wonderful God. You have given us your authority on earth to stand firm against evil and the lies of the devil. I am grateful that "no weapon formed against me will prevail" and my victory is assured because you are with me (Is. 54:17). Guide me this day to remain in your Word and be faithful to your will, that I might be effective in defeating the enemy. In Jesus' name I pray, amen.

SDG

NO WEAPON

Today's Verses—1 John 4:4

You are from God, little children, and have overcome them; because greater is He who is in you than he who is in the world.

Additional Reading: 2 Timothy 4:8; Ephesians 6:10-12; 1 Corinthians 6:19

My Thoughts

Once again, the Word reminds us, here in 1 John 4:4, that the living God is within us. Do you recognize his presence in your life, and are you allowing his power to flow through you? The forces of darkness would rather tell you that he isn't there for you because you are not good enough. They would rather tell you that you don't pray enough and aren't spiritual enough—but that's all nonsense.

God has overcome the world. He has overcome sin and darkness through the death and resurrection of his son, Jesus Christ. So, do you believe the lies of the devil or the truth of his written Word? It's easy to slip into the old self and let self-doubt and fear defeat you. Call on the power of the living God. You cannot fail in him! Use the Bible as your protection against the evil one.

Your Reflections

Prayer

Father God, I look forward to the day when I will receive the crown of righteousness. Help me today, dear Lord, to remain in your strength and to stand firm in your righteousness against the schemes of the evil one. You are with me, and you have overcome the world. Give me victory for your glory. In Christ's holy name I pray, amen.

SDG

NO WEAPON

DAY THREE

Today's Verses—Psalm 91:1-4

He who dwells in the shelter of the Most High will abide in the shadow of the Almighty. I will say to the Lord, "My refuge and my fortress, My God, in whom I trust!" For it is He who delivers you from the snare of the trapper and from the deadly pestilence. He will cover you with His pinions, and under His wings you may seek refuge; His faithfulness is a shield and bulwark.

Additional Reading: 1 John 4:4; 2 Thessalonians 3:3; Romans 8:31

My Thoughts

To truly live the 10X lifestyle, you must believe that God will protect you; that he is, in fact, your refuge and your fortress. Remember those three Jewish boys who would not yield to the king? Read their words in Daniel 3:17-18: "If it be so, our God whom we serve is able to deliver us from the furnace of blazing fire; and He will deliver us out of your hand, O king. But even if He does not, let it be known to you, O king, that we are not going to serve your gods or worship in the golden image that you have set up."

What faith and what courage! I doubt any of us will ever face a fiery furnace, but unfortunately, we let much lesser trials defeat us. The time is now to stand up for the true and living God and boldly proclaim your allegiance to him. Trust in him and him alone. He will deliver you. What are the blazing fires that are holding you back?

Your Reflections

_____

_____

_____

_____

_____

_____

Prayer

Father God, you are my refuge and my fortress, my God in whom I trust. I sing your praises and rejoice in your goodness. Give me the courage, dear Lord, to boldly walk in your path and to boldly proclaim you to all people you put in my path. May my life be a testimony to your love and grace. In Christ's holy name I pray, amen.

SDG

NO WEAPON   DAY FOUR

Today's Verses—Galatians 1:4

Who gave Himself for our sins so that He might rescue us from this present evil age, according to the will of our God and Father.

Additional Reading: Isaiah 50:7; Psalm 138:7-8; 2 Timothy 4:18

My Thoughts

What could possibly keep us from serving our Lord? What keeps you on the sidelines? Is it fear? Could it simply be that you don't believe God at his word? Do you doubt his promises? By now, there should be little doubt in our minds as to the fact that God will deliver us, so why are you not fully engaged?

It's time to move on to what we believe and act accordingly. We ought to act on what we know to be true of our Savior and allow him to give us courage to boldly act according to his will. Our belief must go from our head to our heart to our feet. God expects us in the battle. He will rescue us. Walk with conviction and boldness. He will not fail us.

Your Reflections

_____

_____

_____

_____

_____

_____

Prayer

Father God, you are too wonderful for me to fully comprehend. You are more than my human mind can understand, but this I know: you alone are my God. You have a great plan for all of mankind, and it includes me. I am grateful. Your Word tells me to be bold and courageous to proclaim you to a dark and fallen world. I know you will protect and deliver me. Help me this day, oh, Lord, to walk in you. In the matchless name of my Savior, Christ Jesus, I pray, amen.

NO WEAPON

Today's Verses—Acts 1:8

But you will receive power when the Holy Spirit has come upon you; and you shall be My witnesses both in Jerusalem, and in all Judea and Samaria, and even to the remotest part of the earth.

Additional Reading: Joshua 1:5; Deuteronomy 33:26-29; Philippians 4:13:19

My Thoughts

Finally, we get a clear call to action. Through the power of the Holy Spirit, we are to be people of action. We are called to be witnesses to the true and living God. It starts in our homes and then moves into our communities. You might not get to Jerusalem, Judea, or Samaria, but you can be God's witness to the people he puts in your path.

We mustn't lose sight of our neighbors who don't know the Savior. What a blessed opportunity to be an emissary of the true and living God who offers hope and redemption. He offers healing to the sick and hurting. He offers joy and love. He offers deliverance for a dark and fallen world. Won't you be his messenger?

Your Reflections

_____

_____

_____

_____

_____

_____

Prayer

Oh, Lord, my God, you are my dwelling place. You alone are my refuge in time of trouble. You have empowered us to be your witnesses to a dark and desperate world that is so in need of your healing. Dear Lord, walk with me this day, that I would boldly proclaim your love and grace through my testimony—that others might experience the everlasting waters of salvation through Christ Jesus. In his powerful name I pray, amen.

WEEK THIRTY-EIGHT

PROSPER

PROSPER

DAY ONE

Today's Verses—Joshua 1:7-8

Only be strong and very courageous; be careful to do according to all the law which Moses My servant commanded you; do not turn from it to the right or to the left, so that you may have success wherever you go. This book of the law shall not depart from your mouth, but you shall meditate on it day and night, so that you may be careful to do according to all that is written in it; for then you will make your way prosperous, and then you will have success.

Additional Reading: 3 John 1:2; 2 Corinthians 9:10-12; Proverbs 3:5-6

My Thoughts

Can Christians be rich, or is that just for nonbelievers? Silly question, right? Consider King Solomon's wealth. Matthew 6:20-21 says, "but store up for yourselves treasures in heaven, where neither moth nor rust destroys, and where thieves do not break in or steal; for where your treasure is, there your heart will be also." So, what's the problem? I think it lies with our definition of prosperity. God desires our hearts to be focused on him and his service, not on gaining material prosperity.

Once we focus on serving God and doing his will, prosperity will follow. Prosperity is redefined as God changes our hearts and our minds to match his perspective. It's more about being content in our circumstances and being thankful in them, regardless. This contentment offers us peace and joy in the Lord. There is nothing that can compare.

Your Reflections

_____

_____

_____

_____

_____

_____

Prayer

Father God, I give you praise and thanksgiving for your provisions, which bring prosperity. Help me to be continuously in the Scriptures, that my soul might be in good spiritual health. Keep me focused on you and your calling on my life and not on the things of this world that take me off course. In Christ's holy name I pray, amen.

SDG

PROSPER   DAY TWO

Today's Verses—1 Peter 1:13-16

*Therefore, prepare your minds for action, keep sober **in spirit**, fix your hope completely on the grace to be brought to you at the revelation of Jesus Christ. As obedient children do not be conformed to the former lusts **which were yours** in your ignorance, but like the Holy One who called you, be holy yourselves also in all **your** behavior; because it is written, "You shall be holy, for I am holy."*

Additional Reading: Jeremiah 29:11-13; John 10:10-11; Galatians 6:8-9

My Thoughts

Jesus Christ changed everything! He transformed our lives and gave us a new life in eternity. We no longer live, but, instead, it is he who lives in us. Therefore, our outlook is no longer focused on the things of this world, but, instead, on eternity with our Savior. We are called to be holy because he is holy.

The abundant life and the prosperity we seek is no longer about what we have, what we own, or our wealth; it is about recognizing that we are a part of God's eternal family. We are in the family of the true and living God. All our needs are provided for. Our joy and our hope come from him. Change your focus from what you have on earth to what you have in eternity.

Your Reflections

_____

_____

_____

_____

_____

_____

Prayer

Father God, your Word tells us that you have a plan for our welfare and a future of hope for us. It also tells us that if we seek you, you will be found (Jeremiah 29:11, 13). I am grateful that you, the true and living God, are available to me. I give thanks that my future is secure for eternity as I walk with you. Give me a vision for that future, that I might focus on the glorious life in eternity with you. In Jesus' name I pray, amen.

SDG

PROSPER   DAY THREE

Today's Verses—Deuteronomy 8:18

But you shall remember the Lord your God, for it is He who is giving you power to make wealth, that He may confirm His covenant which He swore to your fathers, as it is this day.

Additional Reading: Romans 8:28; James 1:17; Luke 11:28

My Thoughts

Imagine directly working for Bill Gates or Warren Buffet in a position where they could give you the ability to earn millions. Wouldn't that be cool? Think of the things you could purchase and the freedom you would have. All your worries would be overcome. You could say, "Hakuna matata," for the rest of your days.

Well, this is the best part of serving the King of Kings and the Lord of Lords: he owns it all. All the wealth in the world cannot even come close to the wealth of our Savior. The wonderful thing about our God is that he offers us not only prosperity but also an eternal peace that can never be taken away. His eternal gift is salvation and entrance into the most prosperous family of all.

Your Reflections

_____

_____

_____

_____

_____

_____

Prayer

Gracious heavenly Father, every good thing and perfect gift comes from you. You never waver or change. You are the same yesterday, today, and forever (Hebrews 13:8). I am grateful for the abundance and prosperity you offer your children. Your abundance is of everlasting peace. Your prosperity is the assurance that you will never leave us or forsake us (Deuteronomy 31:6). I give you praise with a grateful heart for your presence in my life. In Christ's holy name I pray, amen.

PROSPER

DAY FOUR

Today's Verses—Philippians 4:19

And my God will supply all your needs according to His riches in glory in Christ Jesus.

Additional Reading: Ecclesiastes 3:13; Psalm 1:1-3; Proverbs 15:6

My Thoughts

OK. Is the message becoming clear? Do you get it? God will supply all our needs. All he is asking from us is our hearts. Our magnificent God not only controls all the wealth of the world but he also possesses a peace and joy that is everlasting.

What do you lack today? Where is your doubt? Do you lack faith that God can and will provide for you? Examine your unbelief. Ask Jesus to transform your heart to one of faith and trust in him. Once you place him at the center of your life and completely yield to him, everything changes. I can't promise you wealth, but I can promise you peace and prosperity in the risen Lord.

Your Reflections

_____

_____

_____

_____

_____

_____

Prayer

Dear Lord, I delight in your law. It keeps me on your path, both day and night. Your Word promises that we will be like a tree, firmly planted by rivers of water, with leaves that never wither, and we will bear much fruit in season (Psalm 1:3). Father, I am grateful that I am planted firmly in your living Word—with you, the living Lord, by my side. Help me to yield much fruit for your glory. In Christ's holy name I pray, amen.

PROSPER

Today's Verses—Malachi 3:10

"Bring the whole tithe into the storehouse, so that there may be food in My house, and test Me now in this," says the Lord of hosts, "if I will not open for you the windows of heaven and pour out for you a blessing until it overflows."

Additional Reading: Daniel 4:27; James 1:4-5; 1 Corinthians 1:4-9

My Thoughts

The richness of God's blessing is without measure. Whether it be material possessions or financial wealth, he provides it all. We must learn to give freely of the wealth God has provided to us. Acknowledge the fact that it all comes from him. You can't outgive God. Once we recognize that our wealth comes from him and we give freely with a cheerful heart, the windows of heaven truly open.

Our prosperity comes from a trusting heart—knowing that God will not only provide for our needs but also create a surplus. I truly believe that God enjoys blessing us with wealth, but he requires us first to surrender to him. Once we learn to walk with him and let it all go, he gives overflowing gifts.

Your Reflections

_____

_____

_____

_____

_____

_____

Prayer

Father God, I rejoice that I have been called into fellowship with your son, Jesus Christ, our Lord. I pray, dear Lord, that I would walk in your righteousness. Help me to gain wisdom and endurance to boldly proclaim your salvation and good news. Create in me, oh, Lord, a new heart that would allow me to see people through your eyes, that I might share your love and grace. In the matchless name of Christ Jesus I pray, amen.

SDG

WEEK THIRTY-NINE

LOVE THE LORD

LOVE THE LORD   DAY ONE

Today's Verses—Luke 10:27

And he answered, "You shall love the Lord your God with all your heart, and with all your soul, and with all your strength, and with all your mind; and your neighbor as yourself."

Additional Reading: Deuteronomy 13:3-4; Joshua 22:5; John 17:26

My Thoughts

"The Bible is God's love letter to us," stated Soren Kierkegaard.[9] God is the epitome of love. He demonstrates it in everything he does. He is the ultimate role model. His love and grace are evident from Genesis to Revelation. We have no excuse not to love him in return.

Think about the very first time you felt romantic love for another person. It was magical and confusing all at the same time. You thought of her every waking moment, and you couldn't wait to be in her presence. You missed her when you were apart, and her very presence brought you joy and excitement.

Do you remember those feelings? Now, how does that compare with your feelings of God? What God requires of us is not the same but much deeper. He longs for your devotion to him, for your desire for fellowship, and an ongoing relationship. The love God has for us is everlasting and will never fade. As we seek him with all our heart and all our soul, his love will fill us for all eternity.

Your Reflections

_____

_____

_____

_____

_____

_____

Prayer

I love you, Lord. You are my King, my comforter, and my protector. Your presence in my life is a daily blessing. Give me ears to hear your voice and help me cling to you. May your great love flow through me to others. Help me to walk in your ways and to keep your commandments. May my love for you be reflected in my actions today and every day. In the wonderful name of Jesus Christ I pray, amen.

---

9   https://quotefancy.com/quote/972026

LOVE THE LORD DAY TWO

Today's Verses—John 14:21

He who has My commandments and keeps them is the one who loves Me; and he who loves Me will be loved by My Father, and I will love him and will disclose Myself to him.

Additional Reading: Proverbs 10:12; 1 Corinthians 13:13; Revelation 2:4

My Thoughts

When you love someone, you naturally do what's best for her. You think about her needs and desires and put her first. Your love is complete when you truly know everything about her and work to please her as an act of your love.

I believe John 14:21 is calling for love in action. If we love God and want to please him, we first must know his commandments. A true 10X lifestyle isn't complete without a daily study and understanding of God's Word. Following God's rules does not come out of fear or guilt, but, instead, it is the ultimate act of love and devotion to our heavenly Father.

Your Reflections

_____

_____

_____

_____

_____

_____

Prayer

Father God, you are love. The Scriptures are a love letter to us. You sent your son to give his life out of love for us. His death and resurrection offer us a path back to your loving arms. Help me this day to be your love ambassador to the people you have placed in my life. Help me model your love, that through me, others might see you. In Christ's holy name I pray, amen.

LOVE THE LORD　　　　　　　　　　　　DAY THREE

Today's Verses—Proverbs 8:17

I love those who love me; and those who diligently seek me will find me.

Additional Reading: 1 John 4:16-18; John 13:34-35; Galatians 2:20

My Thoughts

Proverbs 8:17 reminds us, once again, that God expects us to seek him in all aspects of our lives; seeking him demonstrates our devotion. The wonderful promise is that if we seek him, he is there for us. There is no mystery here. God has made it very simple. Our failure, at times, is that we fail to act—to simply take the first step toward a loving God.

What is keeping us from being totally committed to a life of devotion, study, and service to the King of creation? Could it be fear that if we take the necessary steps, we will have to give up something we really like or enjoy? Are we afraid of having to give all our wealth to his work? Are we afraid to move to Africa to be a missionary? Here's my experience: as I have given my heart to him and yielded to his will, he has changed my heart. I am no longer afraid of what he will ask me to do because, no matter what it is, it's out of love.

Your Reflections

_____
_____
_____
_____
_____
_____

Prayer

Father, you make my heart smile. Your gentle hand comforts me. Your loving arms embrace me and assure me daily of your loving care and your presence. Father, help me this day to remain faithful to your calling and to be obedient—not out of fear but out of love for you, my God. As I abide in you, you abide in me. In the precious name of Christ Jesus I pray, amen.

LOVE THE LORD ────────────────────────── DAY FOUR

Today's Verses—Psalm 116:1-2

I love the Lord, because He hears My voice and my supplications. Because He has inclined His ear to me, Therefore I shall call upon Him as long as I live.

Additional Reading: Matthew 6:24; 1 Corinthians 13:1; 2 John 1:5-6

My Thoughts

A true, loving relationship is founded on trust—knowing that your love will not be taken for granted. Too often, our view of love is based on a love relationship with our spouse or our parents. If we've been hurt by someone in the past, it may cloud our judgment about love.

Whether your experience has been good or bad, it's nothing compared to the love God has for you. He will not forsake you. He will not abandon you, ever. God knows your voice. He hears you and your concerns. He listens to your call. Our love for the Father comes naturally as we learn to trust him.

Your Reflections

_____

_____

_____

_____

_____

_____

Prayer

I love you, Lord. You hear my voice, and you know my needs. You are a loving Father, caring deeply for your children. Through the death and resurrection of my Savior, Jesus, my Lord, I now have a direct line of communication to you, Father God. I rejoice in your goodness and blessings. Help me this day to walk in your will while sharing my love for you with others. I pray that your love would radiate through me and that I would reflect your presence. In the precious name of Christ Jesus I pray, amen.

LOVE THE LORD

Today's Verses—Deuteronomy 7:9

Know therefore that the Lord your God, He is God, the faithful God, who keeps His covenant and His lovingkindness to a thousandth generation with those who love Him and keep His commandments.

Additional Reading: 1 John 4:7-8; Romans 12:9-10; James 2:5

My Thoughts

What a wonderful and loving God we serve. Deuteronomy 7:9 says he is faithful and keeps his promises, not only to us but for a thousand generations to come. It's so comforting to know that he will be there for our children and their children and all future generations. He never changes. He is the same today, tomorrow, and forever (Hebrews 13:8).

God requires two things from us: our love and obedience. We demonstrate our love by being obedient. Examine your heart today. Do you truly love God with all your heart, soul, and mind? Are you sold out for Jesus? The only true path to loving God and being obedient to him is through prayer, study, and dedication. Love comes automatically when you see his true character.

Your Reflections

_____

_____

_____

_____

_____

_____

Prayer

Father God, you are love. Thank you for choosing me and loving me. You created us to love. Out of love, you sacrificed your son to die. Scripture is a testimony to your unwavering love for all of mankind. Your Word says that everyone who loves is born of you (1 John 4:7). I love you, Lord, because you first loved me. Help me this day to walk in obedience, that my love might be a glimmer of your immense love for others. In Christ's holy name I pray, amen.

WEEK FORTY
CALLING

CALLING

Today's Verses—2 Peter 1:10

Therefore, brethren, be all the more diligent to make certain about His calling and choosing you; for as long as you practice these things, you will never stumble.

Additional Reading: Romans 8:28; James 1:18; 1 Peter 2:21

My Thoughts

As a young believer many years ago, I was asked about my "calling," and I thought, *Like calling on the phone?* For many years it remained a mystery to me—not only what *calling* meant but how I would know. For me, it became clearer over time; today, I know it to be God's purpose for my life. Why was I put on the earth in the first place?

God has a very specific plan or purpose for your life, although it might not be clear at first. The Holy Spirit may reveal it immediately, or, as in my case, it might take many years. I don't doubt people who tell me that they knew from the moment of salvation what God had called them to do, but here is what I can tell you: the more you seek him and study his Word, the clearer your calling will become.

The Boy Scouts program exposes young boys to different vocations or areas of interest that often lead to successful career paths. If nothing else, it helps boys develop hobbies and interests. Your calling can best be discovered by studying God's handbook for life, the holy Bible. You learn about his character, his plan for the world, and, ultimately, his plan for you.

Your Reflections

_____

_____

_____

_____

_____

_____

Prayer

Father God, I am so very grateful that you have given me a plan and a purpose for my life in service to you. Keep me, oh, Lord, on that path—in the center of your will—that I might not stumble. Guide me, that I would remain true to your direction and that my actions would glorify you. In the matchless name of Christ Jesus I pray, amen.

CALLING   DAY TWO

Today's Verses—2 Timothy 1:9

Who has saved us and called us with a holy calling, not according to our works, but according to His own purpose and grace which was granted us in Christ Jesus from all eternity.

Additional Reading: Ephesians 2:4-6; 1 Corinthians 1:23-24; Colossians 2:8-10

My Thoughts

What's the message believers need to hear about our calling? We must understand the following: "Jacob was a cheater, Peter had a temper, David had an affair, Noah got drunk, Jonah ran from God, Paul was a murderer, Gideon was insecure, Miriam was a gossip, Martha was a worrier, Thomas was a doubter, Sara was impatient, Elijah was moody, Moses stuttered, Abraham was old, and Lazarus was dead. God doesn't call the qualified, He qualifies the CALLED!"[10]

What is God asking of you? When I first thought of writing this devotional book, I first responded, "Who? Me?" Immediately after that, I said, "But I don't know how to write!" Regardless of your own doubts or fears, God can use you in a wonderful and unique way. None of it is dependent on you. It is about allowing God to use you according to his grand purpose.

Your Reflections

_____

_____

_____

_____

_____

_____

Prayer

Father God, you are rich in mercy. You love us in a great and mighty way. I give you praise for my holy calling, which you have equipped me for. I am qualified to serve you because of the work of Christ Jesus on the cross. Keep me, dear Lord, by your side and in your Word, that I might bring honor and glory to you as I serve others. In the matchless name of Jesus Christ, my Savior, I pray, amen.

---

10   http://livingforjesus.com/god-doesnt-call-the-qualified-god-qualifies-the-called

SDG

CALLING

Today's Verses—Ephesians 4:1-4

Therefore I, the prisoner of the Lord, implore you to walk in a manner worthy of the calling with which you have been called, with all humility and gentleness, with patience, showing tolerance for one another in love, being diligent to preserve the unity of the Spirit in the bond of peace. There is one body and one Spirit, just as also you were called in one hope of your calling.

Additional Reading: John 10:27-30; Luke 22:28-30; Micah 4:2

My Thoughts

Have you ever met, or worse, worked with someone in authority who was a jerk? Perhaps it was your boss or maybe even your parent? There are also many people who talk about their values or ethics yet are the first to abandon them in a crisis or when it is inconvenient. I call this situational ethics.

The 10X lifestyle is neither of these things. Although we walk in the full authority and power of Jesus Christ, we are to act with love and humility. As we reach out to others, we must be willing to show his compassion and grace. Only then are we walking in a manner worthy of his calling. Take some time to really think about what this specifically means to you. What changes do you need to make?

Your Reflections

_____

_____

_____

_____

_____

_____

_____

Prayer

Father God, I rejoice in your goodness and praise your wonderful name. I am grateful for your call on my life to serve others and to speak truth into their lives. Help me this day, oh, Lord, to speak with all humility, gentleness, and patience in love. I pray that my actions would encourage others to serve you in a new and mighty way. In the name of my Savior and Lord, Christ Jesus, I pray, amen.

SDG

CALLING   DAY FOUR

Today's Verses—1 Corinthians 15:50

Now I say this, brethren, that flesh and blood cannot inherit the kingdom of God; nor does the perishable inherit the imperishable.

Additional Reading: John 5:30; Jeremiah 31:9; 1 Thessalonians 4:7

My Thoughts

What on earth is 1 Corinthians 15:50 talking about? Perishable inherit the imperishable? Sometimes, in my early years of study, I would pass over a verse like this and think, I will try to understand this later. Now, I see this plainly and understand it as well. After the fall of mankind in the Garden of Eden, we were separated from God because of our sin. We were dead in our bodies because of the penalty of our sins.

Once we accepted Jesus Christ as our Savior, our bodies were no longer flesh. We became new creations in Christ. Our mortal bodies will still grow old and eventually decay, but our spirits are now eternal. We are no longer perishable, but instead, we are imperishable because of the death and resurrection of Jesus Christ. As such, part of our calling is to walk with him until that final day when we will walk in glory and inherit God's Kingdom. We will be in eternity worshiping the risen Lord.

Your Reflections

_____

_____

_____

_____

_____

_____

Prayer

Father God, you tell us in your Word that you will lead us by streams of water on a straight path where we will not stumble (Jeremiah 31:9). I am grateful for your hand on my life that keeps me on this path. Help me this day, oh, Lord, to seek your will and not my own, that I might fulfill my work for you. I pray that my actions and my life would be a sweet fragrance to you. In Christ's holy name I pray, amen.

CALLING DAY FIVE

Today's Verses—Daniel 7:27

Then the sovereignty, the dominion and the greatness of all the kingdoms under the whole heaven will be given to the people of the saints of the Highest One; His kingdom will be an everlasting kingdom, and all the dominions will serve and obey Him.

Additional Reading: 1 Corinthians 8:6; Ephesians 1:11-12; John 6:44

My Thoughts

OK, so what's all this leading up to? If I follow my calling, what's the endgame here? What rewards are you looking for? Maybe a big house on a hill or on the beach? You may reason, if I am going to give it all for God, don't I deserve a reward? If you are thinking about WIIFM, everyone's favorite radio station, you really missed something along the way. The question is not, "What's in it for me?" but instead, "How will God be glorified by my life?"

Daniel 7:27 does offer us a glimpse of what is to come: we get to rule with Christ over all the earth for eternity. That's the reward for our service, not to mention the peace that comes with fully yielding our lives to Jesus. That's better than anything I can think of! God will prepare you for his call. Are you listening?

Your Reflections

_____

_____

_____

_____

_____

_____

Prayer

Father God, yours is a Kingdom of greatness and dominion. You alone are sovereign. I praise you, my wonderful and amazing God. Your Kingdom is everlasting. And as a believer in Jesus Christ, my Savior, I have the assurance of being part of your Kingdom. Give me the boldness and compassion to share you with others, that they might experience your salvation for eternity. In Jesus' name I pray, amen.

WEEK FORTY-ONE

TREASURED POSSESSIONS

TREASURED POSSESSIONS   DAY ONE

Today's Verses—Malachi 3:17-18

"They will be Mine," says the Lord of hosts, "on the day that I prepare My own possession, and I will spare them as a man spares his own son who serves him." So you will again distinguish between the righteous and the wicked, between one who serves God and one who does not serve Him.

Additional Reading: Ephesians 1:4-5; Matthew 13:44; Isaiah 60:21

My Thoughts

What are the things you value most? Your home, your car, your job, or maybe your family? Here's the bad news: all of this (except for your family) will eventually perish or go away. Our family will always be a source of joy and fond memories—our treasure, if you will. We act accordingly, seeking to preserve the things we value most.

What do you think God values most? Here's exciting news: it's me and you! Once we are accepted into his Kingdom through the redeeming work of Jesus Christ, we become his. Part of God's endgame is that at the end of time we, his children, will be with him in glory. We are his treasured people, and we will be with him in eternity.

Your Reflections

_____

_____

_____

_____

_____

_____

Prayer

Almighty Father, you alone are worthy of our praises. You chose us to be righteous and to possess the land as your holy people. Your treasure is no longer hidden but alive in us through our Lord and Savior, Christ Jesus. I pray, dear Lord, that I would not let this treasure be hidden in me and that I would share it with others. I long for that day when we will be in your presence in glory. In Christ's holy name I pray, amen.

SDG

TREASURED POSSESSIONS   DAY TWO

Today's Verses—1 John 3:1

See how great a love the Father has bestowed on us, that we would be called children of God; and such we are. For this reason, the world does not know us, because it did not know Him.

Additional Reading: Revelation 3:20-21; Isaiah 46:3-4; Colossians 2:2-3

My Thoughts

I don't know about you, but as a parent, nothing is more important to me than my children. They are a source of delight and pride, regardless of how they act. My love for them is unwavering. I cherish the relationship I have with each of my five remaining children and relish the fellowship we enjoy. So, if we feel this way about our children, imagine how much more God loves us.

To be one of God's children is not only the greatest privilege I can imagine, but it is also a wonderful family to be a part of. Being a child of God comes with enormous blessings and privileges. We are his chosen and, as such, his beloved. Do you feel like one of God's treasured possessions? If not, how can you draw closer to him? God never changes. He hasn't moved away from you. Maybe it's time to move closer to him.

Your Reflections

_____

_____

_____

_____

_____

_____

Prayer

Almighty God, I rejoice in the fact that I am your child and that you are my Father. What a blessing to be called a child of the living God. My heritage is rich in history. Prosperity comes from the true knowledge that comes from Christ Jesus alone. Help me to make known your love and share the good news of Jesus with others, that they might walk in your truth. In Jesus' name I pray, amen.

TREASURED POSSESSIONS DAY THREE

Today's Verses—Zephaniah 3:17

The Lord your God is in your midst, a victorious warrior. He will exult over you with joy, He will be quiet in His love, He will rejoice over you with shouts of joy.

Additional Reading: Philippians 4:6-7; Ephesians 2:4-6; Galatians 2:20

My Thoughts

Since I've never been in battle, I don't exactly know how it feels at the end—the joy of victory. Having a precious daughter who played volleyball for several years, I know the joy of watching her do well and win a game or two. As a parent, you feel your child's excitement in the heat of the game, you cheer her on when she does well, and you feel her pain when she makes a mistake or loses to the opponent.

Here's a cool thing that I believe: we may lose a battle or two, but in the end, we will win the war. We can be defeated by our own doubt or fear. We can be defeated by the lies and schemes of the devil. But remember this: with God at our side, we cannot be defeated—unless we try to go at it on our own. He is by our side if we call out to him. He rejoices in our victory.

Your Reflections

_____

_____

_____

_____

_____

_____

Prayer

Dear Lord, you are a wonderful and loving Father who cares deeply for your children. You rejoice over us with shouts of joy. Out of love, you sent your son, Jesus, to die on the cross for our sins, that we might have a relationship with you through his victorious resurrection. We are, indeed, your treasured people. Guide me this day, oh, Lord, to work as your prize, glorifying you in my walk. In Christ's holy name I pray, amen.

TREASURED POSSESSIONS DAY FOUR

Today's Verses—Colossians 3:12
So, as those who have been chosen of God, holy and beloved, put on a heart of compassion, kindness, humility, gentleness and patience.

Additional Reading: Psalm 139:14; Romans 8:1; John 15:4-5

My Thoughts

I am reminded of Mother Teresa when I think about Colossians 3:12. She was truly one of God's treasured who modeled his love. She was the epitome of compassion, kindness, gentleness, patience, and humility. She knew who she was in Christ, but she never put herself first.

As 10X-ers, we are called to exemplify these same qualities to the people God puts in our lives. We are to extend the same to friend or foe. Keep in mind that we are all God's treasures, and he loves us equally. When we show his love to others, they see Christ in us.

Your Reflections

_____

_____

_____

_____

_____

_____

Prayer

Gracious and loving Father, Jesus is the vine, and we are the branches. We abide in him, and he abides in us. Through him, we can produce much fruit for your Kingdom (John 15:5). I am grateful for this wonderful blessing and for the privilege of serving you. Your love and grace overwhelm me. Please keep me this day, dear Lord, near to you, that I might be light in a dark world unto your glory. In Christ's holy name I pray, amen.

TREASURED POSSESSIONS   DAY FIVE

Today's Verses—Deuteronomy 7:6
For you are a holy people to the Lord your God; the Lord your God has chosen you to be a people for His own possession out of all the peoples who are on the face of the earth.

Additional Reading: Matthew 13:52; Isaiah 41:10; 1 Peter 2:9

My Thoughts
At last count, the world's population was 7,500,000,000 people. This number represents many nations, languages, and races. They are all God's children, but not all are chosen. I think the reason Christ has not returned is because God, in his mercy, wants as many people as possible to receive salvation in Jesus, rather than be condemned.

But to be clear, we are God's chosen people, and it is our role to share his love and the good news of Jesus Christ to the world. God's heart aches for this fallen world, but he gives each of us free will to either follow him or forsake him. How can you demonstrate the magnificent plan God has for the life of mankind and model his love?

Your Reflections

_____

_____

_____

_____

_____

_____

Prayer
Father, you are a holy God. You have called us to be a holy people. You have chosen us as your possession as a royal priesthood (1Peter 2:9). We are empowered by your love and grace to share your amazing love and mercy. You have commissioned us to share the hope of our salvation, which is in Christ Jesus. Our walk with you is a journey to hope and joy. Keep me in your presence, that I might walk in you and share you with others. In Christ's holy name I pray, amen.

FINISH WELL

WEEK FORTY-TWO

FINISH WELL

FINISH WELL

Today's Verses—2 Timothy 4:7

I have fought the good fight, I have finished the course, I have kept the faith.

Additional Reading: Philippians 3:12-14; Ecclesiastes 7:8; Colossians 1:9-14

My Thoughts

Have you ever started something but couldn't quite get around to finishing? Is starting but not finishing a habit for you? Or do you see things through to completion once you set your mind to it? Often our motivation for a task comes from the reward of finishing, the prize at the end, or the feeling of accomplishment. Who asked us to complete the task can also be a big factor. We may complete a task for our boss out of fear or a desire to please him yet blow off something around the house.

Maybe you are motivated by the significance of the task, and that's what drives you. Running a marathon is one thing, but what about a one-hundred-mile road race? There would be a big difference in preparation, endurance, and results.

So, what's really at stake in 2 Timothy 4:7 when we think about fighting the good fight and finishing the course? I believe we are talking about the most important assignment of our lives: finishing strong in our pursuit of holiness, in serving Christ while on this earth. One day, we can hear him say, "Well done, good and faithful servant" (Matthew 25:23). We are talking about crossing the finish line, victorious for the cause of Christ. Think about what God is calling you to do and how you can finish strong.

Your Reflections

_____

_____

_____

_____

_____

_____

Prayer

Father, your magnificence surrounds us, as does your amazing love. I give you thanks for the strength that comes from your might. You have given me patience and love, which both allow me to bear much fruit. Keep me close to you, dear Lord, that I might walk in a manner worthy of you. Give me your wisdom and grace, that I might finish strong for your honor and glory. In Christ's holy name I pray, amen.

SDG

FINISH WELL

DAY TWO

Today's Verses—Acts 20:24

But I do not consider my life of any account as dear to myself, so that I may finish my course and the ministry which I received from the Lord Jesus, to testify solemnly of the gospel of the grace of God.

Additional Reading: Philippians 1:6; Luke 14:33-35; Galatians 6:9

My Thoughts

In spiritual circles, we often hear the phrase "die to self," but what does that really mean? I think it means that we no longer can consider our own desires and will for our lives, but, instead, we must surrender it all to Christ. There is no greater calling than to do the work God has called us to do. We must lay our lives aside to serve.

I understand this is a big ask—and even more difficult to live out—but consider what we are working for. As a 10X-er, we must consider the finish line—not the sacrifice to get there. Christ gave his life that we might be able to live in eternity with him. Is it too much to ask of us to give our lives to him?

This is not a sprint but a marathon. It starts by committing to the race because we will get tired, and we will want to give up. Once we are "all in," we must prepare by building our endurance and strength. This comes from a steady diet of God's Word and the ongoing exercise of applying his teaching to recruit others to the race. What is your exercise routine? Are you in shape?

Your Reflections

_____

_____

_____

_____

_____

_____

Prayer

Father God, I give you thanks and praise your holy name. You alone are worthy. Father, you have called me to the race of life, that through your Word and the Holy Spirit, I might draw strength and build my endurance. Keep me diligent in my training, that I might not grow weary and will, instead, finish strong for your glory. In Christ's holy name I pray, amen.

FINISH WELL DAY THREE

Today's Verses—Hebrews 12:1-2

Therefore, since we have so great a cloud of witnesses surrounding us, let us also lay aside every encumbrance and the sin which so easily entangles us, and let us run with endurance the race that is set before us, fixing our eyes on Jesus, the author and perfecter of faith, who for the joy set before Him endured the cross, despising the shame, and has sat down at the right hand of the throne of God.

Additional Reading: Colossians 3:23-24; James 1:2-5; Jeremiah 32:38-39

My Thoughts

Hebrews 12:1-2 reminds me of Peter when he saw Jesus walking on the water. If he kept his eyes on the Messiah, he stayed on top. Once he took his eyes off Jesus, he sank. The message is clear. We must keep our eyes on Jesus. He is our strength. Without him, we are limited.

When we keep our focus on Jesus, he encourages us. He reaches out and helps us overcome our doubt and fear. He is our coach and offers advice on how to win. He has given us our playbook, and he is there by our side every step of the way. Being apart from him is like trying to find your way in a dark room: you stumble and fall. You get up and stumble and fall again because without the light, you can no longer see the path. Christ Jesus is our light. He is our guide and our coach. Get off the bench and get in the game

Your Reflections

_____

_____

_____

_____

_____

_____

Prayer

Gracious Father, you alone are worthy. You alone inherit the praises of your people. I give you thanks that you are my God, and I am your child. I pray, dear Lord, that I will run the race set before me with endurance, fixing my eyes on my Lord and Savior, Jesus Christ—who with joy set before him, endured the cross for us (Hebrews 12:2). Help me, oh, Lord, to finish the race in victory to your glory. In Christ's holy name I pray, amen.

FINISH WELL

Today's Verses—1 Corinthians 9:24

Do you not know that those who run in a race all run, but only one receives the prize? Run in such a way that you may win.

Additional Reading: Romans 8:29-30; Psalm 119:9; Matthew 28:19-20

My Thoughts

Have you ever entered a race you knew you couldn't finish, much less win? Maybe a friend asked you to run a marathon, and you did it as an act of support, knowing all along you couldn't do it. You prepared. You bought the shoes and changed your diet, but there was always that lingering doubt that you couldn't do it. Regardless of the preparation, your heart wasn't in it.

Contrast that to an event or a race you knew you could win, with no doubt in your mind. How did that confidence change your attitude toward your preparation, diet, and exercise? Well, here's the good news: we are assured of victory through the blood of Christ. Although we cannot be defeated, we must prepare. I think of athletes who are willing to change their diet, their sleep patterns, their exercise regimens, and even where they live—all to increase their chances for victory. This 10X lifestyle is no different. You must be willing to be transformed by the Spirit and committed to preparing daily for the race. Are you ready?

Your Reflections

_____

_____

_____

_____

_____

_____

Prayer

Father God, I rejoice in your name. I give you praise for your goodness and blessings. Help me, dear Lord, to adequately prepare for this grand race you have called me to, that I might run with endurance and strength. My victory is assured because you are with me. My victory is a victory for you. May it glorify your holy name. In your holy name I pray, amen.

SDG

FINISH WELL DAY FIVE

Today's Verses—2 John 1:8

Watch yourselves, that you do not lose what we have accomplished, but that you may receive a full reward.

Additional Reading: 2 Timothy 4:7-8; Psalm 65:11; James 1:12

My Thoughts

Anyone who has ever participated in a long race knows there are obstacles along the way. Whether it be the obstacle of poor preparation or of route conditions, you can fall short of your goal.

The Christian walk is no different. Finishing well requires many things. It starts with your motivation and commitment. Keep in mind that even with great preparation, proper planning, and great training, the unexpected can defeat you. Top athletes can be sidelined by injury and can also be removed from play by their actions or misdeeds. To get the prize, we must be prepared for distractions. The evil one will do everything he can to defeat you. Thus, no matter how good your conditioning or how much you've prepared, you must also be aware of distractions such as ambition, fear, lust, or greed. Be on guard!

Your Reflections

_____

_____

_____

_____

_____

_____

Prayer

Father, my words are inadequate to describe your magnificence. As much as I can speak, it comes from knowing you as you have revealed yourself to me. You are the true God who blesses, loves, and protects me. I rejoice in you, my Lord. You are amazing. My prayer is that, someday, I can utter the words of the apostle Paul when he said, "I have fought the good fight, I have finished the course, I have kept the faith; in the future is laid up for me the crown of righteousness, which the Lord, the righteous Judge, will award to me on that day" (2 Timothy 4:7-8). In the matchless name of Jesus Christ I pray, amen.

WEEK FORTY-THREE
CROWN OF LIFE

CROWN OF LIFE   DAY ONE

Today's Verses—James 1:12

Blessed is a man who perseveres under trial; for once he has been approved, he will receive the crown of life which the Lord has promised to those who love Him.

Additional Reading: Revelation 2:10; 1 Thessalonians 2:19; Philippians 4:1

My Thoughts

When I think of crowns, I think of royalty and of kings and queens, maybe a prince. A crown is a recognition of status or high standing. It's a symbol for all to see that the wearer is someone to be respected and honored. It also means a person has power and authority. I can easily see our king, Christ Jesus, with a holy crown as he reins from above. He is the ultimate authority and the only true king.

Here's the cool thing: we get a crown, too! We are a part of God's family, and, thus, we are royalty. The first crown we receive is the crown of life, but it's not an ordinary crown—nor is it an ordinary life. It's an eternal life to live in glory with the almighty God. The responsibly that comes with this crown is to remain faithful and work to his glory, not our own—not like the rich, young ruler who thought it was all about him.[11] Without Christ in our lives, any crown we wear is one of a fool.

Your Reflections

_____

_____

_____

_____

_____

_____

Prayer

Father God, what a wonderful promise you have given us in your Word. We will receive the crown of life. I am grateful, Lord. I am your child, and you love me. My joy is unspeakable as I rejoice in your goodness. Help me, dear Lord, to persevere as I encounter various trials, that I might remain steadfast to your calling and stay true to you. In Christ's holy name I pray, amen.

---

11   https://en.wikipedia.org/wiki/Jesus_and_the_rich_young_man

SDG

CROWN OF LIFE   DAY TWO

Today's Verses—Revelation 3:11-12

I am coming quickly; hold fast what you have, so that no one will take your crown. He who overcomes, I will make him a pillar in the temple of My God, and he will not go out from it anymore; and I will write on him the name of My God, and the name of the city of My God, the new Jerusalem, which comes down out of heaven from My God, and My new name.

Additional Reading: 2 Timothy 2:5-7; 1 Peter 5:1-4; 1 Corinthians 4:5

My Thoughts

God is calling us in James 4:7 to remain steadfast and to resist the devil in his pursuit to defeat us. His primary mission is to lie, cheat, and steal our hope and faith in our risen Savior (John 10:10). If we lose our hope and take our eyes off Christ, we can be defeated. So, muscle up in the Word so you can resist the fiery arrows of the devil.

The wonderful thing about God and his Word is that he has revealed our future and his promises as we serve him. I am excited to know that as we persevere in our quest to serve him and bring others to him, our efforts will be greatly rewarded. Although that's not what motivates me, my place in eternity is a reward that is enough. Think of how we will have a place of honor and how we will receive his recognition. My efforts matter, as do yours. Get in the battle, and, remember, he is with you!

Your Reflections

_____

_____

_____

_____

_____

_____

Prayer

Father God, I rejoice in the glorious hope of Christ's return and look forward to that day, when your followers will receive the crown of glory for faithfully following you. I am grateful to be your disciple, and I pray each day for understanding and wisdom, that I might share, in love, your magnificent plan of salvation with others. Help me to remain close to you, that I would run with endurance and finish the race to your glory. In Christ's holy name I pray, amen.

SDG

CROWN OF LIFE DAY THREE

Today's Verses—1 Peter 5:4

And when the Chief Shepherd appears, you will receive the unfading crown of glory.

Additional Reading: 2 Corinthians 5:17; 1 John 2:28-3:3; Zechariah 9:16

My Thoughts

Often our focus is on this life. We limit our thinking to this mortal mind and body that we have. God doesn't want us to see things this way. He wants our focus to be on eternity. If we limit our thinking to what's possible on this earth, we are being very shortsighted.

When 1 Peter 5:4 speaks of the unfading crown of glory, it means nothing can diminish or remove our crown once we receive it from the Great Shepherd. I am beginning to realize that, at times, my thinking is too focused on the things of this world. I think about my health and my wealth as if those where of utmost importance. Now, I am not suggesting we shouldn't care about these things but, come on—our lives are only a fleeting vapor! In contrast, what we do to receive our crown of glory has eternal ramifications.

Your Reflections

_____

_____

_____

_____

_____

_____

Prayer

Loving Father, you offer us so much hope in the glorious return of Jesus, our Savior. You offer us the crown of glory and the crown of life that will not fade and that will last for all eternity with you. Lord, I know that much is expected of me—to stay the course and to remain faithful to your call. Give me the discipline to stay in your Word, the wisdom of the Holy Spirit, and the boldness to proclaim you in a dark and dying world. Help me to remain pure as you are pure. Guide me this day that your light would shine through me for your honor and glory. In Christ's holy name I pray, amen

CROWN OF LIFE

DAY FOUR

Today's Verses—2 Timothy 4:8

In the future there is laid up for me the crown of righteousness, which the Lord, the righteous Judge, will award to me on that day; and not only to me, but also to all who have loved His appearing.

Additional Reading: 1 John 5:13; 1 Peter 1:3-5; Romans 8:18

My Thoughts

What motivates you to get out of bed in the morning? Is it your career or your business? Is it your family that drives you to get out in the world and do more and be more? For what do we labor? Is it for reward or fame? In the end, what do we seek: fortune and fame or just to have lived a good life? Once again, it's all just stuff; our bodies will eventually stop, and we will be no more.

What if you had a job that you knew would yield immeasurable rewards and recognition? What if those rewards would never end? How hard would you work to do well? I believe that is what God's plan for our lives is all about. We have the greatest calling on this earth: to serve the King of Kings and Lord of Lords. Our reward at the end is the crown of righteousness. Eternal promises of life with the living God is all I need.

Your Reflections

_____

_____

_____

_____

_____

_____

Prayer

Father, I rejoice and give you praise as your plan for my life continues to be revealed through your Word. The Holy Spirit speaks to me and guides me as I follow you. I am grateful that as I grow in you, I begin to better understand how to bring your Kingdom here on earth. Father, please help me to share the living hope that is both imperishable and undefiled, which comes only through the resurrection of my Savior, Jesus Christ. In his holy name I pray, amen.

CROWN OF LIFE   DAY FIVE

Today's Verses—Philippians 3:13-14

Brethren, I do not regard myself as having laid hold of it yet; but one thing I do: forgetting what lies behind and reaching forward to what lies ahead, I press on toward the goal for the prize of the upward call of God in Christ Jesus.

Additional Reading: John 14:12; Luke 14:13-14; Isaiah 62:3

My Thoughts

This is so cool: "I do not regard myself as having laid hold of it yet" (Phil. 3:13). What Paul is saying here is that even after all he has experienced and learned from Jesus, he still hasn't figured it all out. In his quest to serve, he held fast to the future. It is about looking to what lies ahead, leaving the past behind, and always pressing forward to the calling of God in Christ Jesus.

This verse should be a great source of encouragement, and Paul should serve as a model for all of us. Paul reminds us that, first and foremost, we must remain steadfast and keep our eyes on Christ Jesus. There is no other prize we should pursue. Don't let your past hold you back or bring you down. It's all behind you and should remain there. Press on to God's glory, and you will be victorious.

Your Reflections

_____

_____

_____

_____

_____

_____

Prayer

Father God, what a glorious call I have from you. I must press on and be diligent, remaining faithful to you. I no longer consider the mistakes of my past; instead, I walk as a new person in you. Jesus' sacrifice on the cross gave me a new life and a new beginning. Lord, please keep me focused on what lies ahead and the hope of eternity with you. In Christ's holy name I pray, amen.

WEEK FORTY-FOUR

WELL DONE

WELL DONE

DAY ONE

Today's Verses—Matthew 25:21

His master said to him, 'Well done, good and faithful slave. You were faithful with a few things, I will put you in charge of many things; enter into the joy of your master.'

Additional Reading: Colossians 3:23-24; 1 Corinthians 6:19-20; John 5:30

My Thoughts

In the story of the talents in Matthew 25, three servants are given talents: two receive five talents, and one receives two. Until recently, I had never thought of the perspective of the servant who received only two talents. Was he discouraged or did he feel inferior because he only got the two? The master could easily have divided the talents equally and given each four, right? I do believe that God wanted to illustrate a point through this parable.

Most of my life, I identified with the two-talent servant; I never really considered myself as all that smart. As a result, my thinking was limited, and my output for the Kingdom was minimal at best. I would always compare myself to the other five-talent guys and wonder why they had so many. Recently, though, the Lord helped me understand that it's not about how many talents you have—but how you use the ones God has given you. I realized I will never be a person like Billy Graham or Andy Stanley, but I can use the talents God has blessed me with to accomplish his purpose in my life. We all have skills given to us by God. How you use them will determine if you will hear, "Well done."

Your Reflections

_____

_____

_____

_____

_____

_____

Prayer

Father God, thank you for a new day to sing your praises and walk in your righteousness. You are faithful, and your love gives me joy and hope each day. Help me today, dear Lord, to remain steadfast and true to your calling. Keep me focused on your glory that I might be your ambassador, sharing your love and peace. I long for the day when I will enter the joy of my master, my Lord and Savior, Jesus. In his holy name I pray, amen.

WELL DONE DAY TWO

Today's Verses—Psalm 1:2-3

But his delight is in the law of the Lord, and His law he meditates day and night. He will be like a tree firmly planted by streams of water, which yields its fruit in its season and its leaf does not wither; and in whatever he does, he prospers.

Additional Reading: Luke 23:43; 2 Corinthians 5:10; Mark 10:42-45

My Thoughts

God's Word is full of great metaphors that enable us to fully understand the meaning behind his message. I spend a lot of time in the outdoors, and, many times, I've noticed that the biggest and strongest trees are next to streams. The location provides a constant source of water for the tree to grow and flourish. It also allows the tree to be firmly rooted in the soil to withstand strong winds.

Our walk with Christ is very much the same. If we remain close to the Savior and are nourished by his Word, we, too, will be firmly planted. As we grow in the knowledge of God's plan, we can bear much fruit in every season. So, what does that take? It requires drinking the Word of God daily—for your subsistence and learning. How deep are your roots? Can you withstand the winds and storms of this world?

Your Reflections

_____

_____

_____

_____

_____

_____

Prayer

Father God, I praise your wonderful name for the many blessings I receive from you. My desire is for intimacy with you, that I might know your will and act accordingly. I rejoice that you are there to guide me. Help me to delight in your Word and to meditate on it day and night. I pray that I will be like a tree firmly planted, bearing much fruit for your Kingdom. Keep me close. Speak to my heart, that I might magnify your name and honor you. In Christ's holy name I pray, amen.

WELL DONE DAY THREE

Today's Verses—Revelation 3:21

He who overcomes, I will grant to him to sit down with Me on My throne, as I also overcame and sat down with My Father on His throne.

Additional Reading: Luke 12:42-44; Galatians 5:13-14; Matthew 6:24

My Thoughts

This is so cool. We get to sit with our Savior next to the throne. If you are like me, you wish that day would come soon. But in the meantime, we must decide each day to overcome temptation, laziness, and disobedience. Have you ever heard the term "pay your dues"? There are no dues to pay in this case, but God does expect our faithfulness.

Our daily walk isn't "a walk in the park," as the saying goes. It is fraught with obstacles and resistance from the devil. God has fully prepared us for the task, but it's up to us to use our training to stay the course and resist fear and doubt. We need to overcome frustration and disappointment and remember that, someday, we will be ushered into his throne room to join him.

Your Reflections

_____

_____

_____

_____

_____

_____

Prayer

Father God, your son Jesus was sent to deliver us from the penalty of sin, so we might have a new life, a new beginning, a fresh start. I rejoice in your goodness and plan for our lives, that we can spend eternity with you. Lord, help me this day to be mindful of eternity but present in this life. Keep me focused on your will and your righteousness, that others would see you in me for your honor and glory. In the matchless name of our Savior, Christ Jesus, I pray, amen.

WELL DONE   DAY FOUR

Today's Verses—1 Thessalonians 2:13

For this reason, we also constantly thank God that when you received the word of God which you heard from us, you accepted it not as the word of men, but for what it really is, the word of God, which also performs its work in you who believe.

Additional Reading: Mark 9:35; Matthew 23:11-12; Romans 22:1-2

My Thoughts

When I stop to think about all the scholarly work that has been written over the years, it's astounding, from early philosophers, like Socrates to Aristotle, to scientific revolutionists, like Albert Einstein and Stephen Hawking. Intellectual heroes seem to garner a specific following, with each great scholar representing a certain worldview that is often not aligned with a biblical worldview. We might respect these men and others for their advanced thoughts, but the caution here is to avoid taking their philosophies as our own.

Some of these so-called scholars will, at times, cast uncertainty on God's Word. As followers of Christ desirous of living a true 10X lifestyle, we must guard our minds against false teaching and doctrines. God's Word is just that: his Word. It is without error and complete in its instruction. If we understand that the Bible is the inspired Word of God, we will remain faithful to its teaching.

Your Reflections

_____

_____

_____

_____

_____

_____

Prayer

Father God, you are a gracious and loving God. Your Word reveals the mysteries of the universe to those who believe. You clearly give us instructions for daily living and for being transformed by the renewing of our mind (Romans 12:2). Lord, it is clear to me that apart from you, there can be no renewal. Keep me in your will, that I might be a living and holy sacrifice acceptable to you. In Jesus' name I pray, amen.

WELL DONE

DAY FIVE

Today's Verses—1 Corinthians 15:50-52

Now I say this, brethren, that flesh and blood cannot inherit the kingdom of God; nor does the perishable inherit the imperishable. Behold, I tell you a mystery; we will not all sleep, but we will all be changed, in a moment, in the twinkling of an eye, at the last trumpet; for the trumpet will sound, and the dead will be raised imperishable, and we will be changed.

Additional Reading: 1 Samuel 12:24; Joshua 22:5; 1 Peter 1:12

My Thoughts

Do you ever wonder why the Bible is repetitive in its teachings and reminders? I think that it is primarily because we, as humans, tend to forget. If that wasn't the case, God would give us a simple, one-page "Rules to Live By" and that would be enough, right? Unfortunately, we get caught up in the hustle and bustle of life, be it our careers, businesses, families, or a hobby. These things are what the Bible refers to as *perishable.*

We need a paradigm shift in our lives, one that focuses on the eternal. I am in no way suggesting that we shouldn't pursue a career or business. Nor am I suggesting that we shouldn't do our best for our family or pursue a hobby. What I am suggesting is that our focus needs to be on serving our Savior first, keeping in mind that the work we do for the Kingdom is the only thing that has lasting value. If everything you do comes from keeping that in mind, every aspect of your life takes on a different dimension. Is your life in line with a vision of God's Kingdom and of eternity?

Your Reflections

_____

_____

_____

_____

_____

_____

Prayer

Father God, you are the true and mighty God. Your plan for our lives is for us to someday inherit your Kingdom and spend eternity in your glory. I look forward to the day when all who believe will be transformed into imperishable beings. Your blessings are many. You have done many great things in my life. Help me this day, dear Lord, to remain faithful and true to you. Guide me this day, oh, Lord, that I might be your ambassador, offering your love and hope to others. In Jesus' name I pray, amen.

SDG

WEEK FORTY-FIVE

SEND ME

SEND ME
DAY ONE

Today's Verses—Isaiah 6:8

Then I heard the voice of the Lord, saying, "Whom shall I send, and who will go for Us?" Then I said, "Here am I. Send me!"

Additional Reading: John 9:4; Genesis 12:2-3; Hebrews 13:16

My Thoughts

The whole idea behind living a 10X lifestyle is to get off the bench. How long will you sit in the same church pew, listening to the pastor talk about Isaiah 6:8, yawning, and saying, "He can't be talking about me." Guess what? The pastor is and so is God. I can't imagine any sports team that just wants to have a bunch of benchwarmers that show up to practice, go through the motions, and learn the plays but are content in just watching from the sidelines.

Our responsibility is to take the good news of the gospel of Jesus Christ to every corner of the world. You don't have to go to Africa to be effective. It starts in your neighborhood, in your business, or workplace. You don't have to be a missionary to be on mission for the Kingdom. Get in the game today. Share the love and compassion of Christ with every person you meet. Ask the Holy Spirit to give you the boldness to share the hope of eternity.

Your Reflections

_____

_____

_____

_____

_____

_____

Prayer

Father God, I am grateful that you have chosen me as your child and offered me the privilege to serve you. Father, you provide the resources and wisdom I need. Give me a renewed passion each day, oh, Lord, and a boldness to proclaim the good news of Jesus Christ. Teach me to share your love, peace, and joy, that others might see you in me. In Christ's holy name I pray, amen.

SDG

SEND ME   DAY TWO

Today's Verses—Luke 9:23-24

And He was saying to them all, "If anyone wishes to come after Me, he must deny himself, and take up his cross daily and follow Me. For whoever wishes to save his life will lose it, but whoever loses his life for My sake, he is the one who will save it."

Additional Reading: Mark 16:15-16; 1 John 3:17-18; Galatians 6:6-9

My Thoughts

Have you ever met an avid sports fan? You may even be one. The phrase, "He bleeds navy blue and orange," or whatever the team colors are, describes this person. He wears the team colors not just on game day but every day. You even see it in church. Serious fans plaster stickers on their cars and plant signs in their yards. They even go so far as to get a team logo tattooed on their arm. They know all the team stats and rankings and can talk about all the plays for every game for the past ten years. There is no doubting their love for their team.

This is the kind of fan Jesus wants on his team. But here is the big difference: a Jesus fanatic is one who radiates his love and passion for people—not just someone who has an ichthys or a cross on his bumper. Bottom line, God wants us to be so passionate about his Word that we know it as well as any team stats. As Jesus fans, we should be able to site Bible passages and talk about the heroes of the faith. And our wonderful enthusiasm for our Savior should surpass the zeal of the most enthusiastic sports fan we know.

Your Reflections

_____
_____
_____
_____
_____
_____

Prayer

Gracious Father, you are a loving and generous God. Not only did you send your son, Jesus, to die for our sins that we might have a reconciled relationship with you, but you also provide for our every need. I am grateful for your blessings and the richness of my life because of your goodness. Dear Lord, your Word commands us not only to share your love and grace but also to share our bounty with others. Give me your generous heart, oh, Lord, that my love might be a love of action and generosity—not merely words. In Jesus' name I pray, amen.

SDG

SEND ME   DAY THREE

Today's Verses—Matthew 9:37-38

Then He said to His disciples, "The harvest is plentiful, but the workers are few. Therefore, beseech the Lord of the harvest to send out workers into His harvest."

Additional Reading: Romans 12:9-21; Acts 1:8; John 8:12

My Thoughts

Have you ever driven through a wheat field ripe for the harvest or, maybe, a cornfield with bright, yellow corn bursting out of the stalks? What about the fertile fields in Southern California, full of rich, red strawberries? Have you ever wondered what would happen if the workers weren't there to pick the crops? Today, as the world's population grows, the demand for more food is ever increasing and putting pressure for additional production on the nations' farmers.

The Kingdom of God is very similar—except the harvest is not about produce but people! It's estimated that there are approximately 16,600 civilizations in the world, with an estimated 6,700 still unreached with the gospel of Christ. Today, our communities are a mixture of varied religions and beliefs. So, you don't have to go to the far regions of Africa or China to reap a harvest for the Kingdom. Start in your own backyard. The fields are ripe, so put on your overalls and reap a bumper crop for Jesus.

Your Reflections

_____

_____

_____

_____

_____

_____

Prayer

Gracious and loving Father, your Word tells us that we are to rejoice in hope, persevere in tribulation, and remain devoted to prayer (Romans 12:2). Yet in times of trouble, we too often are defeated and rendered ineffective by the challenges we face. Lord, help me to remain in you, that the power of the Holy Spirit would remain in me and that I might rely on your strength and not my own. Give me hope and boldness as I persevere and share your good news with others. Help me to shine your light on a dark world. In Christ's holy name I pray, amen.

SEND ME   DAY FOUR

Today's Verses—Acts 13:47

For so the Lord has commanded us, "I have placed You as a light for the Gentiles, That You may bring salvation to the end of the earth."

Additional Reading: Romans 1:16; Jeremiah 29:11-13; James 1:27

My Thoughts

As a family, we spend a lot of time camping in the great outdoors. One of the many things we love is the night sky in the country. The stars shine brightly, and there seems to be thousands of them. You can identify all the bright stars and constellations you learned in grade school. The first star we always identify is the North Star or Polaris because that one shines the brightest, making it easy to find. When we return to the city, we are often struck by how we can't seem to find the same star. Is it still there? We know it is, but the light pollution from city lights makes it difficult to see stars in the night sky.

I believe that the world today is a lot like the night sky in the city. The stars are there, but we can't see them because of all the pollution of sin and fear. We are called, as believers in Jesus Christ, to be light to a dark and fallen world. Light always wins over darkness, but the light must be strong to overtake it. We are called to stand with other followers of Christ to overcome the darkness in the world. How can your light shine brightly this day?

Your Reflections

_____

_____

_____

_____

_____

_____

Prayer

Father God, your Word is full of your promises that offer us hope, joy, and prosperity. Father, all of this begins with the gospel of Jesus Christ and his sacrifice on the cross for us. My salvation is a result of faith in this gospel. Thus, I am not ashamed to share it with others. Help me, dear Lord, to walk by faith each day with a renewed hope in you. May my life be a living testimony of your righteousness, your hope, and your love, that I might bring others to you. In Christ's holy name I pray, amen.

SDG

SEND ME

DAY FIVE

Today's Verses—Matthew 28:18-20

And Jesus came up and spoke to them, saying, "All authority has been given to Me in heaven and on earth. Go therefore and make disciples of all the nations, baptizing them in the name of the Father and the Son and the Holy Spirit, teaching them to observe all that I commanded you; and lo, I am with you always, even to the end of the age."

Additional Reading: 1 Timothy 6:11-12; John 20:21; Luke 3:11

My Thoughts

In the world of academia today, we see too many times where professors, who are acting under the authority of the college or university, stray from the values that the institution was founded on. They distort the truth and teach based on misguided facts and misinformation. They seek to influence or corrupt the students' thinking and values. This is false teaching. They set their own agenda for instruction and learning without regard for their students.

In contrast, Jesus has given us clear instruction on how we are to live and share him with others. He was given all authority in heaven and on earth, and he is transferring that authority to us. His mandate in Matthew 28:18-20 is clear: first, we must go. Then, we ought to baptize in the name of the Father, the Son, and the Holy Spirit. Finally, we are commanded to teach, keeping in mind that on our walk, we act on his authority and must remain true to his values and teachings. Are you prepared to be his emissary to the world? Are you filled with his knowledge and his Spirit? If so, then go!

Your Reflections

_____

_____

_____

_____

_____

_____

Prayer

Father God, I am grateful for the opportunity that you have given me to share your goodness and love. I am most grateful that I have experienced it firsthand. Thank you. Your unbounded love was demonstrated by Jesus as he gave his life as a ransom for my sins. Lord, help me to pursue righteousness, godliness, faith, love, perseverance, and gentleness. Father, you sent Jesus to model these things. Please send me. In Christ's holy name I pray, amen.

WEEK FORTY-SIX

FELLOWSHIP

FELLOWSHIP DAY ONE

Today's Verses—1 Thessalonians 5:11

Therefore encourage one another and build up one another, just as you also are doing.

Additional Reading: Acts 2:42; 1 John 4:11-14; Matthew 18:18-20

My Thoughts

During most of my early life, I was in the shadows. As what most people would call an introvert, I had trouble in many social interactions. I would rarely start conversations and often ran out of things to talk about once it got past the topic of weather. As a result, fellowship was somewhat foreign to me. Growing up in a dysfunctional family certainly didn't help. We surely had family gatherings, but I never really felt close to my relatives.

As I matured in adulthood, I was forced to "get out more," and I pushed myself to interact with more and more people. Still an introvert, I am not always totally comfortable. But here is the good news: as a part of God's family, once I accepted Jesus Christ as my Lord and Savior, everything changed. I am now a part of this wonderful, loving family that shares my common values and goals. We all seek to become more like Jesus and share his love and grace with others.

Fellowship is now something I look forward to and so should you. I love being surrounded by other believers who love me and have my back. It means having loving people with whom to share hopes, disappointment, and hurts. This fellowship is a bond united by love and our purpose to be living examples of the Savior.

Your Reflections

_____

_____

_____

_____

_____

_____

Prayer

Father God, what a wonderful family you have called me to: one of love, compassion, and true fellowship. What a blessing to be in a family where we seek your wisdom, share your hope, live out your love, and glorify your holy and wonderful name. All of this comes from the love that Jesus Christ shared for us by giving his life at the cross. Lord, help me this day to reach out in fellowship, that my life would be a model of your love and grace. In Christ's holy name I pray, amen.

FELLOWSHIP

Today's Verses—1 John 1:3

What we have seen and heard we proclaim to you also, so that you too may have fellowship with us; and indeed, our fellowship is with the Father, and with His Son Jesus Christ.

Additional Reading: 2 Thessalonians 3:6; Colossians 3:16-17; Romans 16:17

My Thoughts

When I think about 1 John 1:3, my thoughts are on sports fans. In our city, J. J. Watt is a well-liked local hero who plays for the Texans. He is a celebrity of sorts who gives his all—both on and off the field. Now, don't get hung up on this. If you are not a Texans fan, then think about your local sports hero. Think about game day and hanging out with your fellow enthusiasts. You can enjoy each other's company and talk about how great your team is and how they will bring about victory. Now, imagine that during the excitement and anticipation, J. J. himself shows up to your party. The atmosphere is totally ramped up, and you can't believe you are in the presence of one of your heroes. You get to talk with him about strategy and how he plans to bring home the victory.

Okay, now let's take the same scenario, but instead of a sports team, let's consider the game of life. You are rallied together in great fellowship. You share your love and enthusiasm for the Kingdom team. You talk about the Savior and how he can bring about victory. Here's the best news of all: Jesus the Son and God the Father are there with you. They enjoy the fellowship just as much as you do. Better yet, they invite you to come on the field and be a part of this grand game God has for his people. God's got your jersey. Are you ready to enjoy the ultimate fellowship by transitioning from spectator to player?

Your Reflections

_____

_____

_____

_____

_____

_____

Prayer

Father God, thank you that you are amid our fellowship of believers. Father, through our fellowship, we are encouraged and emboldened to reach out with your message of hope, love, and grace. I am grateful for the wisdom I gain from my fellowship with you and other believers. Give me the opportunity to extend this fellowship to others that have lost hope and need your loving transformation and redemption. In Christ's holy name I pray, amen.

FELLOWSHIP

DAY THREE

Today's Verses—Hebrews 10:25

Not forsaking our own assembling together, as is the habit of some, but encouraging one another; and all the more as you see the day drawing near.

Additional Reading: 2 Corinthians 13:11-14; 1 Peter 3:8-9; Galatians 6:1-2

My Thoughts

Why is fellowship important to God? If I believe in Jesus, isn't that good enough? In Genesis 2:18 we read: Then the Lord God said, "It is not good for the man to be alone; I will make him a helper suitable for him." God never intended us to go it alone. In Acts 2:42 we read this: "They were continually devoting themselves to the apostles' teaching and to fellowship, to the breaking of bread and to prayer." Our lives are enriched by being surrounded by other believers that love us, encourage us, and at times hold us accountable.

There is great comfort in a fellowship of individuals who love you and stand with you in bad times as well as good. The fellowship becomes a strand of many cords that will not be easily broken. It can be a refuge or simply a place to get encouragement. It's a safe place to share your fears and doubts. It can also be a place for learning and direction. How strong is your fellowship with other believers?

Your Reflections

_____

_____

_____

_____

_____

_____

Prayer

Dear Lord, you are a wonderful Father; you surround us with your love, and the Holy Spirit offers us true fellowship with you. Your desire for our lives is to live in harmony with other believers that, as a body, we might be a beacon of light and hope set upon a hill. I pray, Lord, the words of 1 Peter 3:8, 9 that call us to be harmonious, sympathetic, brotherly, kindhearted, and humble in spirit and to return evil or insult with a blessing. It is all unto your honor and glory. In Christ's holy name I pray, amen.

FELLOWSHIP

Today's Verses—Proverbs 27:17

Iron sharpens iron, so one man sharpens another.

Additional Reading: 1 John 1:5-7; Philippians 1:3-11; 1 Corinthians 12:24-27

My Thoughts

The beautiful part of being in a close-knit group is that as you get to know one another; you build a bond of trust. That trust then leads to an openness where you have the freedom to share your thoughts. It can also be a great place for learning. Remember the old saying, "People don't care how much you know until they know how much you care."

I have been involved in Bible study fellowship for many years, and it's been a wonderful place for not only fellowship but also learning from others. Typically, there are about two hundred men who gather weekly for one simple purpose: to grow closer to Christ. We spend time getting to know each other, and we share our prayer requests and study God's Word. There are many lively discussions as we each share what we believe a certain scripture or biblical truth is all about. God created us for fellowship. To grow in faith, we need to be around others who share our values.

Your Reflections

Prayer

Father God, the family you have called us to is one of love and compassion. Our fellowship is a place of caring and love for one another that comes from you. I praise your wonderful name for providing such a place where we are safe and can be comforted by other members of your family. Our love for each other comes from you. Help me, dear Lord, to walk in your light, that I might have true fellowship. In you, there is no darkness—only light. In Christ's holy name I pray, amen.

FELLOWSHIP

Today's Verses—1 Corinthians 1:10

Now I exhort you, brethren, by the name of our Lord Jesus Christ, that you all agree and that there be no divisions among you, but that you be made complete in the same mind and in the same judgment.

Additional Reading: Romans 1:12; James 5:15-16; Philemon 1:6-7

My Thoughts

There is nothing that brings about division in a group of believers like disagreement. I have heard of churches splitting over the simplest of issues or very small matters of doctrine. It always disheartens me when I hear stories of disagreement or fighting amongst a body of believers. I recognize that we may have different interpretations of God's truth when it comes to doctrine, but we need to always seek common ground.

There are three simple truths we need to unite around: one, the Trinity; two, the deity of Christ; and three, the inerrancy of God's Word, the holy Bible. Beyond that, it really doesn't matter. Once we have common ground, we can learn from the Scriptures and learn from each other. We can invest in each others 'lives with love, compassion, and service. As a strong body of believers, we can stand strong, united against the devil. A true 10X lifestyle is one of love, service, and consistency in serving others and our Savior.

Your Reflections

_____

_____

_____

_____

_____

_____

Prayer

Father God, the richness of our lives is made full by your immense love for us all and by the diversity of the body of believers. The many facets of our personalities offer us insight and wisdom on how to reach the lost for you. I pray, dear Lord, that when disagreement or conflict comes, we will remain united in the truth and wisdom of your Word and the teaching of the Holy Spirit. In Christ's holy name I pray, amen.

WEEK FORTY-SEVEN
TRAINING

TRAINING   DAY ONE

Today's Verses—1 Timothy 4:8

For bodily discipline is only of little profit, but godliness is profitable for all things, since it holds promise for the present life and also for the life to come.

Additional Reading: Hebrews 5:11-14; Proverbs 22:6; Ephesians 6:4

My Thoughts

When I think of healthy disciplines, two things come to mind: diet and exercise. One excites me, and the other frustrates me. I know what you're thinking: you're frustrated by the latter and excited about the former. But just the opposite is true for me. Don't get me wrong; I love to eat, but the thought of keeping myself strong and fit is very exciting. I do believe it's vital that we follow a healthy diet and exercise regularly to maintain our health—but not at the expense of our time in fellowship with God and other believers.

I have seen many people become fanatical about their exercise and take it to the extreme. I don't see a problem with that if they have the same passion and commitment to their walk with Christ. All David needed to defeat the giant Goliath was five smooth stones and God. Our spiritual knowledge will not only keep us healthy, but it will also lead us to the right path. God wants our hearts and our passion to be set on him over anything else. Your spiritual fitness is the main thing in the game of life.

Your Reflections

_____

_____

_____

_____

_____

_____

Prayer

Gracious Father, you have given us strong, physical bodies that allow us to live with vitality in our work and leisure. But we must rely on the spiritual strength you give to fulfill our true calling. I am grateful that along with our physical bodies, you have given us a sound mind that can understand your wisdom and teachings. Please give me a clear mind, dear Lord, that I might mature in your wisdom and instruction. From this maturity, may I share your wisdom with others, that they might learn your will and calling for their lives unto your honor and glory. In Christ's holy name I pray, amen.

TRAINING   DAY TWO

Today's Verses—2 Timothy 3:17
So that the man of God may be adequate, equipped for every good work.

Additional Reading: Proverbs 4:1-2; Matthew 5:19; Deuteronomy 6:5-9

My Thoughts

"A little knowledge is a dangerous thing" is a quote I've heard many times in my life, and I think this can especially apply to our spiritual knowledge. The holy Scriptures contain everything we need to understand God's plan for our lives and all of mankind. It's a source of wisdom and understanding. It's the ultimate "how to" guide for our lives.

God will put many opportunities in our lives to share the gospel, encourage others with his words, and teach, but if we have little knowledge, we will be ineffective at best. Benjamin Franklin is credited with saying, "By failing to prepare, you are preparing to fail." Our preparation needs to take form in our study of God's Word, in participation in Bible studies, and in learning from others. Your learning will pay dividends when the opportunity to share God's truth presents itself.

Your Reflections

_____

_____

_____

_____

_____

_____

Prayer

Father God, you have provided us with your holy Bible, that we might receive instruction in all aspects of our lives. You offer us teaching with other believers so we can gain greater clarity on your instructions. The Holy Spirit indwells in us that we might have a guide to wisdom and understanding. I give you thanks that in this grand world you have created, we have many resources of wisdom and knowledge. Lord, please help me to seek your wisdom and instruction, that I might learn and prepare for your calling on my life to be equipped for every good work. In the matchless name of Jesus Christ I pray, amen.

SDG

TRAINING   DAY THREE

Today's Verses—Psalm 144:1-2

Blessed be the Lord, my rock, who trains my hands for war, and my fingers for battle; my lovingkindness and my fortress, my stronghold and my deliverer, my shield and He in whom I take refuge, who subdues my people under me.

Additional Reading: Hebrews 12:11; Colossians 3:23-24; Titus 2:1-2

My Thoughts

History is full of examples where soldiers without proper training were easily defeated. The prepared and trained will always overcome. Training begins with the fundamentals and then moves on to strategy and tactics. Soldiers are prepared physically for battle so they might endure harsh conditions or prolonged sieges. Their commanders are skilled in tactics of war and the battlefield. A skilled leader will lead his troops to victory.

As soldiers in God's army, our training is essential. And here's the great news: God is our commander. The God of creation is our strategist and the King of Kings is our battlefield commander. The Holy Spirit resides in us to give us courage and strength. Our responsibility is to apply ourselves to the training. Our battlefield manual, as well as our advanced tactics and strategies, are all we need for basic training. The words in Ephesians 6:12 serve as a good reminder of whom we are facing in battle: "For we are not fighting against human beings but against the wicked spiritual forces in the heavenly world, the rulers, authorities, and cosmic powers of this dark age" (GNT). Even so, God is by our side. We will not be defeated.

Your Reflections

_____

_____

_____

_____

_____

Prayer

Father God, your Word tells us that we must be prepared daily for the battle against the wicked forces of darkness. I rejoice in the words of the psalmist in Psalm 144 that say you are my rock, my lovingkindness, my fortress, my stronghold, my deliverer, and my shield in whom I take refuge as you train me for battle. I pray, dear Lord, that I will remain faithful to your training and instruction, that I might be effective in following your calling and be victorious in you. In the mighty name of my Savior, Jesus Christ, I pray, amen.

SDG

TRAINING   DAY FOUR

Today's Verses—1 Peter 3:15-16

But sanctify Christ as Lord in your hearts, always being ready to make a defense to everyone who asks you to give an account for the hope that is in you, yet with gentleness and reverence; and keep a good conscience so that in the thing in which you are slandered, those who revile your good behavior in Christ will be put to shame.

Additional Reading: Proverbs 18:15; 2 John 1:9; Colossians 2:8

My Thoughts

When I think about sanctification, or being set aside, I think about John the Baptist. Luke 1:80 reads, "And the child continued to grow and to become strong in spirit, and he lived in the deserts until the day of his public appearance to Israel." You can read more about John's story in the earlier verses of Luke, but clearly, God had a plan for him. His heart was truly sanctified to Christ until the point of death.

Training begins with the attitude of our heart. Why do we seek to be sanctified in the first place? For me, it's a function of my desire to unfailingly serve my Lord and Savior, Christ Jesus. If my heart is pure, my motivation will be set on learning his ways, discerning his plan, and willingly following it. My knowledge and understanding will bear witness to the hope I have in Christ. If I am to be an effective witness, I must walk in an upright manner to not dishonor my Lord. Is your walk beyond reproach?

Your Reflections

_____

_____

_____

_____

_____

_____

Prayer

Father God, I am so thankful for your immense blessings and the hope I have in you. Your Word offers us great hope and joy through a relationship with you, the living God. Help me, dear Lord, to sanctify my heart each day, that my hope would be made fresh and my joy would come from you. Help me to continuously seek your wisdom and knowledge, that I might walk in a manner worthy of your calling. In Christ's holy name I pray, amen.

TRAINING

DAY FIVE

Today's Verses—John 14:26

But the Helper, the Holy Spirit, whom the Father will send in My name, He will teach you all things, and bring to your remembrance all that I said to you.

Additional Reading: Proverbs 9:9; Philippians 4:9; Psalm 32:8

My Thoughts

Have you ever seen a TV show or a movie where someone who is ill prepared must answer questions or carry on a conversation and a friend sets up a two-way communication by which the unseen friend can answer questions through a tiny earpiece? Once the question is asked, the friend whispers the answer to his buddy. Invariably, the connection is lost, and the person in the live conversation ends up looking like an idiot.

That will never happen with us because we have the Holy Spirit in us. He is our mentor and teacher. The Holy Spirit gives us greater understanding of the Scriptures, and he clarifies our thinking. It's like having your friend whispering in your ear, but the good news is that the connection will never be broken because he is in you. If we dedicate ourselves to studying God's Word and seeking the Spirit's guidance, then not only will we have better understanding, but we will also have total recall. We are capable of great clarity and supernatural recall if we just ask.

Your Reflections

_____

_____

_____

_____

_____

_____

Prayer

Gracious Father, I am grateful for the helper, the Holy Spirit, you have sent to teach us all things and remind us of your will and instructions. I rejoice in the fact that the Holy Spirit is in me, guides me, and directs me in my daily actions and thoughts. I pray, dear Lord, that I would develop a mind receptive to his instructions, that I might remain faithful to the tasks you have set before me. Help me to remain strong and courageous in the face of adversity, that I might boldly walk in your righteousness for your glory. In Jesus' name I pray, amen.

WEEK FORTY-EIGHT
REFINED

REFINED   DAY ONE

Today's Verses—1 Peter 1:6-7

In this you greatly rejoice, even though now for a little while, if necessary, you have been distressed by various trials, so that the proof of your faith, being more precious than gold which is perishable, even though tested by fire, may be found to result in praise and glory and honor at the revelation of Jesus Christ.

Additional Reading: Isaiah 48:10; 1 Corinthians 3:11-14; John 15:1-2

My Thoughts

We are never promised that our lives will be free of trials or trouble. In fact, these things are part of our journey. The big question is this: how you will react when you face a challenge? Will you remain true to your God or turn to the world for relief? The devil loves to see Christians turn from their beliefs when they face adversity. I don't believe God puts trials in our path to test us, but he does allow them to strengthen our faith.

Many years ago, when my daughter died at the age of twenty-eight after a prolonged battle against Marfan syndrome, I could have been angry at God. I don't understand why my daughter suffered as she did and why her life ended so quickly, but I don't believe God was testing my faith through it all. I do believe it was an opportunity to strengthen my walk and lean more on him. Looking back over the experience, I realize now that I grew in my faith and relied on his strength and not my own. The trial revealed the impurities in my faith. Where do you need refinement in your walk with Jesus?

Your Reflections

_____

_____

_____

_____

_____

Prayer

Father God, I am thankful for the process you have for strengthening our faith. You allow us to experience various trials so that the weakness of our faith might be revealed. As we rely on your strength through our suffering, we are truly being refined. You remove the impurities from our thinking and our reliance on our own capabilities. We emerge from the trial with a renewed confidence in you. Lord, please give me wisdom and courage, that I might be strong as I face various trials and that my faith might be strengthened. I want to honor you in the process. In Christ's holy name I pray, amen.

SDG

REFINED   DAY TWO

Today's Verses—Zechariah 13:9

And I will bring the third part through the fire, refine them as silver is refined, and test them as gold is tested. They will call on My name, and I will answer them; I will say, "They are My people," and they will say, "The Lord is my God."

Additional Reading: 1 Peter 5:10; Matthew 3:10-12; Daniel 12:10

My Thoughts

As I think about the nation of Israel and all that they faced throughout their early history recorded in the Old Testament, I believe God was refining their faith in him. He taught them to put their trust in him alone. They, first, had to put their trust in him to lead them out of Egypt. Then, they had to trust him to help them cross the Red Sea. Each time, God proved his faithfulness, and they still complained and grumbled. The refinement was so severe that they had to wait forty years to enter the Promised Land.

We must examine our own hearts and ask ourselves this: where do we still lack faith and doubt God's power over this world? Where do we need to rid ourselves of bad habits that keep us from serving? Are you stuck in your old self because it is more comfortable? God can deliver you from the past habits. He has already forgiven and forgotten your sins, so don't go back and pick them up. Refinement starts with us and our willingness to allow God to finish the process.

Your Reflections

_____

_____

_____

_____

_____

_____

Prayer

Father God, I feel your mighty hand working in my life. I am grateful that the Holy Spirit is at work in me to bring me into a closer walk with you. I rejoice in the words from 1 Peter 5:10: "After you have suffered a little while, the God of all grace, who called you to His eternal glory in Christ, will Himself perfect, confirm, strengthen, and establish you." Thank you, dear Lord, for this marvelous process in my life, that I might continue to mature in my faith and remain true to my calling. In the matchless name of Jesus Christ I pray, amen.

SDG

REFINED DAY THREE

Today's Verses—Proverbs 17:3

The refining pot is for silver and the furnace for gold, but the Lord tests hearts.

Additional Reading: 1 Peter 4:12-14; Numbers 31:23; Romans 5:3-5

My Thoughts

I wonder sometimes if it would be better to jump into a hot bath to get all our sins, habits, and sinful thoughts washed away. It might take a big bar of soap, but after soaking, scrubbing, scrubbing again, and rinsing, we could just dry off and be pure. However, the refining process of our heart takes time—more time than a good bath might take.

Jesus' death on the cross and resurrection offer us salvation. Once we accept the amazing gift, we are forgiven, and our debt of sin is paid in full. We are no longer under the yoke of slavery to our lust, evil deeds, and sinful nature. The Bible tells us that we are a new creation, but there's a challenge: we are still human, and although the Holy Spirit is in us, the refinement of our hearts and minds takes time.

Once you have accepted God's complete forgiveness, ask him to refine your heart. When you revert to your old ways, you revisit things that do not reflect the image of Christ. Simply ask God to remove this from you. It may take years to overcome sinful habits, but if you are persistent, he is faithful and will slowly refine your heart.

Your Reflections

_____

_____

_____

_____

_____

_____

Prayer

Father God, I rejoice with exultation at your glory. I am grateful for your blessings in my life and your mercy and lovingkindness. You are faithful, oh, Lord, and I rely on you. Lord, as I encounter various trials or difficulties, help me to remain in you. I pray that these issues will not deter me or cause me to doubt you in any way. I recognize that tribulation brings about perseverance, that perseverance brings about proven character, that proven character introduces hope, and that hope does not disappoint—because the love of God has been poured into our hearts through the Holy Spirit (Romans 5:5). Help me, dear Lord, to never lose hope. In Christ's holy name I pray, amen.

REFINED   DAY FOUR

Today's Verses—James 1:2-4

Consider it all joy, my brethren, when you encounter various trials, knowing that the testing of your faith produces endurance. And let endurance have its perfect result, so that you may be perfect and complete, lacking in nothing.

Additional Reading: Malachi 3:3; Isaiah 33:14; Romans 12:1-2

My Thoughts

So, if refinement isn't just a simple cleaning, like taking a bath, how are we refined? The bodies we were born with age over time, and we may see dramatic changes as we grow older. It's a struggle to remain healthy through diet and exercise. No matter how hard we try, we cannot stop the aging process. Although we can control certain elements of our physical bodies, our hearts and minds are a different story.

Although we do have control over our minds and can choose whom to love, there is still so much we cannot do. This is where God steps in. He, through his love and encouragement, is gradually refining us. When we first come to Christ, we are transformed, but we have the same mind, thoughts, and behaviors. As we mature in our faith, the Holy Spirit reveals things to us that we need to change or simply eliminate from our lives. As we give it to God, he can supernaturally remove it from us.

From my experience, the process takes years; it's gradual. As we mature, we find new opportunities to exercise our faith—but along with that come trials. As we pray and work through these various trials with God's help, we grow in our faith. Along with that growth comes courage to take bolder steps in service to the Savior. As new obstacles come our way, we are, once again, taught to trust—and thus, we are refined in our faith. Each time, we grow, but it's an ongoing process.

Your Reflections

_____

_____

_____

_____

_____

Prayer

Dear Lord, I am grateful for this journey you have called me to—a journey of discovery and transformation. Once I became a believer in Jesus Christ and gave my life to him, you gave me a path that provides for my growth and maturity in you. I rejoice in the fact that Jesus is here beside me, along with the Holy Spirit, to teach, comfort, and encourage me along the way. Keep me on your path, Dear Lord. Give me the strength to endure the trials so that my faith would be made perfect and complete—lacking in nothing. In the matchless name of the risen Lord, Jesus Christ, I pray, amen.

SDG

REFINED   DAY FIVE

Today's Verses—Hebrews 12:7

It is for discipline that you endure; God deals with you as with sons; for what son is there whom his father does not discipline?

Additional Reading: Isaiah 1:25; Daniel 11:35; James 1:12

My Thoughts

Without a doubt, laws are intended to protect us and others. Speed limits are set to protect not only the drivers but pedestrians as well—especially when small children are present. Civil and criminal laws are all in place to protect not only our persons, but also our physical property. Throughout the Bible, there are laws and rules to follow. God gives us clear direction on how to live our lives and how we should treat others.

As with our laws here on earth, when God's laws are broken, there are consequences. What would happen if laws were not enforced or if there were no penalties for not following the rules? We would be a lawless society in which no one would be safe.

Jail penalties or fines are put in place to discipline us and to keep us within the confines of the law. God's laws, when not followed, aren't any different. Although we might not be physically incarcerated when we break God's laws, the penalty is far greater: it's separation from God. When we ask for his forgiveness and accept his discipline, we maintain our relationship with the Father.

Your Reflections

_____

_____

_____

_____

_____

_____

Prayer

Father God, you have given us an amazing life—full of hope, joy, and peace. You patiently wait for us to yield to your will and rely on your strength, rather than our own. Your plans are clear, and you have given us instructions for the abundant life in Christ Jesus. I accept your discipline when I fall. Purify me, oh, Lord, that I might walk in your righteousness daily. Help me to be your light, for your honor and glory, in this dark world. In the holy name of our Savior, Christ Jesus, I pray, amen.

WEEK FORTY-NINE
TRUST

TRUST DAY ONE

Today's Verses—Isaiah 25:9

And it shall be said in that day: "Lo, this is our God; we have waited for Him, and He will save us. This is the Lord; we have waited for Him; we will be glad and rejoice in His salvation."

Additional Reading: Psalm 91:1-4; Romans 15:13; Mark 5:36

My Thoughts

Anyone who has lived at all among people—that's most of us—has been let down by them. People we trusted have failed us. It might have been our parents or our spouses. Trust is something we teach our children at an early age by actions—by doing what we say we are going to do. There may be a time in your past where you were the person who violated a trust. You could have broken a marriage vow, or it could have been as simple as not delivering on a promise to a loved one. Once trust is lost, it is very difficult to regain.

Here is what I love about the God I serve: he is trustworthy! As I study the Bible, God has been faithful and trustworthy since the beginning of time. He is always present, and he knows our needs. Just because he doesn't answer right away does not mean he isn't trustworthy. Remember that his ways are not our ways. He will never leave us nor forsake us. Be patient when learning to trust him. In his time, he will deliver you, and you will rejoice and be glad.

Your Reflections

_____

_____

_____

_____

_____

_____

Prayer

Gracious Father, you are an amazing God. I praise your holy name! I have put my trust in you, and you have been true to your Word and your promises. You are faithful. As I grow in you, oh, Lord, you strengthen my trust in you by your steadfast love and presence. Dear Lord, I pray that each day I would walk in your strength with the assurance of protection and provision for my life. Keep me on your path, that I might bear much fruit for you as I walk in you. In Jesus' name I pray, amen.

TRUST   DAY TWO

Today's Verses—2 Timothy 1:12

For this reason, I also suffer these things, but I am not ashamed; for I know whom I have believed, and I am convinced that He is able to guard what I have entrusted to Him until that day.

Additional Reading: Psalm 118:8-9; Hebrews 11:6; 1 Chronicles 28:9

My Thoughts

Think about a time in your past when you were passionate about a leader or, perhaps, a candidate for public office. You put your support behind this individual, campaigned, and gave your time and your finances to his success. You trusted this person because he shared your ideals and values. You urged your friends and family to support him. You believed in him with all your heart and soul, only to learn later that he was not true to his word or the values he espoused. He lacked character and disregarded your belief system.

Once this has happened to you, it's hard to trust anyone again. But 2 Timothy 1:12 is telling us that with God, it's different. We should have the same passion and boldness to share our Savior as our candidate. As you go into the world, you will have critics and naysayers, but stand your ground. Jesus can be trusted.

Your Reflections

_____

_____

_____

_____

_____

_____

Prayer

Father God, your words are clear in Psalm 118:8-9, which teaches us that it is better to put our trust in you than in man or our leaders. Lord, I am grateful that Jesus is my rock and my fortress, whom I can rely on and trust in to deliver me. Lord, I pray that each day, as I am faced with different circumstances, I will turn to you first and not my own human means for wisdom and guidance. I trust in you Lord, in your faithfulness and your presence. In Jesus' name I pray, amen.

TRUST

DAY THREE

Today's Verses—Proverbs 3:5

Trust in the Lord with all your heart and do not lean on your own understanding.

Additional Reading: Mark 9:23-24; Psalm 37:3-6; Joshua 1:9

My Thoughts

I enjoy movies and stories where followers blindly follow their leader into battle. They trust their leader, his command of the battlefield, and his understanding of strategy. The followers lack the knowledge and skills of the leader, but out of the confidence they have in him, they press into battle. They are not leaning on their own knowledge; instead, they rely on their commander.

Our walk with Christ is the same way. It starts with an unwavering trust in the Savior, with a belief so strong that we follow without question. Our faith in Jesus should be just that: unwavering. We don't have to understand everything he is asking us to do, but we can, through the Scriptures, lean on his wisdom and knowledge. He doesn't expect us to understand; he expects us to trust him and follow. It reminds me of the story of Abraham and Isaac when God asked Abraham to sacrifice his son on the altar. Abraham was obedient and trusted God to spare his son, which he did (Genesis 22:1-19).

Your Reflections

_____

_____

_____

_____

_____

_____

Prayer

Father God, I am so thankful that as I walk with you, you remain faithful and are always present. You are the true and mighty God, and you never waver or falter. Father, I know I can blindly follow where Jesus leads me because he is my leader—my Savior and my King. The path before me is clear, and I trust you for guidance as I walk in your strength. Give me the victory this day over the forces of darkness that seek to destroy the work you have called me to so that your light will shine through me. In Christ's holy name I pray, amen.

TRUST

DAY FOUR

Today's Verses—Matthew 6:25

For this reason, I say to you, do not be worried about your life, as to what you will eat or what you will drink; nor for your body, as to what you will put on. Is not life more than food, and the body more than clothing?

Additional Reading: Isaiah 12:2; Hebrews 11:1; Psalm 20:7

My Thoughts

Although we need food for energy and water to remain hydrated, as Matthew 6:25 tells us, it shouldn't be our only focus. This is also true for our careers and businesses, which provide the very resources to buy our food and drink. Unfortunately, we spend entirely too much time worrying and not enough time trusting God. The terrible thing about our anxiety is that it takes our eyes off the Savior. We lose sight of what's truly important: serving him. It also robs us of our joy.

Two years ago, I had the blessing to visit Haiti. During that trip, I witnessed extreme poverty. The villagers had to walk for some distance to the local water well to get their water. Their meager diet wasn't much, and their housing was often four walls covered by a blue tarp. What I witnessed in the people, however, was a sense of peace and a genuine joy for life. The children were especially joyful and content. When we are in the loving arms of our Savior, we, too, can experience the joy of living—free from worry.

Your Reflections

_____

_____

_____

_____

_____

_____

Prayer

Father God, I rejoice in your immense love for me and your children. Your care and provisions are without fail and are ample in supply. Not only do you provide for our daily needs, but you also give us grace that covers us with love and joy. The saving work of Christ at the cross frees us from the burden and penalty of sin. Thank you, dear Lord, for that eternal gift. Lord, through your faithfulness, you have taught me to trust you. Keep me close to you this day. In Christ's holy name I pray, amen.

TRUST   DAY FIVE

Today's Verses—Mark 9:23-24

And Jesus said to him, "If You can?' All things are possible to him who believes." Immediately the boy's father cried out and said, "I do believe; help my unbelief."

Additional Reading: Psalm 112:7; Jeremiah 29:11-13; Isaiah 26:3-4

My Thoughts

The father in Mark 9:23 is a good example of not trusting. The man recognized Christ for who he was, but he didn't trust that Christ would heal his son. Although this doesn't make sense, it reflects the doubt that the man had, despite his need for healing. If the man didn't think Christ would heal his son, why go to him in the first place? However, Jesus doesn't admonish him. He simply questions his unbelief.

I do believe we are a lot like the man in the verses above. We know Jesus is the Son of God and with him all things are possible, yet we still don't trust that he will act on our behalf. What is keeping you from letting go of your hang-ups and doubts to fully trust in the living Lord? Take a closer look and ask God to reveal in your life areas of unbelief. He is ready to deliver you—but first, you must trust and believe. Like one of my favorite hymns says, "To be happy in Jesus, you must trust and obey."

Your Reflections

_____

_____

_____

_____

_____

_____

Prayer

Dear Lord, we read in Isaiah 26:4 your encouragement to us: "Trust in the Lord forever, for in God the Lord, we have an everlasting Rock." I rejoice that Jesus is our everlasting rock. He is my king, who cannot be defeated or dethroned. Lord, I know, at times, I fail to trust you completely and try to do things in my own strength. Forgive me, Lord, when I take my eyes off of you and leave you behind. Keep me in your presence, dear Lord, and strengthen my faith and trust in you, that I might walk with my eternal rock. In Jesus' name I pray, amen.

WEEK FIFTY

KEEP YOU

KEEP YOU DAY ONE

Today's Verses—Deuteronomy 7:9

Know therefore that the Lord your God, He is God, the faithful God, who keeps His covenant and His lovingkindness to a thousandth generation with those who love Him and keep His commandments.

Additional Reading: John 16:33; Genesis 12:3; Ephesians 1:11

My Thoughts

Have you ever known someone who might promise the world but never keeps the promise? It's almost like she is a pathological liar, right? You can never depend on her to be there when you need her or show up when she says she will. You never know if she is being dishonest or is just overcommitted. Either way, it is difficult to have a relationship with a person like this because you don't trust her.

Now, contrast that with a friend who has high integrity and always keeps his word. There is an old saying, "His word is his bond." If he makes a promise, you know you can count on it. You might have had a parent like that, or perhaps it was a friend. In any event, your view of a person is based on your experiences with him—good or bad, right?

Our God is like none other. He never fails and always keeps his promises. He is our model of dependability, and every promise in the holy Scriptures has been kept. His promise to keep us safe and in his care is comforting. His watchful eye is ever upon us. We can count on him.

Your Reflections

_____

_____

_____

_____

_____

_____

Prayer

Father God, you are an amazing and wonderful Father. I rejoice and give you praise. Father, you have given us a model to emulate. You are faithful. You keep your promises. You show us lovingkindness. Dear Lord, help me to walk in this model, to be faithful to your calling, to keep my words for your glory, and to show lovingkindness to those who so desperately need your love and grace. Keep me, oh, Lord, in your presence. In Christ's holy name I pray, amen.

KEEP YOU   DAY TWO

Today's Verses—Zephaniah 3:17

The Lord your God is in your midst, a victorious warrior. He will exult over you with joy, He will be quiet in His love, He will rejoice over you with shouts of joy.

Additional Reading: 1 John 5:18; Genesis 12:3; Ephesians 1:11

My Thoughts

This is so cool! The living God is in our midst as a victorious warrior—not just a warrior but a victorious warrior. This reminds me of the Secret Service agents who protect the president. These men and women are highly trained individuals who are constantly watching out for danger. At any sign of a threat or danger, they immediately surround the president to protect and defend him. They are, in many ways, modern-day warriors who face danger daily.

It would be wonderful if each of us could afford a protective detail like the president's agents, who would follow wherever we went. Well, our protection comes from the holy and living God, and he cannot be defeated. I am not suggesting that we will never come to harm, for we do live in a fallen world. However, I do believe that the protection we are offered is not merely physical but, more importantly, spiritual. Remember: our battle is not against flesh and blood but against the rulers of darkness. Jesus will not only protect us from the forces of evil, but he will also rejoice over us in victory.

Your Reflections

_____

_____

_____

_____

_____

_____

Prayer

Dear Lord, as I recognize your presence is that of a victorious warrior, I am thankful and give you praise. I am so grateful for your love and protection. You are an intimate God. You love each of us with an unfailing love that never ceases or fades. You exult over us and joyfully shout at the sight of our faces. Father, my prayer today is that I will not only feel your presence but also that your joy will be transferred to me—so I might share your joy, love, and peace with others for your glory. In Christ's holy name I pray, amen.

SDG

KEEP YOU

Today's Verses—Jude 1:24

Now to Him who is able to keep you from stumbling, and to make you stand in the presence of His glory blameless with great joy.

Additional Reading: Isaiah 45:5; 1 Peter 2:9; 2 Timothy 2:15

My Thoughts

Think about a time you went to a bowling alley with your kids. To help your family fully enjoy the game, you might have asked that bumpers be put on the lane. This prevents gutter ball after gutter ball and makes the game more fun.

Jude 1:24 speaks of just one of the ways the Holy Spirit protects us. We are certainly protected physically, and there are certainly defenses against attacks from evil, but this goes beyond that. God puts bumpers on our lane so we won't throw gutter balls. It keeps us in play and in the center of the lane he has chosen for our lives. Keep in mind, though: we can remove the bumpers anytime. We do have freewill, after all. A 10X lifestyle mandates that we walk in his presence and follow his will and plan for our lives. I don't know about you, but I like the safety of the bumpers.

Your Reflections

_____

_____

_____

_____

_____

_____

Prayer

Father God, as I read 1 Peter 2:9, I rejoice that you have called us out of the darkness and into your marvelous light. Your light is the light of hope and salvation for eternity. I am grateful that this same light shines through me and offers hope and salvation to a dark world. Father, please keep me from stumbling that I might be an effective disciple who radiates your love and compassion to others. Help me to boldly proclaim you and the gift of salvation through faith in Jesus Christ, my Savior. In his holy name I pray, amen.

KEEP YOU

DAY FOUR

Today's Verses—1 Peter 1:4-5

To obtain an inheritance which is imperishable and undefiled and will not fade away, reserved in heaven for you, who are protected by the power of God through faith for a salvation ready to be revealed in the last time.

Additional Reading: Psalm 91:1-2; John 15:5; 2 Thessalonians 3:3

My Thoughts

When Steve Jobs died, his wife, Laurene Powell Jobs, inherited his wealth of $19.5 billion, making her one of the richest women in the world. Now, that's more than most of us will receive in our lifetimes. I can't imagine what a person could do with that much wealth. I've often heard the phrase, "You can't take it with you." At the end of the day, no matter how much wealth you accumulate, it will mean nothing in eternity. It's all perishable.

There is no doubt that wealth can be used in many good ways and can provide an unbelievable lifestyle, but it pales in comparison to the inheritance we have in Jesus Christ, our Lord. The exciting part is that our inheritance is imperishable and undefiled and will not fade away. So, I guess you can take it with you! Imagine the unspeakable joy of spending eternity with our Savior.

Your Reflections

_____

_____

_____

_____

_____

_____

Prayer

Father God, you are a strong tower and a mighty fortress in whom I can find shelter and comfort. I am so grateful that your divine love for your children provides us with an eternal dwelling place. Our inheritance in you is imperishable and undefiled and will never fade away. Lord, from the beginning, your plan for your people has been to love and protect them—to keep them in your presence. I welcome this fellowship with you daily. Keep me close, that I might find comfort and strength in your mighty arms. In Christ's holy name I pray, amen.

SDG

KEEP YOU
DAY FIVE

Today's Verses—Romans 16:20

The God of peace will soon crush Satan under your feet. The grace of our Lord Jesus be with you.

Additional Reading: Malachi 3:17; John 10:10-11; Ephesians 4:14-15

My Thoughts

I must confess that I am not a fan of superhero movies. The so-called superhero is often defeated by the evil nemesis but, eventually, overcomes the enemy. If they were real superheroes, how could they be so easily defeated? No matter which one you follow, they are always getting kicked around by the villain.

Well, guess what? My superhero is Jesus Christ, the King of Kings and Lord of Lords. He cannot and will not ever be defeated. Now, you may be thinking, If that's true, why am I so easily defeated? That is a good question, and one I cannot answer. I know that I will never fully understand the mind of God or why things happen the way they do, but here is what I am certain about: the God of peace is my protector. We are guaranteed a life of victory in the risen Savior. Stay in the battle and rely on his strength.

Your Reflections

_____

_____

_____

_____

_____

Prayer

Father, I am amazed by you and awed by your majesty. You are the almighty God of peace and grace. Lord, I rejoice in who you are, and I give you thanks, knowing that I am your child and you will never leave or forsake me. Lord, as I walk in your strength, help me to be bold in sharing you with others. Give me a renewed passion and joy in serving you, that I might radiate your love. In Jesus' name I pray, amen.

WEEK FIFTY-ONE

TEACH

TEACH DAY ONE

Today's Verses—2 Timothy 3:16-17

All Scripture is inspired by God and profitable for teaching, for reproof, for correction, for training in righteousness; so that the man of God may be adequate, equipped for every good work.

Additional Reading: Romans 10:17; Matthew 28:19-20; Hebrews 13:7

My Thoughts

Over the course of a lifetime, we will take part in a great deal of schooling. Each subject will have an accompanying textbook that must be read as a part of the learning. In some cases, especially in higher learning, there may be more than one text. Learning never stops, but it's funny how the teaching may change. Take "new math," for example. Math is now so complicated that I struggle to help my kids with their homework.

What if we could simply have one textbook for every course? Wouldn't that make learning easier? What if that same textbook was infallible and never had to be revised or corrected? It's kind of like a magical book you might see in a movie: whatever you ask, the book answers. By now, you should know where I'm going with this. There is such a book. It's called the holy Bible. It was inspired by God and is a complete "how-to" book for our lives. It offers us wisdom and understanding, which equips us for the Lord's work.

Your Reflections

_____

_____

_____

_____

_____

_____

Prayer

Father God, I am so grateful for your perfect plan for our lives, which is without fault or failure. The salvation you offer that comes from accepting Jesus Christ as our Savior gives us eternal life with you. Your holy Scriptures, inspired by you, offer a clear picture of your character and love for us. It offers us wisdom that is guided by the Holy Spirit so we might accomplish your work. You have called us and given us everything necessary to teach others. Dear Lord, please help me to remain faithful to your calling, that I might remain true to your teachings. Help me to boldly share with others, that your mighty name would be glorified. In the matchless name of our Savior, Jesus Christ, I pray, amen.

SDG

TEACH

Today's Verses—Deuteronomy 6:6-9

These words, which I am commanding you today, shall be on your heart. You shall teach them diligently to your sons and shall talk of them when you sit in your house and when you walk by the way and when you lie down and when you rise up. You shall bind them as a sign on your hand and they shall be as frontals on your forehead. You shall write them on the doorposts of your house and on your gates.

Additional Reading: Colossians 3:16-17; John 14:26; Titus 2:7-8

My Thoughts

I have been blessed to have many individuals in my life who have made a considerable impression on my walk with Christ. They have been a great source of encouragement and have shared their passion for serving our Lord Jesus. They have a mastery of God's Word, and they use this knowledge to encourage and share their excitement in intimately knowing the living Lord.

As I have matured in my walk, my love for the Scriptures has continued to grow. I seek the wisdom of the Word and use it as a guide for daily living. My love for Jesus encourages me to be faithful to him and to learn more about him in a quest to become like him. I believe our mandate is to immerse ourselves in God's Word—to learn it and make it a part of everything we do. Once we have captured the Word in our hearts, it will truly be central to all we say and do. As Galatians 2:20 reads, "It is no longer I who live, but Christ who lives in me."

Your Reflections

_____

_____

_____

_____

_____

_____

Prayer

Dear heavenly Father, I pray the words in Colossians 3:16: "Remember what Christ taught, and let his words enrich your lives and make you wise; teach them to each other and sing them out in psalms and hymns and spiritual songs, singing to the Lord with thankful hearts" (TLB). Father, I am so grateful that you have given us your Word. It richly blesses us with your wisdom, and I am equally grateful that you have planted the seed of your Spirit in me and that my love for your teaching has become insatiable. Lord, I pray that I will never grow lazy in studying your Word but will continuously seek your wisdom and guidance. May your Word be ever present in my soul. Let it naturally flow from me, that I might teach others of your love and grace. In the mighty name of my Savior, Jesus Christ, I pray, amen.

SDG

TEACH DAY THREE

Today's Verses—Titus 2:11-13

For the grace of God has appeared, bringing salvation to all men, instructing us to deny ungodliness and worldly desires and to live sensibly, righteously and godly in the present age, looking for the blessed hope and the appearing of the glory of our great God and Savior, Christ Jesus.

Additional Reading: Titus 1:9; Acts 5:42; Ephesians 4:11-13

My Thoughts

Our instruction in 2 Timothy 2:11-13 is to become models of righteousness in all areas of our lives. God offered his son, Jesus, to die on the cross for our sins. In his resurrection, we are offered a new life, free from the debt of sin and death. However, we must walk in a new way—not as the old self but as a new creation in Christ. As teachers of others, we must walk in such a way that it will not bring dishonor to our God.

Our teaching of others must be from God's Word, with the hope for eternity with Christ. We must resist the temptation to return to our ungodly ways. We must forsake worldly desires that can take us off course and render us ineffective in our instruction. We have a responsibility to teach and share our learning with others. It's up to us to disciple the next generation for his work.

Your Reflections

_____

_____

_____

_____

_____

_____

Prayer

Father God, I now realize that our greatest responsibility apart from loving you is to share your wisdom with others and to make disciples. I am grateful for this privilege and calling. You created us to walk in your righteousness as your children and to be living examples of heaven on earth. I now recognize that apart from you, I can do nothing good or of spiritual value. Help me to remain faithful to your teaching and walk in your light, forever a student of your Word, that I might remain in service to our great God and Savior, Christ Jesus. In his holy name I pray, amen.

TEACH

Today's Verses—1 John 2:27

As for you, the anointing which you received from Him abides in you, and you have no need for anyone to teach you; but as His anointing teaches you about all things, and is true and is not a lie, and just as it has taught you, you abide in Him.

Additional Reading: 2 Corinthians 2:17; Matthew 23:8; Jeremiah 15:16

My Thoughts

I believe there are two elements to maturity in Christ: one, the Holy Spirit; second, the holy Scriptures. One without the other doesn't work. Jesus spoke to his disciples in parables, and at times, they were confused about the meaning. Fortunately, Jesus was with them to help his followers understand the meaning for each story. Today, I believe this is the role of the Holy Spirit. He is our guide and interpreter.

The Holy Spirit gives us understanding into the Word and reveals the truth of passages that would remain hidden without his speaking into our minds. God has a wonderful plan for our lives, and the Holy Spirit is there to encourage us and to translate the Scriptures, not only for our understanding but also for enabling us to apply them to our life. Without understanding, we cannot communicate the truths of God's Word to others. Seek him. Spend time in the Bible. Make it a part of your daily diet. Pray for discernment and the boldness to teach others. The Holy Spirit is with you. Lean on him.

Your Reflections

_____

_____

_____

_____

_____

_____

Prayer

Gracious Father, I delight in your loving arms. You are a merciful and loving God. I give you thanks that I have been called by your name, oh, Lord of Hosts. I rejoice that you abide in me and give me hope. You have placed in me a love for your Word and given me a mission to reach others for you. Keep me on your path, dear Lord, that I might speak with clarity and boldness through the guidance of the Holy Spirit. Keep me humble and active in your service. In Christ's holy name I pray, amen.

SDG

TEACH

DAY FIVE

Today's Verses—Romans 2:21

You, therefore, who teach another, do you not teach yourself? You who preach that one shall not steal, do you steal?

Additional Reading: 1 Timothy 2:1-3; 1 Corinthians 3:11; John 6:63

My Thoughts

Have you ever heard the saying, "Do as I say, not as I do"? We are called to teach God's truth, to be servants of Christ, walking in boldness and proclaiming his truth. Faithfulness to the Father requires that we do what we say, we are called to be true to his teachings in the Scriptures. Otherwise, we deny Christ and the work of salvation he offers.

A teacher must develop a certain level of knowledge or proficiency in their chosen field or subject. Additionally, their learning should be reflected in their lives—in their actions. If we believe something to be true, we must act in a manner consistent with our belief. As you grow in your knowledge of the Scriptures, your goal should be set on becoming more like Christ. He was a perfect man who walked on the earth and did not sin. We are incapable of walking in the same manner apart from him. We must walk daily in his strength, in his presence, and in obedience. Only then can we effectively model and teach.

Your Reflections

_____

_____

_____

_____

_____

_____

Prayer

Father God, I give you thanks for Jesus Christ, our Savior, who has laid our foundation for devotion and service to you. He has given us a new life of hope, joy, and peace and eternity with you. Dear Lord, help me to build on this foundation—not in my own wisdom but yours, that I might be an effective witness to your glory. May the Spirit guide me in all manner of wisdom and knowledge, that my teachings would encourage others and bring them closer to you. In Christ's holy name I pray, amen.

WEEK FIFTY-TWO

ACTION PLAN

ACTION PLAN   DAY ONE

East to West

Today's Verses—Psalm 103:12

As far as the east is from the west, so far has He removed our transgressions from us.

Additional Reading: Ecclesiastes 7:20; Luke 7:44-50; Psalm 32:5

My Thoughts

The material for the next five days, beginning today, will be a review of sorts; I want to offer you time to reflect on your learning. My prayer, as you review these five major principles of the 10X lifestyle, is that you will set a course each day to walk in a manner worthy of your calling in Christ, our Lord.

The first principle is East to West, which simple means that your sins are forgiven and forgotten for all of eternity. Do you believe it? How is this truth making a difference in your life? Have you allowed the evil one to convince you that you are still living in sin and darkness? Don't be deceived. You are a new creation in the holy and living God. Live your life free from the past and walk in the light of the living Lord, our Savior, Christ Jesus.

Your Reflections

_____

_____

_____

_____

_____

_____

Prayer

Dear Lord, I am eternally grateful that you are my Father and my God. I give you thanks for the redemptive work of Jesus Christ at Calvary. By accepting him as my Savior, I am free from the penalty of sin. My sins have been removed as far as the East is to the West. Help me each day to walk in your forgiveness and walk in a manner that glorifies you. In Christ's holy name I pray, amen.

ACTION PLAN   DAY TWO

Masterpiece

Today's Verses—Ephesians 2:10

For we are His workmanship, created in Christ Jesus for good works, which God prepared before-hand so that we would walk in them.

Additional Reading: Luke 12:7; Colossians 3:17; Matthew 10:29-31

My Thoughts

As we accept the fact that we are forgiven and our past is forgotten, it gives us a new beginning in Christ. God has a plan for your life—the old self is gone. If you are still walking in the old self with limited belief or doubt about who you are, stop it! God created you for something greater, so get in the game.

Here's the wonderful thing about getting in the game. You were created by God in Christ Jesus for good works. So, it's like the old television show, *The Six Million Dollar Man*, except better. You don't have bionic parts that make you suited for a special mission, but you have the living God in you. The second principle is that you are his workmanship.

As God's own creation, you lack nothing to accomplish his will for you. The Holy Spirit is in you for wisdom and guidance. Jesus, our Savior, is with you to make a difference for the Kingdom. It's up to you now to pick up the cross and do what you were created to do.

Your Reflections

_____

_____

_____

_____

_____

_____

Prayer

Father God, I am grateful for the words in Ephesians 2:10 that tell us, "For we are His workmanship, created in Christ Jesus for good works, which God prepared beforehand so that we would walk in them." Lord, thank you for creating us and placing us on this earth above all living creations and for preparing ahead of time the work you have called us to. Lord, help me this day to walk as your masterpiece and complete the work you set aside for me, unto your honor and glory. In Jesus' name I pray, amen.

SDG

ACTION PLAN | DAY THREE

Abundance

Today's Verses—John 10:10

The thief comes only to steal and kill and destroy; I came that they may have life and have it abundantly.

Additional Reading: James 1:17; Proverbs 3:9-10; Deuteronomy 28:11-23

My Thoughts

Once again, we are reminded who the real enemy is. He won't stop seeking to destroy you as you seek to fulfill God's calling on your life, but this shouldn't deter you. God is aware of this and will provide you with everything you need for the battle.

God's provision through Jesus Christ provides for our welfare as well as our safety. His provision also includes an abundance of wisdom from his Word, the holy Scriptures. You will be supplied with everything you need to live in an abundance of His love and grace. We are called to share this abundance with others along the way. If you lack anything, you simply need to ask, and he will provide. Our Lord will never leave you or forsake you. The principle reminder here is abundance.

Your Reflections

_____

_____

_____

_____

_____

_____

Prayer

Father God, we are reminded in James 1:17 that everything is given, and every perfect gift is from you, the Father of Light, with whom there is no variation or shifting shadow. I give you praise for the bounty I enjoy. Because of your provisions, I rejoice in knowing that you are the same today, tomorrow, and forever (Hebrews 13:8). Keep me focused on my Lord and Savior, Christ Jesus, and not on what I have. Keep me close to him. In his holy name I pray, amen.

ACTION PLAN DAY FOUR

10X

Today's Verses—Daniel 1:20

As for every matter of wisdom and understanding about which the king consulted them, he found them ten times better than all the magicians and conjurers who were in all his realm.

Additional Reading: 2 Timothy 2:15; Matthew 5:13-16; 2 Chronicles 15:7

My Thoughts

Living the 10X lifestyle requires courage and trust to believe that, no matter what, God will provide for and protect you. Throughout biblical history, God has kept his promises to his people. He is faithful and true in every circumstance. The principle here is that a true 10X lifestyle is lived by an unshakable faith in the true and living God.

You must be prepared to stand against injustice, lies, and false teachings. You must have the boldness to proclaim his truth in a dark and fallen world. You will face your share of opposition and challenges, but remember, he will deliver you. Moving from success to significance requires unshakable courage and trust in the living God. How will you answer his call to the 10X lifestyle? Will you walk with the courage of those young Jewish boys in captivity?

Your Reflections

_____

_____

_____

_____

_____

_____

Prayer

Father God, I am grateful that throughout human history, you have never been surprised by the actions of your people or wavered in your righteous rule. You love, teach, strengthen, and protect us. Each of us has a unique calling in how we serve you and your Kingdom. We are called to add flavor to the world but not be in the world (Matthew 15:13). We are called to be the light in a dark and fallen world, but we never act alone, for you are with us always. Dear Lord, I am grateful for your presence in my life. Help me to have the boldness of those young men we learned about in Daniel 1. Help me to be your champion. In Christ's holy name I pray, amen.

SDG

ACTION PLAN

DAY FIVE

Finish Well

Today's Verses—2 Timothy 4:7-8

I have fought the good fight, I have finished the course, I have kept the faith; in the future there is laid up for me the crown of righteousness, which the Lord, the righteous judge, will award to me on that day, and not only to me, but also to all who have loved His appearing.

Additional Reading: Philippians 3:12-14; Jeremiah 32:38-39; Colossians 1:9-14

My Thoughts

Do you ever think about the day when you will stand before our Savior? Do you wonder what will you hear? If you are like me, you want to hear, "Well done, good and faithful servant!" (Matthew 25:23). As we come to the end of this devotional study, what's next? My prayer is that you now have a stronger foundation in the Word and a deeper understanding of how to live a bold and faithful life in service to the risen Savior, Christ Jesus.

It's exciting to think one day we will receive the crown of righteousness from Christ himself. What a glorious day that will be! Our work is not finished until the day we are called home to be with the Savior. Commit this day to finish well, to spend time each day in his Word. Seek the guidance of the Holy Spirit. Walk in his light with boldness, defending the less fortunate. Proclaim his truth in love and grace so that on that glorious day, when you stand before your King, he will welcome you home into his loving arms.

Your Reflections

_____

_____

_____

_____

_____

Prayer

Father God, I am so grateful for the journey you have given me through this devotional study. I have grown closer to you and learned so much about your character. Lord, as I continue this path, I pray your presence and your mighty hand on my daily walk. Keep me faithful and true to your calling so that I might someday hear, "Well done, good and faithful servant." May my life forever be a testimony to your love and grace. In Jesus' name I pray, amen.

SDG

ACKNOWLEDGEMENTS

This devotional took genesis after my friend Greg Leith encouraged me to lead a devotional for our first Convene Chair Advisory Board. Thank you, Greg, for believing in me right from the start. Once that simple devotional was done, I felt a prompting from the Holy Spirit to turn this simple text into what you are holding in your hand today. It's really a partnership, between me and the Holy Spirt. Grateful for a great God that is at work in me.

I want to especially thank to my wonderful wife Sherrill not only for her encouragement but also for tirelessly reading every word. She was faithful and never complained as she read over 47,000 words.

My daughter Charlotte and granddaughter Callie Levine were very helpful in finding verses in God's word that made my research easier. Also Rebecca Li was a great help in not only finding verses but a great set of eyes in the initial editing. Thanks to Charlotte, Callie & Rebecca!

I am grateful for two great editors; Jennifer Hanchey & Angie Kiesling for doing the heavy lifting in preparing my manuscript for publication and the final editing.

Last but not least, the great team at Morgan James I thank you. Especially Aubrey Kincaid for guiding through the beginning steps and Bonnie Rauch for walking with me to the end. I am also grateful to David Hancock founder of Morgan James and Chris McCluskey President of Mount Tabor Media for taking a chance on a first-time author.

ABOUT THE AUTHOR

Carlos Rosales, PDM, CPLC, CPC

Carlos' life mission is to **speak truth into mens' lives and help them be their best selves in Christ Jesus!** He is an avid reader and Bible student and has been an active participant in Bible Study Fellowship International for over 10 years.

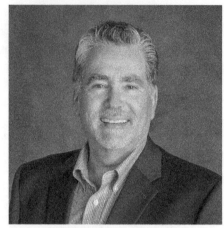

10X4CHRIST is his first devotional book and is based on his life experiences and walk with Christ.

Carlos is passionate about sharing the 10X lifestyle and challenging you to live a bolder more engaging life for Jesus Christ!

Carlos has worked as a professional business coach and consultant since 2007. He is a Convene chair and a Certified Professional Leadership Coach and a Certified Process Consultant. He weaves his faith into every coaching relationship. Carlos has been in business leadership roles for 35 years.

Carlos resides in Spring, Texas with his wife Sherrill, they attend Champion Forest Baptist Church. Carlos has six children and seven grandchildren.

Visit my website www.10X4Christ.org

CPSIA information can be obtained
at www.ICGtesting.com
Printed in the USA
LVHW111817191219
641005LV00005B/11/P